Qualitative Studies of Exploration in Childhood Education

Transitions in Childhood and Youth

Series Editors: Marilyn Fleer, Mariane Hedegaard and Megan Adams

The series brings together books that present and explore empirical research and theoretical discussion on the themes of childhood and youth transitions. Special attention is directed to conceptualizing transitions holistically so that societal, institutional and personal perspectives are featured within and across books. Key to the series is presenting the processes of transitions between practices or activities and their relationship to the person, in contexts such as intergenerational family practices, the processes of care, a person's development, the learning of individuals, groups and systems, personal health, labour and birthing and ageing. All books take a broad cultural-historical approach of transitions across a range of contexts and countries and when brought together in one place make an important contribution to better understanding transitions globally. Books in the Transitions in Childhood and Youth series offer an excellent resource for postgraduate students, researchers, policy writers and academics.

Advisory Board:

Anne Edwards (University of Oxford, UK)
Jennifer Vadeboncoeur (University of British Columbia, Canada)
Anna Stetsenko (City University of New York, USA)

Also available in the series:

Children's Transitions in Everyday Life and Institutions,
edited by Mariane Hedegaard and Marilyn Fleer
Developmental Dynamics and Transitions in High School, Sofie Pedersen
Supporting Difficult Transitions: Children, Young People and Their Carers,
edited by Mariane Hedegaard and Anne Edwards

Forthcoming in the series:

Exploring Young Children's Agency in Everyday Transitions, Pernille Juhl
Pedagogical Transitions in Post-Apartheid South Africa: A Cultural-Historical Approach towards Inclusive Primary Education, Joanne Hardman

Qualitative Studies of Exploration in Childhood Education

Cultures of Play and Learning in Transition

Edited by Marilyn Fleer, Mariane Hedegaard,
Elin Eriksen Ødegaard and Hanne Værum Sørensen

BLOOMSBURY ACADEMIC
LONDON • NEW YORK • OXFORD • NEW DELHI • SYDNEY

BLOOMSBURY ACADEMIC
Bloomsbury Publishing Plc
50 Bedford Square, London, WC1B 3DP, UK
1385 Broadway, New York, NY 10018, USA
29 Earlsfort Terrace, Dublin 2, Ireland

BLOOMSBURY, BLOOMSBURY ACADEMIC and the Diana logo are trademarks of
Bloomsbury Publishing Plc

First published in Great Britain 2022
This paperback edition published in 2023

Copyright © Marilyn Fleer, Mariane Hedegaard, Elin Eriksen Ødegaard and
Hanne Værum Sørensen and Bloomsbury 2022

Marilyn Fleer, Mariane Hedegaard, Elin Eriksen Ødegaard and Hanne Værum
Sørensen and Bloomsbury have asserted their right under the Copyright, Designs and
Patents Act, 1988, to be identified as Author of this work.

For legal purposes the Acknowledgements on p. xvii constitute an extension
of this copyright page.

Series Design by Joshua Fanning
Cover image © SDI Productions/Getty Images

All rights reserved. No part of this publication may be reproduced or
transmitted in any form or by any means, electronic or mechanical, including
photocopying, recording, or any information storage or retrieval system,
without prior permission in writing from the publishers.

Bloomsbury Publishing Plc does not have any control over, or responsibility for,
any third-party websites referred to or in this book. All internet addresses given
in this book were correct at the time of going to press. The author and publisher
regret any inconvenience caused if addresses have changed or sites have
ceased to exist, but can accept no responsibility for any such changes.

A catalogue record for this book is available from the British Library.

Library of Congress Cataloging-in-Publication Data
Names: Fleer, Marilyn, editor. | Hedegaard, Mariane, editor. | Ødegaard,
Elin Eriksen, editor. | Sørensen, Hanne Værum, editor.
Title: Qualitative studies of exploration in childhood education: cultures of play
and learning in transition / Edited by Marilyn Fleer, Mariane Mariane,
Elin Eriksen Ødegaard and Hanne Værum Sørensen.
Description: London; New York, NY: Bloomsbury Academic, 2022. | Series: Transitions
in childhood and youth | Includes bibliographical references and index.
Identifiers: LCCN 2021023533 | ISBN 9781350199422 (hardback) |
ISBN 9781350199460 (paperback) | ISBN 9781350199439 (pdf) | ISBN 9781350199446 (epub)
Subjects: LCSH: Early childhood education–Research–Case studies. |
Child development–Case studies. | Play–Psychological aspects–Case studies. |
Learning, Psychology of–Case studies. | Vygotskiĭ, L. S. (Lev Semenovich),
1896-1934–Influence. | Developmental psychology–Case studies.
Classification: LCC LB1139.225.Q35 2022 | DDC 372.21072–dc23
LC record available at https://lccn.loc.gov/2021023533

ISBN: HB: 978-1-3501-9942-2
PB: 978-1-3501-9946-0
ePDF: 978-1-3501-9943-9
eBook: 978-1-3501-9944-6

Series: Transitions in Childhood and Youth

Typeset by Integra Software Services Pvt. Ltd.

To find out more about our authors and books visit
www.bloomsbury.com and sign up for our newsletters.

Contents

List of Illustrations	vii
List of Contributors	ix
Preface	xv
Series Editors' Foreword	xvi
Acknowledgements	xvii

1   Cultures of Play and Learning in Transition *Marilyn Fleer, Mariane Hedegaard, Elin Eriksen Ødegaard and Hanne Værum Sørensen*   1

Part I: Macro-transitions within and across Educational Cultures: Children's Explorations as a New Conception in Transitions

2   Ideas for a Radical-local Approach to Care and Support for Children's Playful Exploration in Preschool and Transition to School *Mariane Hedegaard and Naussúnguag Lyberth*   19

3   A Pedagogy of Collaborative Exploration *Elin Eriksen Ødegaard*   41

4   Play Exploration and Active Learning in a Chinese Kindergarten: An Educational Experiment into How Teachers Meet the New Societal Demands of the Educational Reform and Transition into New Play Practices *Marilyn Fleer and Liang Li*   69

5   Children with Disabilities Growing Up and Exploring Life as Adults – Sociocultural Challenges around the Transition to Adulthood *Louise Bøttcher*   97

Part II: Children's Explorations during Microgenetic Transitions within Activity Settings

6   Crisis as Microgenetic Developmental Transitions: Using Explorative Activities in Micro-transitions to Recognize Opportunities for Development between Young Children and Their Fathers – A Cross-national Study *Rita Chawla-Duggan and Rajani Konantambigi*   117

7	Babies in Motion within Daycare Transition: (Co)construction of Locomotor Exploration in a Brazilian Case Study *Natália Meireles Santos Da Costa and Katia De Souza Amorim*	147
8	Transitional Activities: Children's Projects in Finnish Pre-primary Education *Jaakko Hilppö, Teemu Suorsa and Anna P. Rainio*	163
9	Moth Funeral: Exploring Issues of Life and Death in Early Childhood Education *Lasse Lipponen, Jaakko Hilppö and Antti Rajala*	183
10	Micro-transitions in Outdoor Playtime in Kindergarten: Conditions for Children's Exploration and Cultural Formation *Åsta Birkeland, Hanne Værum Sørensen and Min He*	197

Index   218

Illustrations

Tables

2.1	Different perspectives on early childhood education	21
2.2	The seven standards for early childhood education: Effective pedagogic	25
2.3	Different perspectives in educational activity	26
2.4	General suggestion for how to work with the way families live and the extended family	33
3.1	Seven features of collaborative explorative practice	56
6.1	Families in England	122
6.2	Families in Mumbai, India	123
6.3	Father-child activity settings in the cluster families in England	126
6.4	Father-child activity settings in the cluster families in Mumbai	127
6.5	F2 England: Participant video data: Activity setting/social situation: Bedtime routines	128
6.6	F2 Mumbai-India: Participant video data: Activity setting/social situation: Playing Games – Scene 1	132
6.7	F2 Mumbai-India: Participant video data: Activity setting/social situation: Playing Games – Scene 2	133
6.8	F2 Mumbai-India: Participant video data: Activity setting/social situation: Playing Games – Scene 3	134

Figures

1.1	Hedegaard's wholeness model (2012)	3
2.1	The relations between society-practice and persons with cultural traditions and activity settings as mediating links	20
4.1	Model for conceptualizing new institutional practices for introducing activity setting for exploration in play	77
4.2	Whole group role-play	84
4.3	Collectively solving the problem in the play	85

4.4	Model of play and learning for the Chinese Kindergarten	91
6.1	Bea and her father enjoying the book together	128
6.2	Father looks at Bea	129
6.3	Father gives Bea a good night kiss	130
6.4	Sonia points to the blue group	134
6.5	Dad picks up the pillow and points to the red flower, and then picks up a red cube	135
7.1	Illustration of first excerpt	153
7.2	Illustration of second excerpt	154
7.3	Illustration of third excerpt	157

Contributors

Katia de Souza Amorim is Professor at the Department of Education, of the Faculty of Philosophy, Sciences and Letters of Ribeirão Preto, of the University of São Paulo, Brazil. She is the coordinator of CINDEDI (Centre for Research on Human Development and Early Childhood Education). Her research is related to the fields of human developmental psychology and early childhood education and care, and her interests are on zero-to-three-year-old children. She coordinates diverse funding projects in the central areas of her research, which are carried out in different contexts, as at home, daycare centre and institutional shelter. She is the Brazilian main researcher of ISSEET (International Studies of Social Emotional Early Transitions) group.

Åsta Birkeland is Professor of Education at Western Norway University of Applied Sciences, Norway, and a key researcher at KINDknow – Kindergarten Knowledge Centre for Systemic Research on Diversity and Sustainable Futures (HVL). Her research interests are cross-cultural studies on teachers' cultural formation, kindergarten practices and cultural formation ideals, conditions for children's exploration and education for sustainability. She has contributed with systematic comparative and intercultural studies of Chinese and Norwegian approaches to early childhood education. Birkeland has been project leader for partnerships projects for several years, financed by the UTFORSK programme, including researchers from Beijing Normal University, China, East China Normal University, China, HVL and kindergartens from both countries. She is also a key researcher as co-leader within work package 6 'Conditions for children's exploration'. Birkeland was honourable Professor at Beijing Institute of Education, China, in 2018.

Louise Bøttcher is Associate Professor at Aarhus University, Denmark. She is a member of the research programme *Future technology, Culture and Learning*. Her research interest has focused on the interplay between neurobiological and social and cultural conditions for development. Her research departs in Vygotsky's idea about disability as an incongruence between the natural and the cultural line of development and is aimed at the investigation and further theoretical understanding of children and youth with disabilities and neurobiologically based impairments. She is co-author of *Development and Learning of Young Children with Disabilities* (2016). In her current research, she focuses on the role of social conditions and communicational technologies in the development of independence and exploration of young people with multiple impairments and no verbal language.

Rita Chawla-Duggan is Associate Professor in the Department of Education at the University of Bath, UK. Originally trained as a middle-school teacher, then as an educational ethnographer, she has conducted ethnographic-oriented research with children in a number of countries and has a long-standing history of research with children in India, dating back to more than twenty years. Her research focuses on qualitative research methodology, especially the use of photography and video in research with children and families, educational quality, poverty alleviation programmes for young children and families, the study of pedagogic relations and child socialization, early childhood learning and development and the social influences on young children's learning, especially fathering. She recently completed leading an international methodological project funded by the British Academy entitled Using Digital Visual methods in Cross National Research with Young Children: The Case of Paternal Engagement in Home Learning Environments. The project was conducted with young children and families in England, Norway, Hong Kong and India. She is author of *Fathers, Education and Child Development* (forthcoming) and co-editor for the series *Qualitative and Visual Methodologies in Educational Research*.

Marilyn Fleer is Laureate Professor and the Foundation Chair of Early Childhood Education and Development at Monash University, Australia. She was awarded the 2018 Kathleen Fitzpatrick Laureate Fellowship by the Australian Research Council and was a former president of the International Society of Cultural-historical Activity Research (ISCAR). In addition, she holds the positions of an honorary Research Fellow in the Department of Education, University of Oxford, UK, and a second professor position in the KINDKNOW Centre, Western Norway University of Applied Sciences, Norway, and has been bestowed the title of Honorary professor at the Danish School of Education, Aarhus University, Denmark. She was presented with *the 2019 Ashley Goldsworthy Award* for Outstanding leadership in university-business collaboration.

Min He is Associate Professor at East China Normal University, Shanghai, China. She holds a MA in Early Childhood Education and a BA in Physics Education.

Her research interests focus on space and time in early childhood education, children's life course in kindergarten, young children's science education and education for 0 to 3 years. She is an experienced teacher in early childhood teacher education in China since 1998. She has been to Japan and Norway as visiting scholar and has joined in international research with scholars from Norway, Denmark and Japan. She has published articles and chapters of books in Chinese, and some articles in international journals in English.

Mariane Hedegaard is Professor Emerita in Developmental Psychology at the University of Copenhagen, Denmark. She has also been Professor II at the Western Norwegian University of Applied Sciences, Norway. She is doctorate honoris causa at the University of Pablo Olavide in Seville, Spain, and she holds a senior research fellowship at the Department of Education, University of Oxford, UK. She has authored and co-edited twenty-nine books, of which fifteen are in English. These include *Radical-local Teaching and Learning; Vygotsky and Special Needs Education; Motives in Children's Development; Learning, Play and Children's Development; Children, Childhood and Everyday Life, Children's Transition in Everyday Life and Institutions and Supporting Difficult Transitions* and *Children's Exploration and Cultural Formation*. She has also written a number of articles in journals such as *Mind, Culture and Activity; Outlines: Critical Social Studies; Culture & Psychology;* and *Learning, Culture and Social Interaction*.

Jaakko Antero Hilppö is a University Lecturer at the Faculty of Educational Sciences, University of Helsinki, Finland. His current research focuses on children's projects as manifestations of their agency in and across different settings and especially on compassionate projects and the learning taking place within them. This work directly builds on his previous research on children's sense of agency and interest development as well as doing co-participatory research with children. He has also studied compassion in children's peer interactions and cultures of compassion in early childhood and care contexts.

Rajani Mohan Konantambigi is Professor and Dean at the School of Human Ecology, Tata Institute of Social Sciences, Mumbai, India. Her research focuses on childcare and early years education and the socialization of children. Currently her interests are in learning environments, emotional socialization and school-based counselling. Exploring qualitative methodology for her research, she has worked on transition and adjustment of children in Grade I, teaching strategies for first language and mathematics for Grade V children, and intervention researches to improve classroom learning of all children (including children with learning disabilities) and enhancing resilience in adolescents has been the work guided of PhD scholars by her. She has received The Rockefeller's Team Residency Fellowship (at the Bellagio Study Center, Italy) and the Fulbright Post-Doctoral Fellowship which she completed at the School of Education, University of Georgia, Atlanta, USA.

Liang Li is Senior Lecturer in Early Childhood Education at Faculty of Education, Monash University, Australia. Her research focuses on cultural-historical studies, infant-toddler's education and care, children's play and pedagogy, family studies, teacher education, visual methodology and STEM in play-based contexts. She has recently involved in the early childhood care and development evaluation programme in China, Vietnam and Nepal. She publishes widely in international journals such as *Learning, Culture and Social Interactions*, *Early Years*, and *International Journal of Early Years Education*.

Lasse Lipponen is Professor of Education, with special reference to early childhood education, at the Faculty of Educational Sciences, University of Helsinki, Finland. His research work is directed to emotions and emotional practices in ECE from sociocultural perspective. He has authored over 100 research articles on teaching and learning. He has have received several awards, such as the first price in the educational technology competition of the University of Helsinki 1999 for the 'Future Learning Environment', and 2008 he was the recipient of the Helsinki University 'Good Teacher' award. He has numerous international and national responsibilities, and assignments.

Naussúnguag Lyberth is Head of the daycare area in Sermersooq Municipality, Greenland and, until December 2019, director at the Center for Early Childhood Education, Department of Education, in Greenland. She is leading research with Mariane Hedegaard related to the national curriculum development, studying the play and learning needs of children in Greenland.

Anna Pauliina Rainio is a University Researcher at the Faculty of Educational Sciences, University of Helsinki, Finland. She is also a Senior Lecturer in Class Teacher Education Program on Educational Psychology and a Vice Chair of The Finnish Society for Childhood Studies, Finland. She has conducted participatory ethnographic and intervention research with children and adults in educational programmes from early childhood education to youth work. Her publications investigate how play and arts-based activities can support and enhance student engagement and agency in educational interaction.

Natália Meireles Santos Da Costa is a Psychology PhD student from the Faculty of Philosophy, Sciences and Letters at Ribeirão Preto from the University of São Paulo, Brazil. She is a researcher at CINDEDI (Centre for Research on Human Development and Early Childhood Education), a referential study centre in early childhood studies in Brazil with international projection. Costa's work focuses on locomotor socio-perceptual development in under-twos taking place in relational everyday living, mainly in group-based educational contexts. Her studies privilege the qualitative analysis of naturalistic visual material and are underpinned by the cultural-historical approach of the Network of Meanings, using notions of dialogism, embodiment and ecological perspectives. She is currently part of the Brazilian team of the ISSEET (International Studies of Social Emotional Early Transitions) group.

Teemu Suorsa is a researcher, teacher and psychotherapist in the Faculty of Education at the University of Oulu, Finland. His research focuses on theoretical, methodological and practical questions of psychological and educational-psychological research on subjective experience and everyday practices. In addition to systemic, subject-scientific and cultural-historical approaches to psychology and multi-professional collaboration, he has examined Heideggerian phenomenology, psychoanalysis and solution-focused psychotherapy in his books and articles.

Hanne Værum Sørensen is Associate Professor at VIA University College, Aarhus, Denmark. She holds a MA in Child Psychology and a BA in Social Education. Her research interests focus on conditions for children's outdoor playtime, children's explorative activities and children's important peer relationship in the transition from kindergarten to school. She is an experienced teacher in early childhood teacher education in Denmark since 2001, and in Norway, where she has four years of experience from doing research and teaching within the area of ECE education. She has published articles in Danish, Nordic and International Journals as well as book chapters in Danish, English and Norwegian.

Elin Eriksen Ødegaard is Professor and Director of KINDKNOW – Kindergarten Knowledge Centre for Systemic Research on Diversity and Sustainable Futures at Western Norway University of Applied Sciences, Norway. She is also Professor

II at UIT – The Arctic University of Norway, Norway. She completed her doctoral thesis in 2007 at University of Gothenburg, Sweden. Since then, she has published extensively on children's exploration and cultural formation, play and collaborative narrative meaning-making and 'becoming'. Her research embraces global and local perspectives and teachers' pedagogies and changing practices. She received research grants from Research Council Norway (RCN) (2007, 2009–2014, 2018–2023) and was supported by Nordic Council of Ministers (2015, 2016, 2017). Her latest books include *Exploration and Cultural Formation* (2020) and *Childhood Cultures in Transformation* (2021).

Antti Rajala is Postdoctoral Researcher at the Faculty of Educational Sciences, University of Helsinki, Finland. He is currently working in the project Constituting Cultures of Compassion in Early Childhood Education (funded by Academy of Finland, 2016–2020). His other research interests include dialogic pedagogy, global education as well as learning, agency and activism in education. He is Associate Editor in Frontline Learning Research; Co-Editor in Outlines: Critical Practice Studies; and Book Reviews Editor in Mind Culture and Activity.

Preface

The contributors to the book have presented their work at an event specifically focused on children's explorations. The event was the **Cultural-Historical Approaches to Children's Development and Childhood (CHACDOC)**. The CHACDOC 2019 meeting was held in Bergen, Norway in May, with the theme: ***Exploration in Early Childhood Education.***

Western Norway University of Applied Sciences (www.hvl.no) and the research centre *KINDknow* hosted the CHACDOC event. Participants from all over the world enjoyed the inspiring presentations and conversations and new networks were built during the meeting. The meeting inspired and challenged delegates with building more knowledge and asking more questions for future research. All keynotes, papers and posters focused on national traditions, institutional practice and children's development in different parts of the world, and the orientation of the meeting was related to the theme *Exploration in Early Childhood Education* from different perspectives.

Importantly, cultural-historical theory underpins the narrative that frames the structure of the book and this framing acts as the theoretical glue to bind the different contributions. All authors who have contributed to the book draw on the concepts of children's exploration as either macro or microgenetic transitions.

Series Editors' Foreword

In this book series we have chosen to focus on transitions through the lens of cultural-historical theory. Specifically, transition is conceptualized to encompass the changes in daily activity settings, the changes in everyday moves between different institutional practices and the changes on entering new practice through life course trajectories, such as going to school, leaving school, entering the work force or entering into parenthood. Through transition into new practices, children and young people meet new challenges and demands that may give them possibility for development.

Important for a cultural-historical conception of transition is the person's agency or intentions, which can be used as analytical tools for gaining the person's perspective during microgenetic transitions between activity settings within an institution, such as indoor play, lunch and outdoor activities in kindergarten, in daily moves between home and kindergarten, school or work, and during macro-transitions that involve new practices. As the person or people take forward their intention within the daily transitions or the new institutions that they attend, a dynamic interplay between the person and the institution can be observed. Cultural-historical studies of transitions across a range of contexts and countries are brought together in this book series, where they can make an important contribution to better understanding transitions globally.

Marilyn Fleer, Mariane Hedegaard and Megan Adams
Series Editors

Acknowledgements

We would like to record our appreciation to Dr Antionette White who supported the final stages of the production of this book through her careful attention to the presentation of the works, and Mark Richardson from Bloomsbury Publishing for his continued support of this volume and the series as a whole. We acknowledge the support from Tanya Stephenson in preparation of the final manuscript. We also acknowledge the contributions of the various funding bodies, universities and participants of the studies reported. They have collectively made possible the foundational research reported in the chapters that follow. Finally, we acknowledge the reviewers who have contributed to the quality of this volume through their comments and suggestions. We are excited by the new concepts and the respective research that makes up the body of this volume on transitions from a cultural-historical perspective.

Chapter 3

A special thanks to the staff in the case-kindergarten that allowed me to reuse the material and gave additional rich new narratives, explanations of their work and thinking in a follow-up study. Thanks also to Mariane Hedegaard for critical-constructive feedback on earlier versions that enabled me to think with the concept of transition.

Chapter 4

Special thanks to the principal, teachers and children who participated in the project and to Ms Xianyu Meng for her translation and administrative support.

Chapter 6

Funding: The study was funded by the British Academy/Leverhulme Small research Grants SRG 2016 [grant numbers: SG160083]; Entitled: 'Using Digital

Visual Methods in Cross-National Research with Young Children: The case of paternal engagement in home learning environments'. The funding source had no other involvement in the project.

Chapter 7

We acknowledge scientific support and funding received by FAPESP, CAPES and CNPQ:
CNPq Research Foundation, grant 304351/2016-4
Grant 2016/24466-7, São Paulo Research Foundation (FAPESP).
Grant 2016/24717-0, São Paulo Research Foundation (FAPESP)

Chapter 9

We wish to thank Nimco Noor for her valuable comments on the article. Our thanks go also to the Academy of Finland project no. 299191 for the financial support for preparing the article.

1

Cultures of Play and Learning in Transition

Marilyn Fleer, Mariane Hedegaard, Elin Eriksen Ødegaard and Hanne Værum Sørensen

Exploration is a vibrant activity in young children's development. In the everyday life children approach new experiences with curiosity and when supported and encouraged, children's exploration creates conditions for emotional, social, intellectual, bodily and ethical development. In a cultural-historical framework, both the biological and cultural dimensions of life develop through the conditions created in families, educational institutions and societies at large. Exploration is the process of seeking new positions in the cultural spaces that children, families and teachers inhabit. Exploration is the process through which humans find and refine a solution during the many transitions they meet in everyday life and over their life course. Exploration takes different forms in different cultural age periods and we bring out this diversity through the collection of studies reported in the two sections of this book: Section I: Macro-transitions within and across educational cultures – Children's explorations as a new conception in transitions; Section II: Children's explorations during microgenetic transitions within activity settings.

The core content of this book is cultures of play and learning in transition and specifically how exploration takes place in educational contexts and changes over time. The book addresses the formative development of children in ways that ensure holistic development and agency. In taking this perspective, the societal values and conditions where children live are brought forward, as will be shown in the pages of this book. This brings out new content as we create research conditions to see the world from the child's or young person's perspective. If we are to support children's exploration in play and learning in different life phases, we need research designs that provide both micro and macro perspectives, as well as the dynamic between these.

The practice of care and education changes when societal conditions change. As children grow up, they will experience continuously changing conditions in family life, as well as in the institutions they inhabit. In addition, as societies change, this can directly sway children's lives, such as when they experience events that inspire or provoke them through crises. Crisis can also come suddenly, for instance in the family (i.e. the death of a family member, a sudden accident), in daycare (i.e. as peer violence) or at the societal level (i.e. as a pandemic). Major crises at the institutional or societal levels may create new conditions that institutions respond to with new ways of interaction and setting new regulations. Such crises that children, families and educators may experience may contribute to new conditions for children's development. Also, children may experience minor crises in their everyday lives, such as the loss of tooth or when they enter into a new setting in home or daycare. These smaller crises are also important for the development of children. They are of interest because children's exploration can be studied in the moment-to-moment microtransitions that are occurring in everyday practices, thereby giving new insights into young children's opportunities for development.

The purpose of this book is to conceptualize and present studies on the complexities and dynamics of children and young people's exploration. It also seeks to illuminate empirically and theoretically how children contribute and change with their transition through their life course, as well as within daily transitions. The book offers a unique collection of cultural-historical studies where the analysis broadens and deepens our understandings of how children's development and young person's transition into adult life is always entangled in multi-layered processes of personal, situational and societal conditions.

A Holistic Frame: Different Perspectives on Children's and Young Peoples' Everyday Life across Institutions

To accomplish the analyses of transitions between different values, practices and activity settings that interweave in children's/young people's lives and contribute to their life course, as well as their daily activities, we draw on Hedegaard's wholeness model (Figure 1.1).

In this model, children participate in several different institutional collectives, family, daycare institutions, school and afterschool programmes throughout their childhood, and they also attend different institutional collectives in their everyday life. Each of these institutional collectives is oriented towards shared traditions in society. This can be seen when children start kindergarten and when they begin school. Even though families can be quite different in a society,

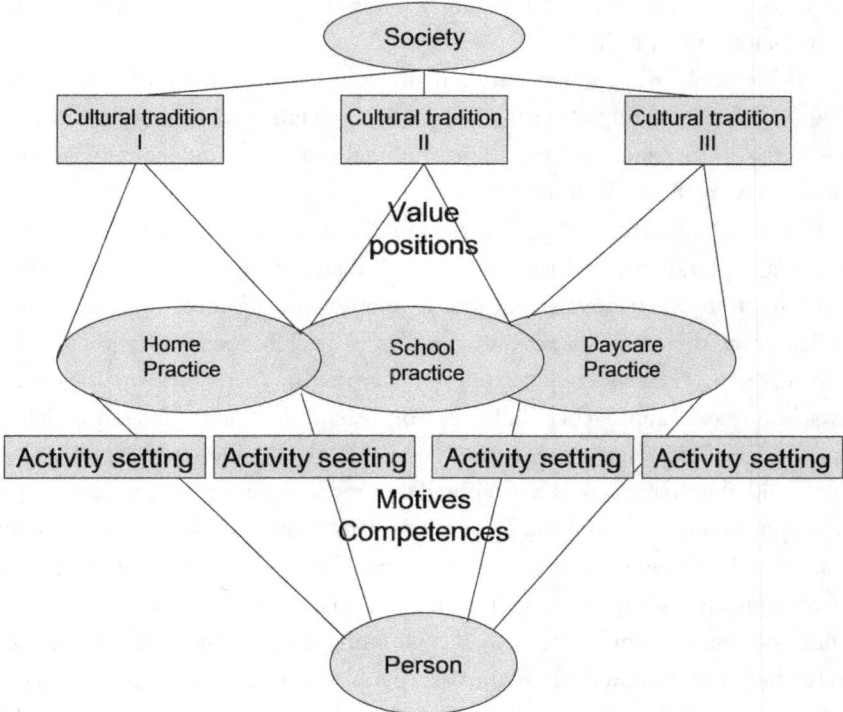

Figure 1.1 Hedegaard's wholeness model (2012).

they also have a shared background because several societal conditions are commonly experienced, that is, the health-care system, the school system, TV and other media communication system, the transport and mercantile systems etc. But how these conditions contribute to realizing a single family's everyday activities, and how these other institutional conditions influence children's learning and development, varies. In addition, what children learn at home and what knowledge and competences they bring into daycare, school and work preparation can be different.

In a holistic model children's life course may be seen as a transition between the different institutional practices. At the same time children in everyday life may also transit between different practices, coming from home or going to daycare or school. In a single institution there will be daily transitions between activity setting, for example, the activities that take place in daycare, such as arriving in the morning in, having lunch, outdoor activities etc. In the same way we can find traditions for activity settings in families, such as getting ready for school. But there are also transitions between home and school, as children move between institutions.

In this book, the relation between the activities that are outlined in each chapter is understood within the holistic interpretation of Hedegaard's model, where both societal conditions, institutional practices and activity settings (such as play time or lunch in daycare, and subject matter teaching and breaks in school) are used to analyse the conditions for children's and young people's explorative activities and their play and learning. In this analytical interpretation, we are aware that today we often see a dichotomization of play and learning that often shapes the agenda of early childhood education practice and research. The tendency is to define learning in terms of formal learning, as school-based approaches that focus on teacher-led, goal-directed activities and documented knowledge, or to define play as activities led by children as open-ended activities. This conceptualizing reduces both play and learning to stereotypical dichotomization. This binary distinction has ruled the field of early education for decades. As previous researchers have pointed out, learning is not an outcome, primarily of instruction and teaching, as children also learn through bodily communication in the form of exploration and play and therefore we need to further describe and theorize the basis of holistic development for a pedagogy responsive to children's embodied ways of playing, exploring and learning (e.g. Fleer & van Oers, 2018; Hedegaard & Ødegaard, 2020; Pramling et al., 2019; Volden, Pettersen & Ødegaard, 2016). This book goes beyond binaries because the contributors have individually, and therefore collectively, taken a holistic conception of children's explorations and a cultural-historical theorization of transitions.

The Core Theoretical Concepts

This book draws on Vygotsky's (1998) cultural-historical theory and the understanding that children's cultural formation takes shape as part of a dialectic relation between children's/young people's interests and motives and the actual institutional and community practices they participate in.

Central to the content of this book is how all the chapters contribute to better understanding how exploration relates to transitions. What is different across the chapters is how this relation is analysed. The content of the book is presented in relation to two important distinctions: (1) *major transitions* and (2) *microgenetic transition*. In the former, transitions are shown as transitions in pedagogical practices, transition between institution; and in the latter, the *microgenetic transitions* are shown between daily life activities, and as transitions in activity settings. Both macro- and microgenetic transitions influence children's everyday lives, and these different transitions give different or new possibilities for the play, learning and development of children and young people.

The concept of transition is used as the common framework for the empirical studies of children's process of being and becoming active learners, when moving between and within institutional practices into different activity settings. Transition seen in the chapters of this book as a life course perspective, which takes place when a child moves from home to daycare and starts in nursery or kindergarten. In the various chapters, different values dominate the different practices, both formally as regulations and laws for parents' responsibilities for their children, and laws for the regulations of daycare as well as laws for the kind of pedagogy that teachers have to live up to in daycare and school. Transition between practices takes place when new educational projects are pointed out (Hedegaard & Lyberth Chapter 2 argues for changes in pedagogy related to family and community traditions). These possible changes may contribute to children's life perspective because it gives new possibilities for development. In Ødegaard's Chapter 3 we can follow how change in societal values related to national symbols also influences and extends activities in kindergarten. In Fleer and Li's project (Chapter 4) we can follow how changes in national regulations for preschool activities influences concrete practices of kindergartens and leads to a change in the preschool teachers' values about the importance of play.

The concept of transition towards new practices points to changes that create new conditions for a child or young person's participation in activities, where new demands and possibilities arise (see Chapter 5, Bottcher; and Chapter 7, Meireles Santos da Costa and de Souza Amorim). Such a transition may result in new demands on the child's or young person's capabilities and may result in one or multiple crises for a child. These new conditions change a child's/young people's relation to his or her environment. The crises can take many different forms, depending on how well the child/young person has been prepared for the new demands and possibilities, or how they imagine new forms of participation for themselves. If the child/young person is oriented to exploring the new possibilities there may still be crisis, but the form may take another pathway, rather than it being experienced as an abrupt change, as noted for the young people in Bottcher's study (Chapter 5).

Transition can also be understood within a daily or weekly movement between home, nursery and other institutions, visit to grandparents, participation in weekly arrangement, such as clubs, gymnastic, music or church events, or transition during the day within the single institutional practice and follow what this means for children's activities and learning.

Children's exploration is a new concept for guiding studies of children and childhood and this concept frames this book on transitions. In this book we draw attention to the many forms of exploration that can take place within the varied forms of transition. A major transition may take the form of an educational planned transition projected to promote exploration to support children's play, learning and development, as several of the chapters show through the studies presented (Chapters 2, 3, 4, 7). If these transitions give room for children's exploration, they may support children's development of imagination and reflection about their own activities, and the activity settings they participate in.

Minor transition may also take place as children's exploration that just happen as part of the coordination of families, schools or other everyday activities. This is the case in Chapter 7, where the interaction between father's and children promotes exploration, or in Chapter 9, where a teacher's sensitivity towards children's interest initiates a moth's funeral and thereby promotes discussions about the theme of life and death. In other projects the exploration is a planned part of the preschool curriculum, as seen in Chapter 8 where children's imaginary exploration was promoted through shared projects. Chapter 10 demonstrates how culturally diverse values and traditions influence children transition between indoor and outdoor activities.

Exploration is a vibrant condition for young children's development. Children approach new experiences with curiosity and when supported and encouraged, children's exploration creates conditions for emotional, social, intellectual, bodily and ethical development. In a cultural-historical framework, both biological and cultural energies develop and become human activity through the conditions created in families, educational institutions and societies at large as seen in the societal goals for play in Chapters 4 and 10. Cultures of exploration open possibilities for young children's emotional well-being and joy as well as for the capability to strive for transformation when life conditions are uncaring.

Each chapter contributes knowledge and understanding about how children and young people are both shaping themselves and are being shaped through their explorations during times of transition. The volume brings out through the different studies and their respective insights, how children and young people engage in explorations during times of microgenetic and macro-transitions, where emotions and motives central for living and development change and transform. The book collectively brings together

a) research into how local cultures of exploration change over time in response to societal changes.
b) theoretical analyses and empirical studies of children in the process of being and becoming agentic persons within and through transitional changes in their life context.
c) how children's exploration influences different forms of activities and educational cultures, and how families and teachers influence children's cultures of exploration.

Section I: Macro-transitions within and across Educational Cultures – Children's Explorations as a New Conception in Transitions

The first section of this volume shows new ways of capturing the transition points in relation to the co-explorations of the participants and this gives a new way of framing research. The focus of the first section in this book is centred around three key conceptions of the material conditions, co-explorations and agency. We believe these concepts give new directions for the close study of transitions in institutional practices while being anchored in country specific contexts.

Central to Section I is how *the societal values can be seen in the material conditions of the institutions that children and young people participate in as part of their everyday lives.* Greenland (Chapter 2), Norway (Chapter 3), China (Chapter 4) and Denmark (Chapter 5) have their own societal values, laws, environments and cultural traditions for education. How these are seen in the practices of the institutions emerges when the material conditions of the participants are studied, and these material conditions give different possibilities for exploration and the cultural formation of the child and young person in a particular country.

In Chapter 2 (Hedegaard and Lyberth) we follow how everyday life may be realized in a new curriculum in Greenland through new principles for selecting content and through play pedagogy. New and different conditions for play and learning are opened up for young children in kindergarten or daycare. A change in the practice tradition may change the material conditions, and this may create different developmental possibilities for children in Greenland. The goal in this new curriculum is no longer the formal learning of school knowledge abstracted from the realities of everyday life, but rather it is to connect children and educators to valued local knowledge, such as 'places where children can experience how a seal is brought to shore and how it is parted and distributed'. This gives content for 'supporting play about these events of hunting for food and distribution of food through stores or through community sharing' (Hedegaard and Lyberth, Chapter 2) and this in turn gives possibilities for the development of children's motives for learning and may change their social situation of development. This is also the orientation found in the research of Fleer and Li (Chapter 4) who study how teachers and children transition into new practice traditions by following the Government curriculum guidelines for more play in Chinese kindergartens and daycare centres. The expectation is that teachers in China will create activity settings where exploration in play becomes available to the children. The Government's goal in China is for less formal kindergartens and whole group instructional teaching, and towards activity settings where children are given opportunities to play. The importance of local knowledge is also reported in the study by Fleer and Li where puppetry is seen as a key community practice tradition that should be included in the curriculum of the kindergarten and as a vehicle for learning. The focus of this chapter is how local traditions and values create a base for transition from formal learning into play exploration. Their study shows how new material and new activity settings of play give condition for children's development. As noted by Hedegaard (2020), 'The first step in an approach to learning in early childhood education is to orient children to the content of their everyday life, which implies a move away from a functional approach' (p. 20). Both chapters make contributions to showing how children and educators' transition into new activities, which in the case of China gives more room for children's initiatives in play exploration in puppetry and theatre production, and in the case of Greenland, gives more localized content for exploration in play. *Studying the material conditions of the community that children and young people participate in as part of their everyday lives is a new direction for future research interested in children's development.*

Ødegaard in Chapter 3 demonstrates how new material conditions become important to understand the transition points for developing new practices related to teachers/carers and children's explorations. The study is connected to the concept of transition and the concept of collaborative exploration (co-exploration). Co-exploration is shown as the central activity in the kindergarten practice. The study focuses on the societal values in Norway that creates national identity in a context of ongoing cultural diversity, and the results show how this influences type of play material found in the kindergarten. National celebrations of Norwegian Constitution Day influence kindergarten practice through the personal and local use of specific artefacts which are symbols of longstanding societal traditions. Through the concept of co-exploration, Ødegaard moves beyond a passive and individualistic conception of exploration by showing how kindergarten teachers and children gradually take over local artefacts. In the study, this is shown as examples of Norwegian embroidery/dress where a collaborative explorative activity begins with personal engagement in this artefact, which extends through a collaborative investigation and exploration of how the diversity of symbols that constitute Norwegian society today can be used in the institutional practice of the kindergarten. The author argues that to realize the diversity of artefacts, stories and activities as conditions for a collaborative explorative practice in the kindergartens across Norway, it is necessary to continue to study this type of material and at the same time create new digital platforms with images of artefacts. Ødegaard argues that transitions may be realized through co-explorations where the institutions themselves change and thereby support transition processes in the formulation of new developmental conditions for the children. The contradictions created by the cultural diversity within the Norwegian Constitution Day, as found across Norwegian kindergartens, become a motivating force for transition of practice as co-exploration. In her research the participants did not know at the beginning what the end goal will be. Ødegaard argues that transition in this way is not a zigzag or linear path but has to be seen as a spiral.

Related to this are the new material conditions and co-explorations that Bøttcher (Chapter 5) discusses as young people with disabilities transition into adult lives in twenty-first-century Denmark. How material conditions become available to the participants, for both the carers and the young people with disabilities, and how they meet the transition points/moments/continuum in very different ways, is also not linear. Expected pathways for transitioning are often incongruent with the unique developmental conditions and diverse pathways needed in a diverse community for what constitutes a good life. Exploration is socially mediated and pathways are uniquely individual for young people with disabilities. However, there is a shared motive and value position for transitioning into adult life for both young people with disabilities and non-disabled peers. The shared motive is to find their social position as an adult, and as uniquely co-created with carers and others in the community for realizing the motives of the individual. *This research brings out the co-exploration of participants in a period of transition into adult life.*

Exploration also captures the way societies give agency and invites the initiative of children and young people for contributing to their own developmental conditions. How this happens is shown in the studies presented in the chapters across the first section of this volume. In Denmark young people with disabilities have a lot of room for contributing to their own developmental conditions, in China and Greenland children's initiatives are seen through how they can be anchored in local traditions as content for play exploration, and in Norway the kindergarten communities give agency to families and their children for co-exploration of what Norwegian Constitution Day means in a culturally diverse society. The new concept of exploration brings out something very important about children's development, and it is through deploying this concept in the different studies that we can see how the different societal values and very different institutional practices give very different conditions for children's initiative and agency.

As an analytical concept, exploration is in line with van Oer's (2013) concept of degrees of freedom for understanding child agency in schools in the Netherland. The concept of exploration expands the concept of exploration, because degrees of freedom show the 'space' for children's initiative. But the concept of exploration in contexts of transition gives insights into the activity settings and the agentic activities of children for particular institutions and societies that as a whole are in a state of change. Although the societal values can be seen through the practices of the different institutions being researched (Greenland, Norway, China, Denmark), it is difficult to understand what this means for children's development when practice in institutions is transitioning due to new societal demands, such as for new curriculum, or a desire by different communities to develop new traditions to celebrate National Day. The term 'exploration' as an analytical concept can bring out the way societies give agency and invite the initiative of children and young people in contributing to their own developmental conditions. But also, exploration can show the different kinds of developmental possibilities during the process of institutional transition, as a direct result of societal change in values (Denmark and Norway) or new Government directions (China and Greenland).

Section II: Children's Explorations during Microgenetic Transitions within Activity Settings

The second section gives considerable attention to the child's exploration as an *embodied* transitional change process. Through close studies of minor transitions, the chapters in this section add to our current knowledge with key contributions that illustrate how *mind, body, relations and local activity settings* play out in a dynamic entity informed by cultural-historical theory. With these dynamics the studies in this section give substantial contributions to our understandings of a holistic approach to children's development, an approach that includes both the contextual conditions and the agency of the child in the different activity settings.

The concept of microgenetic transition is grounded in Vygotsky's (1998) cultural-historical theory of development and points to the change in the pedagogical practices that create new conditions for a child's participation in activities, when old and new demands and possibilities arise and provoke children, families and teachers. A transition may result when new demands on the child's capabilities are made, and this may create one or multiple crises (or conflicts) for a child. These new conditions change a child's relation to his or her environment and will thereby change the conditions for the family and the teachers and peers in the institution.

A key contribution that is made across the studies in this section is the rich descriptions and sophisticated analyses which illustrate how children's exploration unfolds in microgenetic moments (transition points) and how exploration and transition are embodied. This is a vital contribution since developmental change processes are not easy to observe and describe. In traditional research designs, such microgenetic moment by moment processes may have been overseen, since they do not necessarily involve a direct observation of change while it is occurring (Lavelli et al., 2005). By studying micro-transitions, the researcher closely observes processes of change, instead of products. Here moment-by-moment changes are observed within a short period of time in an activity or series of activities. This approach makes it possible to capture fine-grained information that is necessary for understanding change processes. Observing and understanding changes at the micro-level of real time are fundamental to understanding changes at the macro-level of developmental time (Lavelli et al., 2005, p. 40). This is exactly what the studies in this section offer.

In the chapter authored by Chawla-Duggan and Konantambigi (Chapter 6), they examined the opportunities for development emerging from the micro-crisis situations in a family in Mumbai and in Great Britain. Through a fine-grained analysis, they enabled insights into how fathers created moments of testing as an instructional strategy, with fewer explorative activities, and therefore fewer opportunities for development. In moments where a moment of exploration was emerging, they found that siblings intervened in the activity. They reflect this by contextualizing cultural aspects of what Indian fathers considered, 'kala' (time), as important. This means that fathers, following a cultural tradition, more easily focus on enhancing the cognitive capacities of the children, rather than the affective, to accommodate competition in the context of education and future career opportunities. As the fathers became more engaged, the concept of fathering was explored and changed. In the transition to being fathers, their new role took a more important place in the children's lives. And as a result of the new father-child interactions, the children's family situations were moved to become more holistic developmental conditions. The authors discuss this element as akin to the prescribed traditional role and they raise questions, grounded in their findings, about how traditional ideas of fathering and the Hindu traditional as associated with potential in the individual are two sides of the one coin, and that the dialectic between them, nevertheless may pave a way to realizing exploration for some children in families in India.

Another example is the analysis provided by Meireles Santos da Costa and de Souza Amorim. In their study of *Babies in motion within daycare transition: (co)construction of locomotor exploration in a Brazilian case study*, they illustrate how the structuring of space and relational experiences constrain a baby's locomotor exploration within a sociocultural-historical context when entering the institutional space. Their fine-grained analysis illustrates the processes of postural positioning and locomotor activity in under one-year-old babies, whether produced by others or by their own autonomous action, plays out as an inter-corporal process and modulates exploratory possibilities and outcomes. In describing the infant, Isabela, her continuous exploration of her new everyday life through an embodied back-and-forth movement strategy from the well-known to the new and unknown situation was identified. In this most important contribution, the analysis brings adults' mediation, spatial organization, peers' interaction to the forefront and they lift understandings by reflecting on how biological aspects simultaneously broaden and limit possibilities, potentially leading to transformations in such locomotor exploratory processes, through time and experiences. Their video analysis design allows new understandings of developmental change to emerge as embodied, both biological and culturally situated. The level of details in the analysis opens up understandings in how conditional factors are intertwined and embodied in practices and thereby in the infant's possibilities to explore.

These moment to moment explorations are also featured in Chapter 9; *The Moth Funeral: Exploring Issues of Life and Death in Early Childhood Education*. In this chapter the authors bring together the mind and body in relation to an emotional crisis involved a decision of life and death of a small suffering creature, a moth, found in the kindergarten. Lipponen, Hilppö and Rajala introduce us to a case of how emotions and exploration can be entangled in the everyday life of

Finnish kindergartens. Their fine-grained analysis allows us to understand how the daily flow of activities can be broken down when something overwhelmingly unexpected breaks the daily routines. Such a situation of crisis can open for expanded exploration. Unexpected happenings can create opportunities for us to learn about ourselves and others. Sometimes, mundane disruptions in the flow of our daily activity have repercussions at an existential level and can challenge us to reflect on our being in the world. This case contributes to our knowledge of how emotions and exploration can be enmeshed in the everyday life of Finnish kindergartens. This study further adds to how small crises can be identified and how these create agentic moments. How these moments are taken forward by the children and teachers gives us insights into understanding exploration in educational institutions.

How day-to-day routines, whether disrupted or not, as in the case study of *The Moth Funeral*, give different development possibilities for children's explorations in educational contexts is important to study. These everyday routine practices within the institutional settings are often invisible in research because they are simply taken for granted rather than studied. For example, in Chapter 10 Birkeland, Sørensen and He identify how micro-transitions during the day in kindergarten – from inside to outside – are related to the activity setting. There is an interplay between children's exploration and community policies and values, and this interplay is framed according to the structures and organization of the pedagogical practice. The movement is practical but experienced differently. For instance, transitioning from inside to outside is shown to be collectively organized in one country (China) and in another it is presented as open for individual children's motives (Norway), where having more time in the transition process to finish dressing up or playing outside is allowed. The study shows how micro-transitions in kindergarten provide conditions for children's explorative activities and thereby their cultural formation. The authors examine how the micro-transitions related to the activity setting of outdoor playtime interplay with children's exploration in different institutional settings which have different traditions related to community policies and values in China and in Norway.

Children's projects as part of the activity settings within the institutional practices of the kindergarten also give opportunities for the close study of exploration in educational settings. A theoretical contribution is developed by the authors Hilppö, Suorsa and Rainio, as they explore the notion of children's projects (Hilppö, 2017) in Chapter 8; *Transitional Activities: Children's Projects in Preschool*. Their study has theoretical and empirical importance for the development of cultural-historical activity theory. The context of the elaborate theoretical arguments is illustrated with an example of a children's project from a Finnish primary education group. Their analysis illustrates how children's projects emerge through children's agency and the opportunities these projects offer for supporting children's learning and development. Such projects are *transitional activities* and the authors examine how they are related to the leading activities in children's development, such as sociodramatic play and school learning.

When taken together, the studies in Section II of this book showcase methods that give insights into how the small crises emerge within the activity settings in which children participate. The concept of microgenetic transition that has come from the seminal work of Vygotsky (1998) gives a theoretical framing to the study of transitions. Vygotsky's original cultural-historical theory of development and concept of crisis does not show what this looks like in the practice of research. Therefore, this section is informative because it brings out the conditions for a child's participation in activities, but also shows how research works when studying one or multiple crises. Therefore, microgenetic research can bring to our attention a change in a child's relation to his or her environment. This new relation is difficult to study, and in finding the different ways to illuminate crisis, we can better understand how a change in the conditions of a family or educational setting affords development for a child.

Going Forward

In this book we conceptualize and present studies on the complexities and dynamics of children and young people's exploration by illuminating empirically and theoretically how children contribute and change with their transition through their life course (Section I), as well as within daily transitions (Section II). We look closely as how local cultures of exploration change over time in response to societal changes and in so doing, we advance the concept of exploration in play and learning.

In this book we showcase through studies of children and young people in the process of being and becoming agentic persons within and through transitional changes in their life context the different ways in which research can be formulated – as microgenetic and from a societal, institutional and child-orientated perspective. This dynamic model gives insights into how to study small crises, while also examining large crises within society as a whole.

A synthesis of chapters in Sections I and II identify how children's and young people's exploration influences different forms of activities and educational cultures, and how families and teachers influence children's cultures of play exploration. These are not unsubstantial daily moments or invisible routines, but are the engine which brings forward the developmental conditions of children. Transitions capture the broad and small-scale moments, and exploration gives a theoretical concept for capturing the degrees of freedom that are made available to a child within educational settings and family homes or to young people transitioning into adulthood. But also, the child's/young person's agency or degrees of freedom afforded are created by the children/young people as they enter into the new activity settings and meet the new demands. The concept of exploration as advanced in this book gives a conceptual analytical frame, methodology and method for the study of young children and young people in transition in play and learning.

References

Fleer, M., & Van Oers, B. (2018). International trends in research: redressing the north-south balance in what matters for early childhood education research. In M. Fleer & B. Van Oers (Eds.), *International Handbook on Early Childhood Education, Volume 1* (pp. 1–31). Dordrecht, The Netherlands: Springer.

Hedegaard, M. (2014). The significance of demands and motives across practices in children's learning and development: An analysis of learning in home and school. *Learning, Social Interaction and Culture*, 3, 188–94.

Hedegaard, M. (2020). Children's Exploration as a Key in Children's Play and Learning Activity in Social and Cultural Formation. In Mariane Hedegaard & Elin Eriksen Ødegaard (Eds.), *Children's Exploration and Cultural Formation* (pp. 11–27). Springer

Hedegaard, M., & Ødegaard, E.E. (2020). (Eds.). *Children's Exploration and Cultural Formation*. Springer.

Lavelli, M., Pantoja, A., Hsu, H. Messinger & Fogel, A. (2005). Using microgenetic designs to study change processes. In D. M. Teti (Ed.), *Handbook of Research Methods in Developmental Science*. Blackwell Publishing.

Lawrence, C. (2010). Historical key words – Explore. *The Lancet*, 375, 1.

Pramling, N., Wallerstedt, C., Lagerlöf, P., Björklund, C., Kultti, A., Palmér, H., Magnusson, M., Thulin, S., Jonsson, A. & Pramling Samuelsson, I. (2019). *Play-Responsive Teaching in Early Childhood Education*. Dordrecht, Netherlands: Springer.

Tharp, R. G., Estrada, P., Dalton, S. S. & Yamauchi, L. A. (2000). *Teaching Transformed: Achieving Excellence, Fairness, Inclusion, and Harmony*. Westview.

Van Oers, B. (2013). Educational innovation between freedom and fixation: The cultural-political construction of innovations in early childhood education in the Netherlands. *International Journal of Early Years Education*, *21*(2–3), 178–91, DOI: 10.1080/09669760.2013.832949

Volden, M., Pettersen, G. O. & Ødegaard, Elin Eriksen. (2016). Ida och kuben - att utforska matematik och surfplatta på et lekfullt sätt. [*Ida and the Cube – Exploration of Playful Mathematics and Pads*] Studentlitteratur AB, pp. 199–227.

Vygotsky, L.S. (1998). *The Collected Works of L.S. Vygotsky: Child Psychology.* (Vol 5). (M.J. Hall, & R.W. Rieber, Trans.) (Ed. English translation). Kluwer Academic and Plenum Publishers.

Part One

Macro-transitions within and across Educational Cultures: Children's Explorations as a New Conception in Transitions

2

Ideas for a Radical-local Approach to Care and Support for Children's Playful Exploration in Preschool and Transition to School

Mariane Hedegaard and Naussúnguag Lyberth

In the Nordic approach to early childhood education and care (ECEC) play has been seen as central. In the tradition in Denmark a central activity has been free play (uninterrupted by adults) (Andersen, 2004). Such an approach contrast with an orientation to ECEC where focus is on preparing children for school with activities oriented to math and reading abilities, that has entered the tradition (Hedegaard, 2017).

Our aim in this chapter has been to show a third way and formulate principles for ECEC that support children's exploration through play that also may prepare children for transition to school without creating schoolification activities in kindergarten or daycare (e.g. to create activities that support children's social and cultural formation without drawing school activities into kindergarten practice).

We will argue that caregivers through care and cooperation should support children's playful exploration of the local community and nature building images of the central activities here. The inspiration to transcend both the new wave of schoolification and the tradition of 'free play' has been the radical-local approach to education (Hedegaard & Chaiklin, 2005) that forwards a double move between local experience and general understandings. Another inspiration comes from Davydov and Kurdriavtsev's (1998) theory of development of images as central in play and important for later concept learning in school. We will argue, building especially on Lisina's research (1985), that caring support through practical situated communication and play are the way to support children's explorative activities, learning and development in ECEC. How these ideas can be combined to a new approach for ECEC we will formulate in relation to daycare and kindergarten practice in Greenland[1] building on the existing programme that has been promoted there the last ten years as *effective pedagogue* developed in cooperation with *Centre for Research in Education, Diversity and Excellence* (CREDE) (Tharp et al., 2000). To accomplish this, we draw on the conceptual relations Hedegaard's (2014) wholeness model depicted in Figure 2.1, and outline in Table 2.1.

The societal condition for practice may be seen both in the laws, the material and human conditions that society provide for ECEC in kindergartens and daycare. Preschool education is closely connected with *societal values* (Hedegaard & Munk, 2019; Johansson et al., 2018). In the approach presented here the values for preschool education are connected to ideals in the Nordic countries of a good life for children, for family life and to the value of society's investment in kindergartens. These values are explicated in the laws and regulations that the government formulates for preschool practice.

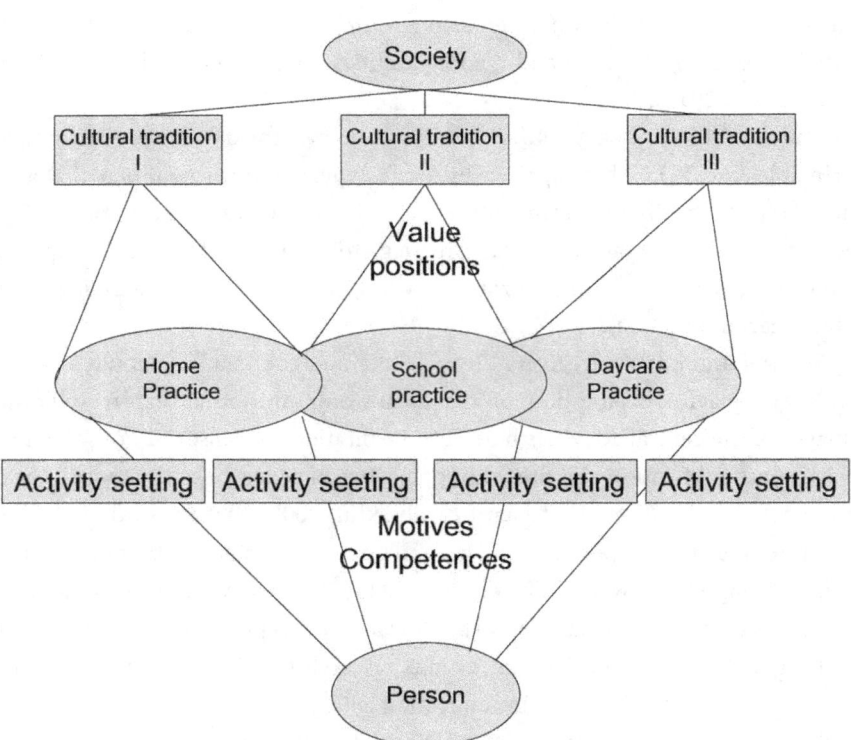

Figure 2.1 The relations between society-practice and persons with cultural traditions and activity settings as mediating links.

Table 2.1 Different perspectives on early childhood education

Perspective	Process/Demands	Dynamic
Society	Societal traditions and value demands	Societal conditions/needs
Institution	Practice demands for type of participation	Value goals/objectives/motives
Activity settings	Social situation demands on both child and others	Situated motivation/engagement/interests
Person	Reciprocal demands for ways of participating in an activity	Motive orientations/intentions

Source: M. Hedegaard (2014) [Modified]

The practice in kindergarten reflects the societies *objectives/value motives* with daycare institutions that over historical periods are reflected in the different kind of practice that the tradition had promoted. This makes different demands in the different periods for how the concrete practice is realized. In *concrete institutions* in a given period variation may be found between the specific institutions as well as in a given institutions between the staff's values for children's care and education.

The activity settings in the Nordic ECEC institutions value cooperation, play and exploration, as central for children's personality development and life capabilities but also for preparing them to school life (Hedegaard & Munk, 2019; Hedegaard & Ødegaard, 2020; Johansson et al., 2018). In this chapter we will concretize these aspects in concrete suggestions for activities.

For children and caregivers, the activities in daily life create both demands for the children and demands upon the staff but should also give possibility for children's motive development through the staffs support and care.

The chapter will conclude with an outline for a *radical-local* curriculum oriented towards practice development in daycare and kindergarten in Greenland, aimed at orientation the educational activities towards local community practice in everyday life including music, drama, art and science that support children's capabilities and motive development oriented to school activities.

Radical-local Education Related to Children's Development in Preschool and School Age

In the cultural-historical tradition children's development is conceptualized as a life course through qualitatively different institutions (Hedegaard, 2009). Based on the conception of different age periods in children's life course

(Bozhovich, 2009; Elkonin, 1999a; Lisina, 1985; Piaget, 1955), children in each age period acquire different capabilities that are connected to societal ideals for the specific periods. The transition from kindergarten to school marks a qualitative change in children's development through the change in the institutional activity settings that children participate in. Kindergarten and school create different learning settings because their objectives, traditions and practices are different. These differences offer different possibilities for activity settings, making new demands on the participants. For some children the transition from kindergarten to school will be smoother than for others. Nonetheless, it will imply some kind of rupture because of the difference in demands in the different activity settings.

The conception in the cultural-historical approach (Davydov & Kurdriavtsev, 1998; Elkonin, 1999a; Hedegaard & Munk, 2019; Vygotsky, 1998; Winther-Lindqvist, 2019) is that the transfer from kindergarten to school should *not* be seen as (a) continuity, *neither* as (b) accommodating the social and pedagogical task of preschool education to the requirement of and characteristics of school instruction (i.e. by pressing reading and calculating into systematic activities in kindergarten). Nor should educators in school use an approach of further developing the elementary body of knowledge and skills that children bring from kindergarten.

Education should *not* according to Davydov and Kurdriavtsev (1998) become directed at conceptual learning in ECEC but instead be oriented towards imagination and play activities. Davydov and Kurdriavtsev point to the discontinuity in children's development between preschool and early school age and to the importance of the development of images through role play to prepare children for school. This at the same time comes to create crises for the young child, when experiencing his or her own lack of capacity for acting the way the adults do. The radical-local approach (Hedegaard & Chaiklin, 2005) that is developed in relation to school practice may from this perspective be relevant for preschool education if we take the difference in preschool children's leading activities (e.g. practical situated communication and play) into consideration and see preschool education as aimed at children's development of their images of events and activities. The main point in this approach is that radical as the root or general aspect of knowledge becomes connected to local knowledge. This means that the preschool child's experiences, through imagination, are directed towards general images of activities. Davydov (1982) argues that knowledge and thinking in school should be theoretical which implies an understanding of the relations between core concepts in subject areas (i.e. in biology that animal species are connected with their habitat) and methods to study and explore relations.² These new demands in school presuppose children's capabilities acquired in preschool of imagining activities and events for their acquisition of theoretical knowledge and thinking.

> In the process of cognition, theoretical thinking and productive imagination perform a *unified* function. They enable the person to comprehend the universal principles governing the development of things and events, and to transform and make sense of the world as a whole in accordance with them. The only difference is that in thinking, these principles are grasped in the form of abstract concepts, whereas in imagination they are grasped in the form of special images whose content derives from the contradictory unity of the universal and the individual, the necessary and the random.
>
> (Davydov & Kurdriavtsev, 1998, p. 42)

Caring Social Relations and Play as Core in Early Childhood Education

Lisina's (1985) research has oriented us to focus on emotional interactions and caring demands as foundation for how different periods in early childhood may unfold. A development where the child is active and exploring does not take place alone by the child's direct contact with the environment (as Piaget's, 1955, theory depicts). Neither do we see play as natural activity that are biological determined but it is through the relation to the adult that the child's playful exploration of the environment is created and by the adults attention and demands to the child's interaction that new capabilities develop.

It is important, Lisina writes (1985), that the adult builds up a communicative loving atmosphere around the young child and communicate with the child about the daily practical activities. This way of loving and caring interactions is the foundation for the young child's orientation to play and language development. Infant's simple object-play Lisina characterizes as *situated cooperation* that may result in the child's first forms of *imagination* that led to a child's further capabilities to transcend to the next phase of development characterized by *practical cooperation with role play as a central activity*. Other children also become central in a child's practical cooperation when it turns into play activity.

Fleer (2013) points out the importance of collective imagination in children's play activity. In play children attach new meaning to objects and actions and may together create imagined worlds. Analysing social fantasy play, Schousboe (2013) points out that there are three spheres in play structures that vows in and out of each other. These are the sphere of reality and the sphere of imagination and combining these two is the sphere of staging or planning. Through moving in and out of the three spheres in collective play children both explore reality and build capacity and find new ways to contribute to a shared imagination. In the sphere of planning the child build images of activities, as described by Davydov and Kurdriavtsev (1998). Through joint play activities and negotiation in play children also learn to control themselves (Elkonin, 1999b), a capability that school demands. Adults support children's development of play by giving material possibilities. They can also directly initiate an imagined world in play as in the Golden Key approach (Kravtsov & Kravtsova, 2009). The playworld approach formulated by Lindquist (1995) and developed by Fleer (2019) demonstrates another way for how adults may enter into the play and support building images of activities. Elkonin (1999b) points out that it is through the relation with adults and imagining adults' activities that preschool children's motive for learning and for school activities evolve.

So to conclude it is important to support play activity in a communicative atmosphere, and to support children to engage in playful exploration, so they may develop images related to activities in their everyday community. These images become central in children's learning activity when they transcend to school, to learn in different subject areas oriented to theoretical knowledge.

The Tradition for Early Childhood Education in Greenland

The above ideas about playful exploration, we will exemplify in relation to practice development in kindergarten and daycare in Greenland. To engage in practice development in early childhood education one need to have a good impression and knowledge of the practice tradition one wants to develop. This section will therefore contain a short outline of ECEC in Greenland.

The history of ECEC in Greenland should be seen in relation to the Danish colonization of the country. The preschool institutions and practices are modelled after the Danish system with focus on free play and the last year in kindergarten towards preparation for school. When home rule was established, the Greenlandic Government created their laws for ECEC (Landstingsforordning nr. 10, 2008). The same formulation of goals for preschool children's education was kept in the law from 2012 at the establishment of self-rule. This states that daycare should support children's development and their acquisition of respect for parents, the local culture and nature, other cultures as well as human rights and freedom. The strong focus on the local community and nature transcends the Danish tradition, though being central in the law in Greenland for ECEC it is not yet completely realized, as we have experienced through observation in several kindergarten and daycares in Greenland in connection with creating a screening material for three- and five-year-old children (Hedegaard & Lyberth, 2019).

When home rule was established in Greenland the tradition from CREDE was introduced by inviting Ronald Tharp as a consultant for development of the practice in both school and daycare/kindergarten. The CREDE tradition, based on Vygotsky's educational ideas (Tharp et al., 2000), was introduced into daycare practice in Greenland, after it first being introduced in school formulated as five standards. These five standards were transferred to guide preschool education with two new standards added (S6 and S7) (see Table 2.2) that especially took the Danish tradition in the Greenlandic daycare practice into consideration and was named Effective Pedagogic.

The adding of S6 and S7 in the new educational approach for daycare and kindergarten practice in Greenland was important reflecting Vygotsky's idea that education in preschool should orient children to play and imagination and follow children's interest (Vygotsky, 1987). S3 was also reformulated to focus on the everyday activities. The three other standards S2, S4 and S5 were oriented to prepare children for school. In the following we will argue for a new interpretation of the pedagogic in ECEC in Greenland oriented to the radical-local approach to overcome the problems of schoolification that several of the standards of effective pedagogic implies.

Table 2.2 The seven standards for early childhood education: Effective pedagogic

S1) joint productive activity
S2) language development and emerging writing and reading skills
S3) contextualization (e.g. transition of knowledge between kindergarten home and community)
S4) promoting complex thinking through questions
S5) instructional conversation
S6) modelling, visualizing, demonstrating
S7) following children's interest to initiate shared activity

Source: M. Hedegaard & N. Lyberth, In *Supporting Difficult Transitions. Children Young People and Their Carers* (Bloomsbury Academic, 2019).

Traditional Activity Settings in Kindergartens in Greenland (and Denmark)

A day in kindergarten may start 7 am and end at 5 pm. In general, in most kindergartens in Greenland like Denmark, in the morning sessions from 8 to 12, the activities mostly go on inside. In the morning the children arrive 'peu en peu' as it fits with the parents work hours. The staff meet the children and parents and take care that the arriving child get care to settle down. The children often are activated in the first hours in the morning with different games that are put out on a table or by paper, pencil and crayons so they can draw. Toys are also available. At around 10 am the children and staff are gathered, and it is time for the circle activity, where children are sitting on pillows or small chairs together with the staff in a circle. One from the staff records the children and then takes up a topic that different children are asked to respond to. After the circle dialogs the children in general play with each other or play games until lunchtime. Around 11.30 they eat lunch, in some kindergarten they have warm food for lunch, eventually three out of five days.

After the lunch meal the children are asked to go outdoor to play in the yard except in bad weather. Outside the children have three-wheled bikes and other play equipment. Sometimes the staff takes children on tours, where to, depends on where they live in Greenland, it may be up in the mountains or to the harbour. They have fruit at 2:30–3 pm. and then they have activities with a staff member or play again. When the staffs play with the children it is mostly inside with two to four children, and then the staff may use the ideas of the seven standards in their communication with the children.

The activities in the kindergarten can be evaluated both from (1) a societal perspective of creating a daycare practice, (2) the perspective of the staff (the pedagogical perspective) and (3) the perspective of the children. The different

Table 2.3 Different perspectives in educational activity

	The societal perspective	The staff's (pedagogical) perspective	The children's perspective
Process	Practice	Activities/Demands	Actions/Intentions
Type of interactions	Traditions	Tasks/Demands	Interaction/Demands
Dynamics	Objectives/Challenges	Objectives	Motive orientation/Conflicts

perspectives are presented in Table 2.3, and the differences perspectives are differentiated into type of interactions, dynamics and demands.

In the following example taken from a kindergarten in Greenland the focus will be on the pedagogical perspective analysing the staff's and head-teacher's activities.

Exemplifying a Concrete Morning in a Greenlandic Kindergarten

Extract from Observation, 9 September 2014, 8.30–11.30, observer Mariane Hedegaard.

The children's names are anonymized. Teacher B (the leader of the kindergarten) speaks both Danish and Greenlandic. In most kindergarten Greenlandic is the primary language. In this kindergarten they use both Danish and Greenlandic. Focus on teacher B.

1. When the observers arrive 8.30 am the teacher B is playing Calaha with Inuk. When finish she exclaims YES, and asks who won today? Together with the child she counts the pieces. She counts '1,2,3' and the child repeats. Teacher B names several times the Danish number for four (fire), finally the child says 'vier' (he cannot pronounce the f).
2. Two children that arrive approach teacher B. She puts her arm around Andy2, and asks if he got clean trousers with him in his kindergarten bag, and tells him that he shall remember to say when he needs to pee, so she can help him to go out (to the toilet) to pee.
3. The teacher has now changed her position to the other side of the table and starts a new play with the same child, another child Sabine joins to participate.
4. Now there are five children in the room (Inuk, Sylvest, Andy2, Luna and Lise) but rather soon there are ten.
5. Andy2 is playing with Lego blocks together with Lise.
6. Sylvest has been sitting with electro picture lottery, approximately half an hour. Now he finishes.

    Hansine (staff) plays Kahlua with Cinderella.

    Luna, who is sitting at the table in front of me, uses a Lego block as mobile phone at the same time she also colours in a colouring book along with Tupparnaq.

    Andy2 comes and puts a toy-dog down at the table in front of me.

    Sabina and Inuk play Kahlua for a short time.

    Andy1 still plays with big Lego blocks.

7. The observer notices, that it seems that Andy2 needs to pee and says so to Julie (staff). She takes him to the toilet.
8. Teacher B's mobile phone rings and she goes out of the room.
9. When she is back, she sits down and talks with the two girls who are colouring in the colouring book and asks about the pictures in the book. She counts the arms of a squid that Luna is colouring and explains that it has eight arms. Luna smiles and tells about a starfish. Teacher B asks another adult to tell her the name of a starfish in Greenlandic.
10. Teacher B is now sitting at the big table in the middle of the room, Inuk, and two other boys and Lise and Julie are also placed there.
11. At the small table where they play Kahlua there are now three girls. Teacher B talks with them from her position at the big table.
12. All the children have now been seated at the different tables.
    The circle activity starts.
13. A staff member holds the paper with children's names to record their attendance. This is done in Greenlandic. Each child is asked to tell their full name, where they live and their father and mothers name.
14. Teacher B asks what day it is.
15. Then a staff member points at the days in the calendar and a child has to point at the day number, when the children in chorus say the day's name.
16. Teacher B has taken Inuk on her lab.
17. Luna gets the task to point at the day number, but she points faster than the children can pronounce the name.
18. Teacher B hands Inuk over to Hansine (staff) and helps Luna to point by supporting her arms and counting aloud together. They count to thirty-one.
19. Then teacher B points at the month, January, February, that she names together with the children's chorus.
20. When the circle activity is finished the children want to go outside, but teacher B says they can forget that since it is raining, as they can see, and she points to a new girl who came late in the morning and still has raindrops on her cloth.
21. The new girl got a bun when she came in.
22. The children can now again play with the puzzle, Lego, Ludo etc.
23. Teacher B asks Sylvest: 'What do you say, should we play Ludo together?'
24. Five children want to play with teacher B.
25. Sylvest finds the game.
26. Cinderella, Spiderman, Inunngua will play Luna too with Sylvest and teacher B.

27. Teacher B goes away, and the kids sit quietly waiting.
    Hansine plays a kind of card with two of the children.
    Teacher B brings milk to the new girl, she still has the bun, she got when she arrived, but she didn't really eat anything.
    Teacher B comes back and plays Ludo with the Ludo group.
    The new girl has now found a colouring book and a colour pencil and starts colouring with the pencil; she is still sitting at a table for herself.
    The new girl asks teacher B about something in the colouring book, she sits on a chair adjacent to teacher B, but with her back to the table.
    Now Inunnguaq leaves the Ludo game. Teacher B says: 'What! Do we not play Ludo?

Analyses of Teacher B's Activities

Activities

Teacher B welcomes children. She plays both Kahlua and Ludo with children, she leads the circle activity.

Motives/Demands

By welcoming children she shows she *cares* for them as shown through the way she greets Andy2 and at the same time making *demand*s that he shall remember to tell when he has to pee. It can also be seen in relation to the new girl, when she gives her a bun, and a little later a glass of milk and take care she gets to play, and when she talks with the two girls about the pictures that they are colouring in a colouring book. This is also demonstrated when she plays Calaha with Inuk and Ludo with a group of children. *The demands she put on the children* is to tell when they need to go to the toilet and to *finish the game* they have started. The demands can also be seen in her expectation that the children respond in the circle activity.

Objectives

When she plays, she tried to do it as an equal partner, but she has an *educational aim* as we see in her interaction with Inuk, where she gets him to count. Also in her interaction with the girls around the colouring book, she ends up counting, she counts the arms of the squid and does not extend the girls' comments that she knows a starfish, so the possibility to talk about water animals is not taken. It seems as her main interest is that children should be able to concentrate over longer period when they participate in the different games and from the circle activity that they get number and counting knowledge. In the circle activity she orients the children to number and month of the year that are factual knowledge. There is no support for role play. It is the *schoolification aspects of the activities that are forwarded*. The daycare law that was stated in 2008 has not yet had much influence on the chosen content in the pedagogical interactions.

Curriculum Ideas for a Radical-local Approach in ECEC

If we follow the theoretical points made earlier about what is important for children's development in ECEC, we found that it is adults caring relations to promote explorative play activities through practical cooperative communication. When adult's activities function as models for children's play children may develop images of activities that give them wishes for starting school to achieve the capabilities for activities in real life (Davydov & Kurdriavtsev, 1998; Elkonin, 1999a; Lisina, 1985). A curriculum around practical cooperative communication and play in kindergarten/daycare includes both support and caring demands.

Effective Pedagogic with its seven standards has been used in education of preschool teachers locally all over Greenland. Four of these standards may fit with the theory for ECEC advocated in this chapter. These are (S1) joint productive activity; (S3) contextualization; (S6) modelling, visualizing and demonstrating; and (S7) following children's interest to initiate shared activities. These four standards we will use to concretize the theoretical analyses formulated by Elkonin, Davydov and Kurdriavtsev and Lisina, about how to communicate and interact with children, oriented to local content and directed towards playful exploration.[3] So what we suggest in the following is to build on these four standards from the Effective Pedagogic system and forwards the local knowledge even more than has been done in Effective Pedagogic using the radical-local approach. Thereby we intent to create an outline of a curriculum for ECEC in Greenland supporting children's development of capabilities to play and create images of activities and learn to respect the family, local culture and nature. The inspiration from the radical-local approach reflects the ideal of orienting children towards local content and through cooperative demands creates an oscillation between concrete experiences and general understandings.

An example of how to relate local knowledge with general knowledge is visiting shops to relate concrete knowledge of where and how to buy food with an understanding of the relation between a shopkeeper and a customer. This can be done by the care persons supporting children to play shops in the kindergarten and talk about events connected to visiting shops. Furthermore, the educational task is then to help children to get these different events connected to more general understandings of humans' relation to each other and to nature. A way to do this is through either novel reading or further excursion (i.e. to places where children can experience how a seal is brought to shore and how it is parted and distributed), and supporting play about these events of hunting for food and distribution of food through stores or through community sharing.

For children in preschool the general knowledge should take form as imaginations through pictures and narratives. Davydov and Kurdriavtsev write that the difference between preschool children's and school children's knowledge is that preschool children build images. '[I]mages whose content derives from the contradictory unity of the universal and the individual, the necessary and the random' (Davydov & Kurdriavtsev, 1998, p. 42). This way of acquiring knowledge in ECEC as images of activities based on experiences from visits, pictures, narratives and literature songs and music reflected in explorative play activity an drawings is a preconditions for school children's knowledge acquisition that draws on these experiences and images of activities but are oriented to learn the real stuff to become able to participate in real-life activities.

To care for and educate a group of preschool children the preschool teacher should build collective activities for acquiring experiences and play (Stanek, 2017), supporting social fantasy play (Fleer, 2013), to build collective images. This may be found in the ideas for play-world activities (Fleer, 2019). A play-world activity setting may stretch over some days. Through this approach it may be possibly for children to create collective coherent images of activities when participation over time in explorative play activities that develop around a theme. The way it has been realized in the projects by Fleer is that the activity takes departure in children literature. We would suggest that such an approach also may take departure in real events that can be played through, as in Elkonin's (1999b) example of visits to Zoo, or in excursion to nature (Sørensen & Birkeland, 2019) or drama activities in local institutions (Ødemotland, 2020).

The ideal learning curriculum/learning programme for ECEC is that children are both learning how and learning what in relation to a theme, where they learn to cooperate with each other and adults in the activities. Therefore, when we in the following suggest a curriculum for preschool children, the activities take place as cooperation between children and adults with the adults also as possible play partner but always as supporting and guiding the children in their exploration within the actual themes. In relation to the Greenlandic preschool law the result should be that children learn to act respectfully but also build more general images/understandings of how and why to act in relation to family, nature and community.

An Idealized Example for a Preschool Curriculum

To build a curriculum for preschool children based on the theoretical principles outline earlier in this chapter, we suggest four themes[4] to structure the curriculum for a period of a year each lasting three to six month, depending on how easy it is to realize for the staff in daycare/kindergarten to engage the children. Each theme relates to children' close environment (i.e. family, nature and community):

1. The way families live and the extended family
2. The sea and its inhabitants and human's relation to the sea
3. Community and its work life
4. Nature and animal life in the artic

Each theme should be announced with a big sign in the period, where drawings from children about the theme also may be presented. The staff should in the period orient to the dominating theme hopefully supported by the parents. Each thematic period could involve some parents in the morning session that volunteer to contribute to workshop related to the theme of the period. The children should have the choice of accepting to participate in the morning workshop or just want to play or draw with available play material related to the theme of the period.

Activity Settings in Kindergartens

The day in a kindergarten has traditionally been split up in different activity settings, this tradition has developed through necessity and should be kept, but content should be modified to create continuity in children's play and exploration. Therefore, children should not clear away the material they use for play or exploration after each session. Instead they should be allowed to leave the sessions where the staff helps them organize their play material so they can continue the next day if they have not finished their play. Playful exploring activities preferable last some time for children to come acquainted

Table 2.4 General suggestion for how to work with the way families live and the extended family

Activity setting	Content	Teacher's activity	Children's activity	Standards
Parents may lead morning activity oriented to exploration	Workshops for children oriented to family or community activities	Making room for parents, supporting their activity	Contributing with ideas. Getting task in the workshop	Joint productive activity (S1). Modelling (S6)
Circle time and musical activity	Starting with musical activity relevant for the family relations. Reflection over last afternoons novel. Discussing the mornings' workshop	Starting with musical activity and guiding the activities and supporting children to participate	Learning to participate in musical activities and singing. Remembering and reflection about content	Joint productive activity (S1). Contextualization (S3). Both staff guided, modelling (S6) and child guided (S7)
Play/Drawings/Games	Children's choice	Supporting with material and otherwise	Children's initiative	Child guided activity (7). Modelling (S6)
Lunch	Local food and tradition around eating. Conversation	Conversation about the food and traditions. Taking care to include all children	Participating in the conversation, while eating	Modelling (S6)
Afternoon activity	Grandparents' parents' activities and relation to children	Taking care of children. Leading drama play for all children or supporting child group initiated play	Playing	Joint productive activity (S1). Contextualization (S3). Drama play (S6)
Fruit	Cooperation	Taking care that they share the fruit	Learning to share and take care of each other	Modelling (S6)
Novel reading	Sibling, grandparents and uncle and ants in families and their relations and activities	Taking care that the content engages the children to listen and comment	Engaging and commenting	Contextualization (S3)

with a thematic area so they can develop stable images of activities and events connected with different themes. General suggestions for how to work with a theme that will be used in the activity session in a kindergarten are illustrated in Figure 2.4, for the theme: 'The way families live and the extended family.'

Reformulating the Use of the Standards of Effective Pedagogic

Since the standards of effective pedagogic are well-known in daycare/kindergarten in Greenland, though they are mostly used in small groups, we will point out how we suggest they are interpreted in relation to a radical local approach. We see (S1) joint productive activity as central in all settings in kindergarten/daycare in such an approach except when receiving the individual child in the morning. To accomplish this, it is important with a shared theme, that children can engage in, especially when the staff has to take into consideration also the standard (S7) of following children initiatives and suggestions. The standard (S3), 'contextualization', is for us the key standard in the daily activities. To use this standard means to widen children's experience from their home with new experiences. In the concrete practice this activity may reach out to parents and grandparents, so they may be included in some of the activities in kindergarten. In the standard (S6), modelling, visualizing and demonstrating, we find the possibility for the staff to support explorative play where the adults also may participate, not through instructing the children but by participating on equal foot with the children in explorative play activities. The (S7) following children's interest to initiate shared activities is important for engaging children, especially combined with the standard of contextualization (S3) as may take place through visits to parents' workplaces or other places in the community. By using the standards (S7) and (S3) together to create activities it may be possible to focus on the relation between people in dramatized play activities (Ødemotland, 2020) so children get ideas of how their community functions and relations between people and animals (i.e. the shopkeeper and the customer, the police and the one who asks for help, the teacher in school and the pupil, the hunter and his sled dogs). Since five of the standards were formulated originally in relation to school activities, we will suggest not to attend to three of these in ECEC but to leave these for later school activities. These are (S2) language development and emerging writing and reading skills, (S4) promoting complex thinking through questions and (S5) instructional conversation. These three standards (S2, S4, and S5) may be responsible for the schoolification one finds in many kindergartens/daycares in Greenland. We advise to leave these activities out of

ECEC practice and instead support explorative play and to promote children's image building of activities.

Conclusion

The aim in this chapter has been to discuss how to formulate principles for ECEC that support children's exploration and social and cultural formation that also may prepare children's transition to school without creating schoolification activities in kindergarten or daycare (e.g. to create activities that support children's development without drawing school activities into kindergarten practice). To accomplish this one needs to orient to the conditions the state gives and demands for the practice. In the concrete case, of Greenland the government support ECEC by giving conditions for all children to participate in kindergarten/daycare, but also demands for respecting the local culture and nature. It has both led to developing the ECEC by introducing the ideas from the CREDE to Greenland but since the CREDE standards have been originally formulated for school the use of these standards in kindergarten/daycare practice has also introduced schoolification into this practice. This may also connect with the idea that the transition to school has to be smooth. Ideas that dominate the Danish traditions that also influence the daycare/kindergarten practices in Greenland (Hedegaard & Munk, 2017; Winter-Lindqvist, 2019).

Vygotsky (1987) pointed out that in early childhood education the social relation in the concrete everyday life and play activity are the foundation for children acquisition of capabilities. Capabilities as Davydov and Kurdriavtsev (1998) characterized as abilities to relate to the world through playful exploration and acquisition of general images for activities, a capacities that for young children and preschool children, Lisina (1985) showed, are dependent of caring and loving support and demands.

Children's transfer to school creates a break in their daily lives and may lead to minor or major crises. Such crises can be met in two ways, either as borderlands, that have to be bridged, or as completely new life practice that has to be celebrated as a rite of passage (Garpelin, 2014). The tradition in Denmark and Greenland builds on the bridging ideas. Based on the theories presented in this chapter, we will argue for that transition to school should be handled as a break from the earlier way of preschool education.

A transition to school, we have argued, has to change children's activities from exploring and play activities to real learning activities. Children should in school be supported to use their acquired capabilities from preschool of playful exploration and imagining activities to learning within different subject areas. The transition that takes place should go from children's experiencing the close environment building general images of activities to enter into a learning environment where they have to acquire methods and use concepts from different subjects to analyse and explore relations between matters. Development implies qualitative changes in children's social relation, and new motives for orientation to the world (Hedegaard, 2019). Therefore, this transition should be celebrated as entering a new practice necessary for a child's development.

The inspiration to create a practice that allows such a break and at the same time prepare children for the transition through their acquisition of capabilities for further development in school comes from several sides. From the importance of collective play for children's imagination to evolve (Elkonin, 1999b; Fleer, 2013; Schousboe, 2013). It also comes from Elkonin's (1999a) theory about how adults' serve as models for children's orientation to transition based on their experience of adults activities that at some point is not enough to play out, instead they come to wish to be able to do and control these activities.

How to formulate a concrete curriculum took departure in the radical-local approach of Hedegaard and Chaiklin (2005). The concrete example has been the educational practice in kindergarten and daycare in Greenland where Effective Pedagogic (based on the CREDE tradition) already has started to change the kindergarten and daycare practice. The idea has been to modify the Effective Pedagogic approach that already influence ECEC in Greenland and draw on the standards in CREDE that fit with the radical local approach presented in this chapter, which implies that children's acquisition of images of activities becomes more related to the local cultural and nature seen as a whole.

Notes

1 In Greenland, the government has institutionalized education and care for all preschool children. In the cities it takes place in kindergartens, but since the population is sparse at the settlements, it takes place as daycare in a daycare house, with local women as the staff.
2 This has been contrasted by empirical knowledge as categorical or factual knowledge based on abstractions (see Hedegaard & Chaiklin, 2005).
3 The way this national education of staff has been organized locally by the Center for ECEC under the department of Education in Greenland to promote the seven

standards is quite impressive implementing practice development in concrete institutional practice through educating staff locally and using coaching as a method to reach all (Wyat & Lyberth, 2011).

4   Other themes can also be used, the idea is just that it should relate to the local environment.

References

Andersen, P. Ø. (2004). Daginstitutionernes indhold og pædagogik i historisk belysning. In T. Ellegaard Og A. H. Stanek (red.), *Læreplaner i børnehaven*. Vejle: Kroghs forlag.

Bozhovich, L. I. (2009). The social situation of child development. *Journal of Russian and East European Psychology, 47*(4), 59–86. https://doi.org/10.2753/RPO1061-0405470403

Davydov, V. V. (1982). Ausbildung der Lerntätigkeit. In V. V. Davydov, J. Lompsher & A. K Markova (Eds.), *Ausbildung der Lerntätigkeit bei Schülern* (pp. 37–44). Volk und Wissen.

Davydov, V. V., & Kurdriavtsev, V. T. (1998). Developmental education: The theoretical foundation of continuity between the preschool and primary school stages. *Russian Education and Society, 40*(7), 37–64. https://doi.org/10.2753/RES1060-9393400737

Elkonin, D. B. (1999a). Toward the stages in mental development of children. *Journal of Russian and East European Psychology, 37*(6), 11–30. https://doi.org/10.2753/RPO1061-0405370611

Elkonin, D. B. (1999b). The development of play in pre-schoolers. *Journal of Russian and East European Psychology, 37*(6), 31–70. https://doi.org/10.2753/RPO1061-0405370631

Fleer, M. (2013). Collective imagination in play. In I. Schousboe & D. Winter-Lindqvist (Eds.), *Children's Play and Development: Cultural-historical Perspectives* (pp. 73–88). Springer.

Fleer, M. (2019). Children and teachers transitioning in playworlds. The contradiction between real relations and play relations as a source of children's development. In M. Hedegaard & M. Fleer (Eds.), *Children's Transitions in Everyday Life and Institutions* (pp. 185–206). Bloomsbury Academic.

Garpelin, A. (2014). *Transition to School: A Rite of Passage*. Springer.

Hedegaard, M. (2009) Children's development from a cultural-historical approach: Children's activity in everyday local settings as foundation for their development. *Mind, Culture, and Activity, 16*, 64–81. https://doi.org/10.1080/10749030802477374

Hedegaard, M. (2014). The significance of demands and motives across practices in children's learning and development: An analysis of learning in home and school. *Learning, Culture, and Activity, 3*, 188–94. https://doi.org/10.1016/j.lcsi.2014.02.008

Hedegaard, M. (2017). When daycare professionals' values for transition to school do not align with the educational demands from society and school: A practice developing research project for daycare professionals' support to children's transition to school. In A. Edwards (Ed.), *A Cultural-historical Approach to Collaboration* (pp. 247–64). Cambridge University Press.

Hedegaard, M., & Chaiklin, S. (2005). *Radical-local Teaching and Learning*. Aarhus University Press.

Hedegaard, M., & Lyberth, N. (2019). Radical-local screening of preschool children's social situations of development: From abilities to activities. In M. Hedegaard & A. Edwards (Eds.), *Supporting Difficult Transitions: Children Young People and Their Carers* (pp. 91–112). Bloomsbury Academic.

Hedegaard, M., & Munk, K. (2019). Play and life competences as core in transition from kindergarten to school: Tension between values in early childhood education. In M. Hedegaard & M. Fleer (Eds.), *Children's Transitions in Everyday Life and Institutions* (pp. 21–46). London: Bloomsbury Academic.

Hedegaard, M., & Ødegaard, E. (2020). *Children's Exploration and Cultural Formation*. Springer.

Johansson, E., Emilson, A., & Puroila, A-M. (2018). *Values in Early Childhood Education*. Springer.

Kravtsov, G, & Kravtsova, E. (2009). Cultural-historical psychology in the practice of education. In M. Fleer, M. Hedegaard & J. Tudge (Eds.), *Childhood Studies and the Impact of Globalization: Policies and Practices at the Global Levels. Word Yearbook of Education 2009*. New York: Routledge.

Landstingsforordningen nr. 10, 2008, om pædagogisk udviklende tilbud til børn i førskolealderen.

Lindquist, G. (1995). The aesthetics of play: A didactic study of play and culture in preschools. *Acta Universitatis Upsaliensis. Uppsala Studies in Education, 62*, 234. http://dx.doi.org/10.1080/0957514960170102

Lisina, M. I. (1985). *Child-Adults-Peer*. Progress Publisher.

Ødemotland, S. (2020). Exploration through process drama with kindergarten children. In M. Hedegaard & E. Ødegaard (Eds.), *Children's Exploration and Cultural Formation* (pp. 173–87). Springer.

Piaget, J. (1955). The construction of reality in the child. Routledge & Kegan.

Schousboe, I. (2013). The structure of fantasy play and its implication for good and evil games (12–28). In I. Schousboe & D. Winter-Lindqvist (Eds.), *Children's Play and Development: Cultural-historical Perspectives* (pp. 13–27). Springer.

Sørensen, H. V., & Birkeland, Å. (2019). Children's explorative activities in kindergarten playgrounds: A case study in China and Norway. In *Children's Exploration and Cultural Formation*. Springer.

Stanek, A. H. (2017). *Børns fælleskaber og fælleskabernes betydning*. Roskilde Universitetsforlag.

Tharp, R. G., Estrada, P., Dalton S. S., & Yamauchi, L. A. (2000). *Teaching Transformed: Receiving Excellence, Fairness, Inclusion and Harmony*. Westview Press.

Vygotsky, L. S. (1987). *Problems of General Psychology: The Collected Work of L. S. Vygotsky* (Vol 1). Plenum Press.

Vygotsky, L. S. (1998). *Child Psychology: The Collected Works of L. S. Vygotsky* (Vol 5). Plenum Press.

Wyat, T., & Lyberth, N. (2011). Addressing systemic oppression in Greenland's Preschools: The adaptation of a coaching model. *Equity & Excellence in Education*, 44(2), 221–32. http://dx.doi.org/10.1080/10665684.2011.558421

Winther-Lindqvist, D. (2013). Playing with social identities: Play in everyday life in a peer group in day care. In I. Schousboe & D. Winther-Lindqvist (Eds.), *Children's Play and Development: Cultural-historical Perspectives* (pp. 29–54). Springer.

Winther-Lindqvist, D. (2019). Becoming a school child: A positive developmental crisis. In M. Hedegaard & M. Fleer (Eds.), *Children's Transitions in Everyday Life and Institutions* (pp. 47–70). Bloomsbury Academic.

A Pedagogy of Collaborative Exploration

A Case Study of the Transition from a Monocultural Entity in National Celebration Rituals to a Multi-layered Informed Pedagogical Practice

Elin Eriksen Ødegaard

Introduction – Co-exploration[1] through Institutional Transitional Events

Children and teachers possess the human capacity to explore, discover and create, as well as form and be transformed in ecological interplay with the local community and society in which they live. In this chapter, exploration is considered a driving force in human activity and of special interest to early childhood education. Approaches towards education that begin from a real-world scenario in the form of case studies – in which the problems are not well defined and where children and/or teachers and caregivers are encouraged to build on personal historical histories when shaping their own directions of enquiry – are not new in the field of education. They operate in a wide critical and socio-epistemological field (Ødegaard & Krüger, 2012) and can be seen in practice developmental and practice transformative methodologies such as praxiological approaches (Oliveira-Formoshino & Forrmosinho, 2012), open-ended and relational approaches (Davies, 2011; Fleer, 2013; White, 2016), change-laboratories approaches (Paavola et al., 2004) and radical local approaches (Hedegaard, 2020). The literature on early childhood education within this wide socio-epistemological field all shares a steppingstone of a situated sensitivity and a process of open-ended methodology when understanding, provoking and developing practices. However, the literature is less developed when it comes to descriptions of how exploration unfolds in practice, how artefacts play a significant role, and how the dynamics involved, can be regarded as transitional practices over time.

Through a case study, this chapter investigates transitional events leading to a more nuanced pedagogy where children's and pedagogue's *co-exploration* is the central practice in kindergartens. The chapter adds to our understanding of the notion of exploration, artefacts and transition in the context of early childhood education, by searching for features through a three-dimensional case analysis. The empirical base of this study is a project was called kindergarten as an arena for cultural formation and learning.[2] The idea was to document transitions while working together with staff to build a higher awareness of the teachers' cultural values and the content practices of kindergartens. This partnership research was inspired by German *bildung* and Nordic *didaktik* tradition where practices circle around an interest (a content). According to Pramling et al. a typical Nordic way of understand didactics is connected to the German bildung tradition that presupposes a critical analysis of the choice of content and forms of teaching, what in Nordic countries is known as 'communicative didactics' (Pramling et al., 2019, p. 16). Friedrich Fröbel called this content of interest *the invisible third* (Eikset & Ødegaard, 2020; Fröbel, 1885), referring to the *something* that binds the teacher and the child in a joint focus. In this chapter this will be referred to as a *curricular space*, meaning the dynamics of societal structures, the personal and participatory space, and the content (artefacts, action, reflection and imagination) (Ødegaard & Krüger, 2012).

Moreover, the research design was directed at the transformation of everyday activities to become more co-explorative while at the same time identifying the empirical processes of cultural formation through documenting and analysing the processes and outcomes. The research design was created to bring new knowledge and insights into the content and values in everyday practices. At the same time the project supported higher awareness for the kindergarten staff of the local aspects of culture and learning by focusing on the relation between values and the curricular space. The participatory design secured systematic observations and co-creation of data at the same time as kindergarten teachers were encouraged and provoked to explore, imagine, change, describe and reflect.

This chapter clarifies the notion of exploration in the context of early childhood education through a three-dimensional enquiry space, *Exploration, transition and artefact*. The object of the analysis is

a) *The concept of exploration.* The notion *to explore* often holds positive connotations, such as to investigate, to enquire and to be curious in education – it is a positive verb signifying a process of the agentic child's play, learning

(Nilsson et al., 2018) and cultural formation (Hedegaard & Ødegaard, 2020). Still there is a lack of clarity to the concept of exploration in the context of early childhood education. The aim of the case analysis is therefore to look for features of *collaborative exploration* (co-exploration) in the case.

b) *The transitional events in practice,* as *transition* is often studied in relation to mayor transitions like leaving preschool and entering school, we need more in-depth studies into the *micro-transitions* during the everyday life. In the context of Norway, the micro-transitions connected to celebration of Norway's constitutional celebration and its connected activities are described and analysed. In the current study, this is a shared activity in a manifold sense, first in the sense of collaboration between the staff and researchers and then among the staff. Moreover, it becomes a shared activity between the staff and the children, intertwining with the local culture. The aim of this aspect of analysis is to unfold the processes of transition in their relationship to the cultural affordances given through cultural practice, artefacts, symbols and dialogue.

c) *The significance of artefacts* to understand the content dimension of early childhood education. Artefacts carry symbols and meaning and bring affordances and conditions for the curricular space and how exploration is enacted and performed. Artefacts can also be important thinking tools for transition. The aim of this aspect of analysis is to reveal how the personal and local use of specific artefacts creates the conditions for children's formative development.

The interest here is both theoretical and oriented towards practice. As I see it, exploration entails a dynamic process and captures the relational nature of exploration necessary to achieve quality early childhood education (Ødegaard, 2020) and it is therefore important to study how these dynamic processes are intertwined. A useful way to do that is through unfolding details via a case analysis. The study is framed in a cultural-historical approach to give the appropriate conceptual and analytical tools to describe and understand a change of practice through what I propose as *institutional transitional events*. The case shows how a collaborative study between researchers and kindergartens elicited one of the staff members, Susanne's story, performance and initiatives in 2012; she responded to a task, given by the researchers, that was designed to elicit personal stories, local heritage, imagination and new practices. What happened can be described as an institutional transitional event. Many years later, another staff member, Anne recalls more events that sum up a series of transitional events. The institutional practice transformed over the years to more a context- and co-explorative-oriented practice.

Here, transitions are holistically approached and are regarded as a process of change in institutional settings over time. In line with Vygotsky's conceptualization of human development as 'history of behaviour' (1997, p. 43) when outlining his thinking of 'higher' mental functions as cultural-historical rather than biological in their origins, the current study regards *institutional transitional events* as a 'history of changing practices' in early childhood institutional settings. From this line of thought, human development is not a linear process. Rather, development is a complex process where mental (psychological) functional variations are followed by structural reorganizations (Kellogg & Veresov, 2019, p. 10). Vygotsky (1997) presented development as both natural regularities and cultural-historical laws, both being achronological and disproportionate. In short, this means that the development of separate psychological functions in humans does not correspond with chronological time. In a perspective of cultural formation, development is rather uneven and cyclical; the time of change is more like an uneven wave or a spiral than like a simple linear function. A Bakhtinian metaphor of the *loophole* (Bakhtin, 1973) can indicate how a transition in an institutional context is not at all a process where a certain input results in a certain output. This metaphor of a loophole indicates the moves and manoeuvres, the responses to provocations, the always changing *journey* that the professional teacher must go on to learn from what happens in events (Ødegaard, 2020). Being interested in creating awareness of the local with a respect for diversity and tension the dynamics in education adds to the loop. These different waves of practices, imbalanced as they can be, will be clustered as *institutional transitional events*.

There is a robust stream of literature on action research methodology that highlights the suitability for early childhood educational institution to do collaborative action research with academics and for academics to do participatory design with practitioners. When used as an ongoing method, these epistemologies make it possible for teachers to analyse and reshape their content and programme effectively (Tekin & Kotaman, 2013). Collaboration between academics and practitioners is often described as uneven and a struggle to find knowledge forms and languages that connects them (Fleer, 2013). Few studies document the transition and long-term transformation of practices within the context of early childhood education and content. Hence, there is robust research on partnership methodology that focuses on the success and challenges in working together; however, less research describes the processes and transitions by exploring and expanding on the values, symbols and politics embedded in local culture and practices (Hedegaard &

Munk, 2019). Hence, the current case study will elaborate on the transition within a curricular space.

First, the chapter briefly outlines the concept of *exploration* and the current research studying exploration in the context of transitions in early childhood education. This is followed by a presentation of the analytic concept of *artefact*. Furthermore, the chapter describes the participatory project over time, its procedures and process, followed by a rich case description and analysis. *Transitions* are investigated holistically, actualizing pedagogical practices, as transitioning and transformative practices. To sum up the case analysis I present a table of seven features of collaborative exploration found through the case analysis. The table also sums up how artefacts play a crucial role in expanding processes of collaborative exploration, and how these dynamics enter loops of what I call *institutional transitional events*. The chapter ends with reflecting and further deepen our understanding of the historical and societal meanings in the in-depth case presented.

Co-exploration as Participatory Activity and Knowledge Creation

The concept of exploration is derived from the Latin *explorare*, which entered the English language around the fifteenth century and can be etymologically traced to the meaning of investigation and examination (Lawrence, 2010). In his studies of Russian children and their cognitive development, Lev Vygotsky (1978) uncovered the links between processes taking place in society and the mental processes taking place in the individual. Mariane Hedegaard further expanded on Vygotsky's perspectives to develop and refine the cultural-historical theory of children's development and participation, emphasizing the lives and activities within the institutions and the transitions between them (Hedegaard, 2008, 2011, 2020). Within this line of cultural-historical theory, the child is regarded as an apprentice in a culturally defined, socially organized world. Inspired by the wider works of Vygotsky (Khinkanina, 2014; Vygotsky, 2004) and his followers (e.g. Rogoff, 2003) new inspirations from childhood studies (Fleer et al., 2009; Kjørholt, 2007; Ødegaard, 2007) and studies of social sustainability (Boldermo & Ødegaard, 2019; Hedegaard & Ødegaard, 2020) nuanced the notion of apprenticeship by bringing in more nuances, for example, diversity and a larger focus on the children's emergent interests and motives, their agency and their play imaginations and how these are facilitated, neglected or denied within an institutional frame. As important as the recognition that relationships with adults are a crucial condition for children's development is the argument that artefacts, for example, signs and symbols, landscapes, local customs and diverse heritages are affordances nourishing the formative development of a child.

As mentioned in the Introduction, the concept of exploration often refers to a play- or curiosity-related action, a social situation that affects what and how objects and relations are explored. However, exploration can also be differentiated from play and curiosity but never with clear distinctions (Ødegaard, 2020). Prior literature often has conceptualized *exploration* as a fixed sequence of behaviours with relatively stereotyped patterns across situations and species, as well as being an open concept preceding curiosity and play (Schoggen & Schoggen, 1985). Exploration and curiosity have similar definitions because both imply seeking knowledge and initiating actions that can be vague to others or identified as more explicit performance. Exploration can be a line of thought of philosophical character in a person's mind and, thereby, invisible to others until the line of thought is made explicit, such as when a child is drawing and talking or trying to figure out an inspiration or experience.

The urge to explore can be considered a trait, a driving force for performative and philosophical actions in individuals (Schoggen & Schoggen, 1985). In recent years, the literature on the ontological view of the child as an agentic and responsive – not only a responding human being – has expanded. The newborn will imitate what the newborn will meet (responding), but at the same time, development and cultural formation will be conditioned through a dialogical and collaborative exploration where the newborns start the exploration through the bodily senses and drive agentic and responsive behaviours (Gradovski et al., 2019; Rogoff, 2003). Exploration, however, is not an action belonging to the children alone. Humans of all ages and under all conditions are inspired to explore materials, thinking and relations when the basic needs of living are taken care of. Early childhood researchers have investigated how shared intentional interactions between educators and infants, or *joint attention episodes*, have the potential to support collaborative exploration. Studies in pedagogy for early infancy open new possibilities by taken children's curiosity seriously in early childhood pedagogy (Degotardi et al., 2017).

Three recent studies of how exploration have been used in educational literature revealed that exploration was first and foremost used as a verb, without being theorized as a concept, but used to indicate actions, traits and activities such as *enquiry, investigation, curiosity, open-ended pedagogy, creativity, imagination, play* (e.g. play exploration), *learning and improvisation* (Eikset & Ødegaard,

2020; Ødegaard, 2020). These words are often used in relation to exploration or used to signify similar processes. The third study unveiled the similarities and differences in a comparative study of Confucius (China and Hong Kong) and Nordic (Finland and Norway) perspectives when it comes to how the concepts of play and learning are used and contextualized in their respective early years frameworks; in the study, the authors proposed exploration as a bridging concept (Hu & Ødegaard, 2019).

Therefore, being co-explorative is not obvious, nor is it easily done. The cultural context, that is, the values, matter for what is regarded as acceptable and enriching pedagogy. The pedagogy of being co-explorative needs to be elaborated and discussed. Therefore, the features of the pedagogics of exploration are important to investigate further.

Adults, as any other humans, are easily intrigued to explore situations where they are curious and triggered by an urge to find out more. The elaboration of the concept of exploration given in the current section is a pedagogical premise for how the participating team works in shared practices. In the following section, it will be described how artefacts are material and how symbolic affordances are intertwined in practice.

Artefacts – Material and Symbolic Affordances in Activities

Our perceptions and experiences are *informed* and shaped by the cultural tools (artefacts) made available to us. We experience and understand our world in terms of the tools of our culture, and these can be considered key to the development of what Vygotsky (1978) referred to as *higher mental functions*, such as remembering, imagination and understanding symbols, signs and conceptions. Wartofsky questioned the notion that human perception is *natural* and argued that it is an activity that is mediated by artefacts such as tools, language and models (Wartofsky et al., 1994). These mediating artefacts, Wartofsky argued, have to be seen as objectifications of human needs and intentions 'already invested with cognitive and affective content' (1979, pp. 205–6). Here, we are talking about a practice involving multimodal processes and multiple forms of awareness. Wartofsky categorized artefacts in three forms of perceptual and performative activities, as follows:

1) Primary artefacts: used in production and labour, such as for a hammer, a needle, scissors or a camera

2) Secondary artefacts: relating to primary artefacts (such as a user manual for a camera or instructions for an embroidery pattern)
3) Tertiary artefacts: representations of secondary artefacts, symbols, theories and models (imagining new ideas)

Regarding the tertiary artefact, Wartofsky wrote about representations of 'imaginative practice' (1979, p. 207). Michael Cole (2019) exemplified how a certain pedagogical approach can be a tertiary artefact in this regard, explaining that the tertiary artefact can be embodied as alternative canons of representation; once the visual picture can be *lived in*, perceptually, it can also come to influence and change our perception of the *actual* world. A representation of imaginations can open possibilities not presently recognized. Tertiary artefacts enable aesthetic perception, planning and revising of practice (Cole, 2019). This category will serve as a thinking tool in the pedagogical task given to teachers in the current study.

An artefact, whether a manual tool, a sign, model of thinking or language or all these at the same time will entail a history and come with connotations and rules of use and can bring up feelings. Here, we can use a flag as an example. A flag is a national symbol often used in constitutional celebrations and political meanings. As an artefact, it can be used in ways that are based on various understandings and differences in political opinions and can create misunderstandings and tensions at a relational level. This realization has an important consequence for our understanding of the pedagogy of co-exploration in the institutional curricular space. This tension means that an artefact cannot simply be internalized by the child in a ready-made form (Ødegaard & Pramling, 2013). It also means that exploration and learning do not necessarily take place as intended by the teachers if the artefacts are presented by the teacher and made available to the child. Ideas, sensations, emotions and actions are intertwined in the curricular space.

Starting out with local *anchoring* can elicit within the child and teacher the motivation for exploration, as can the new objects and events. The process of gradually taking over and being able to use a tool or artefact is referred to as appropriation (Rogoff, 2003). Still, because appropriation is not passive internalization, the artefact can easily turn to unexpected and novel use, and here, we are in the pedagogy of co-exploration. This implies dialogue and negotiation between the agents on how to use the artefact and what makes meaning in the frame of the current activity and how to take inspiration and resources from one activity setting into another (transition).

Long-term Transition through Collaborative Exploration

In this section, we describe how researchers and early childhood practitioners worked together first over a year in 2012. This is followed by a description given by a kindergarten teacher in an interview when the researcher revisited the kindergartens eight years later. Since I, for this study, was interested in the three-dimensional aspects of exploration, artefact and transition, how exploration is supported, encouraged by staff, over time; how pedagogical practices potentially can be long-term transformative, I decided to revisit a kindergarten, chosen for the two reasons of being a previous participating research kindergarten and for being motivated towards transitions and quality development. By going back to a kindergarten, I knew had developed a local awareness through the intervention study about enhancing awareness of cultural formation and the content of learning, I expected to get new insight in the long-tern transition of pedagogical practices. I could reopen research data and add new data to these particular study aims.

From an open call in 2012, highly motivated kindergartens applied to take part in the project. The project had a clear participatory design and had strong expectations that in the kindergartens, all staff would partake in the project. Each kindergarten appointed a lead team that was led by the manager of the kindergarten, and one teacher and one assistant from each kindergarten joined. The main project came to include teams from eleven kindergartens and five main supervisors and researchers. The project was carried out over a period of eleven months in 2012 and 2013 with two whole-group sessions (300 participants) and three project-group sessions (40 participants); each kindergarten had at least three supervising sessions where at least one of them was carried out in the kindergarten. The project allowed the kindergartens to hire extra staff for the periods of the project seminars and project teams; this allowed the researchers to spend time in the kindergartens to coordinate the project and write up the case studies. A safe digital platform was established for sharing tasks, presentations from kindergartens and researcher- and volunteer-written documentations. No portrait photos of the children were shared. In addition, participatory writing groups were established in 2012, and later, some of the kindergartens were further followed up (Schei & Ødegaard, 2017).

As a project leader at that time, I build on research concerned with the new critique of the Nordic model. New evidence revealed a dissonance between the policy aims and the structures for inclusive practices, and studies showing weakness in the model. Open-ended and play-oriented practices seem to function well for children of high- and middle-socio-economic backgrounds, while children of low socio-economic background seemed to be ignored (Jensen, 2009). Studies also showed a crucial aspect explaining differences between high-quality and low-quality kindergartens, namely the personal involvement and engagement from the staff (Birkeland & Ødegaard, 2019; Bjørnestad & Os, 2018; Kallestad & Ødegaard, 2013). Also, some studies raise critique of the ambiguity of globalization and marketing pressure on children, families and early childhood institutions (Ødegaard, 2015; Sutton-Smith, 1986; Zipes, 1997). I was working on the research design with the goal of empowering the kindergartens through research at the same time my role of the researchers was threefold – supervisor, main investigator and collaborator. These manifolds roles in research create strengths such as deepened access to complex problems and processes, at the same time a manifold and close engagement between the researcher and the participants, also can possess unique characteristics, compared to other respondents, so that the case study comes with a unique signature. In this case, validity will mean that the research is highly detailed and can shed light on situations that are difficult to study in other ways. This study can be said to have high ecological validity, as it can tell us a lot about real-life practice over time.

Central to the 2012 study was a series of tasks related to participatory (children and staff) explorations into local resources by taking photos (photo expeditions), writing narratives, asking questions, exploring and experiencing new ways of doing things, implementing new artefacts found in the local community, collaborating with families and establishing new activities. The teachers' processes of presenting a personally important artefact revealed their own attitudes, habits and common ways of doing things (Schei & Ødegaard, 2017).

From this main project, new questions were raised regarding existing empirical documentation, and for the purpose of expansion, a new follow-up study was conducted. The new study searched for features of pedagogy of co-exploration. One of the accounts originated in the local community and was chosen for reanalysis. To elaborate on the ecological processes in the kindergarten team, I contacted the kindergarten and conducted a retrospective interview[3] with Anne, a teacher who was a participant in the project in the first round. She had organized the pedagogical developmental work in this kindergarten over the study's time frame. The interview was rich in narratives. Anne remembered in detail Susanne's contributions and the changes that were set off through the project, along with a series of new transitions that were developed in the years after and that today constitute a profile of the kindergarten regarding nature and cultural sensitivity and awareness. Notes were taken from the interview and immediately transcribed after the interview ended and additional information (public documentation) was added to the empirical base.

Unfolding Institutional Transitional Events – Becoming Locally Sensitive

In the research material from 2012, there was a biographical narrative and a photo Susanne showing a photo of herself; she was holding a doll wearing a local folk costume and a piece of embroidery, a chest piece belonging to her own folk costume. The photo and narrative were followed by a short imaginative text where she reflects on how her personal engagement with this artefact could inspire future practice. This narrative, this photo and this short text are here regarded a tertiary artefact, following Wartofsky's reference to 'imaginative practice' (1979, p. 207) and Cole's explanation (2019) of tertiary artefacts as embodied, alternative representations, for example, a visual picture can be *lived in*, and influence and change our perception of the *actual* world, as tertiary artefacts enable aesthetic perception, planning and revising of practice. A tertiary artefact also adds to understand the dynamics of the what and how of content; the curricular space (Ødegaard & Krüger, 2012).

This process initiated by researchers allowed her to use her resources, both material and mentally, to develop ideas that was shared with colleagues, children and researchers. The case was fore fronted by the researchers to the staff at the time, as an example of a case with high potential to work with cultural heritage and formation. Revisiting the kindergarten later revealed that this case, in fact today served as a thinking tool (a tertiary artefact) for them. The kindergarten used the case as a model case and an inspirational idea, when expanding their content and practice as the following description will reveal.

The doll's costume had the same embroidery as the chest piece – patterns associated with her home village, where she also worked as a kindergarten teacher. Susanne sat on a chair with the embroideries exhibited on a table in front of her. The photo was taken by a colleague, Susanne wrote the story of the doll being a gift from her grandmother when she was a child. Her grandmother had embroidered the patterns on the doll's costume, and Susanne had embroidered the chest piece for her own folk costume and a belt. In her text of imagine new practices, she wrote that she would like to introduce to the children the local women's culture in her village, creating folk costumes (*bunad*). It was the bead embroideries belonging to folk costumes she had in mind. Susanne learned to embroider these local patterns at the age of thirteen, and encouraged by this self-presentation, she and her colleague invited the children to a collaborative in an investigation of the local patterns found in the *bunad*. She and her team created an activity in the kindergarten to create this type of pattern with pearls, responsive to their age range of three to six years. The kindergarten already had plastic beads in a variety of colours and ready-made templates of geometrical figures. Together with the children they explored new variations with inspiration from the patterns on the doll's costume and the chest piece – an institutional transitional event of inspiration from local heritage (patterns from embroideries) emerge as co-creation.

The spring of 2019, the children were again invited to study the embroideries found on the local village folk costume, and inspired by these, they used plastic beads to play and explore with the patterns, regardless of whether it was to replicate or redesign. New this year, according to Anne, was their families being more involved, resulting in a widened perspective on and knowledge about the folk costume tradition in Norway and the historical change of this tradition. Inviting families (more families from diverse background attended the kindergarten in 2019, than in 2012) to the activity, also expanding participants of the co-creation of content.

Revisiting the kindergarten eight years later made it evident that the initiating project and Susanne's narrative, photo and imagination had been a catalyst to a series of new transitional institutional events. Anne remembers Susanne's narrative well and says that every spring since 2012, the topic of the local folk costume comes up. Spring is the time of the year when the folk costume tradition is actualized because people would wear them in spring, especially on Norwegian Constitution Day (May 17) and at other spring rituals such as baptism, confirmation day, weddings and in Christian and non-religious rituals. The folk costume tradition is not a marker of religion. Instead, wearing a folk costume is a marker of economical or cultural difference, a distinction between people who can afford a folk costume and (or) who can undertake long-term planning for the tailoring of it. This handicraft work takes time, and some will inherit the *bunad* from earlier generations. Ideas (tertiary artefact) are expanding, no longer limited to *bunad*, but the theme of local heritage was connected to associated artefacts and events of further local, national and international relevance. Today the kindergarten, profile their work as a *Cultural* kindergarten, meaning using local resources to elaborate on their practice.

In an increasingly diverse society, such a practice creates ambivalence but has also been a symbol for transitions, as pointed out by Anne. Over the last years, they have picked up the old and new ways of using the folk costumes and had to manoeuvre and balance between handing over a national heritage and being sensitive to diversity in heritage. The folk costume has appeared on the political agenda many times over the last years, for example, when immigrants celebrated the transition into becoming Norwegian citizens by making and wearing Norwegian folk costumes, when women initiated political actions against midwifes being centralized at the largest hospitals and when woman protested against high-power masts in the fjords close by their local communities. In some of these protests, women were carried away by the police, and the events were a magnet for the media, hence being very powerful. These societal events created transition points for the staff, especially because the actions took place and affected their local community and the region where they lived.

The kindergarten works with the children's families to identify the heritage of the folk costumes used in their families, for both men and woman. The staff bring their own folk costumes and wear them in the kindergarten to *show-and-tell* sessions. This storytelling includes personal stories about the person's relation to the clothing, including who had created the different parts of the costume, valuing the handicrafts of the women, noticing what kinds of patterns are present in the costume, what the patterns look like in other variants of the folk costumes and what colours are present in the embroideries. Anne continues talking about how the pattern in the local costume created in her village has the same colours as the Norwegian flag. They would give attention to the flag, and as in most Norwegian kindergartens, the flag is present in kindergartens at celebrations such as Constitution Day and birthdays. To study the flag is one of the opportunities used pedagogically in this kindergarten to search for colours and patterns and to go on expeditions to find answers. They visit the local museum and the local handicraft workshop and gallery to learn more about the history of the local *bunad* and the variants for summer and winter and for men and women, better understanding why some of the costumes worn by women include a head cover, some of them with resemblance to what can be seen in other cultures, such as the hijab. Primary artefacts (Wartofsky, 1979) like folk costumes and flags are intertwined with symbols derived from them and attached to the storytelling.

More transitions took part over the years; these were related to the themes of the *bunad* and Constitution Day, including food traditions connected to celebrations. Today, they often cook this food in the kindergarten, and its preparation follows many paths. Children participate in the making of porridge made of sour cream, bake the traditional bread (*flatbrød*) and taste the salted, smoked and dried local meet from sheep (*fenalår*). Moreover, they listen to singing and song in sessions of traditional songs originating from composers born in their village and their life stories. Also, local traditional dances are introduced to the children. These dances include a ring dance accompanied by local songs made for a locally made violin (*Hardingfele*). They also sing the Norwegian national anthem *Yes, We Love This Country* (*Ja vi elsker dette landet*).

Because a transition to school in many kindergartens means working with academic competencies and social regulation, this kindergarten made their own additional transition ritual by repeating the two first choruses of the anthem until the oldest children learned them by heart before leaving kindergarten for the summer before starting primary school. In this way they added a specific national content to the curricular space of transition to school.

Anne mentions more events developing a local and national anchored content. They took yearly expeditions to a local farm, where they can try baking in the baking hut and see the sheep when they give birth to their lambs. They later revisit the farm when the lambs and sheep go out to play and eat. She continues to talk about their project of making a local sweet brown cheese (*dravle*) and how the children love the taste of it. Another year, they started to grow potatoes, and from these, they make a local cake (*potetlompe*) that is popular to eat with butter and sugar or plain. Every autumn, they used to pick berries from the bushes in their kindergarten and from berries in the neighbouring woods; however, in the previous years, they have expanded this activity by working in a more elaborate way with concepts and talking about a year's cycles, the calendar, while picking berries and making jam.

Another transition was the project to introduce the children to the local construction custom in their region. They became involved in building a traditional hut used to store food. This hut is built with a construction technique that is many centuries old; it includes a tower with a bell used to call for meals and announcements. They explore the different building styles and architecture by visiting the local museum and the houses of some old farms. Today, the kindergarten articulates their statement on their webpage:

> *For our kindergarten, culture is considered part of our heritage and our future. The culture we want to convey to the children is a fundamental value in Norwegian society. Our goal is also to convey folk traditions and art. It is also important to get to know cultures other than our own because today we live in a multicultural society.*

Anne emphasizes how their pedagogical practice today holds a stronger awareness of diversity in language, valuing local dialects and all the languages present in the kindergarten. She exemplifies how they use local and specific concepts when introducing the folk costume, such as the skirt on the folk costume, which is not referred to as the everyday concept of *skirt* (*skjørt*) but rather as (*stakk*), a more precise concept signifying a long, thick, black, woollen *stakk*, hard-pressed in a way that will make the *stakk* swing a certain way when dancing. The same concept of awareness applies to the naming of artefacts and handicrafts, what they encounter and experience when visiting local farms and landscapes and learning about different animals, architecture, food and music.

It is obvious that Anne's story coming forward in the interview is also a story containing a series of institutional transitional events. It is a multitude of short stories all of which support the main story of the kindergartens increasing local awareness and an increasing sensitivity to cultural and historical differences. The first initiative by Susanne, encourage by research, has today become an institutional culture of valuing a variety of local cultures and being a part of a changing society. The case can illustrate how the first case developed through the participatory research project, served as tertiary artefacts function, a modelling example of using local heritage for cultural formation and learning. In following, I will clarify why this case also illustrate collaborative practices of exploration.

Seven Features of Collaborative Explorative Practice in Pedagogy

To sum up the case, Table 3.1 illustrates how artefacts enable explorative practices and transitions, here looking at seven features of collaborative exploration and how this in interwoven in the cultural dynamics described above. Table 3.1 considers the aspects and features of explorative practice in the narratives depicted in the spectrum of content, including artefacts and symbols. As mentioned above, primary artefacts can be tools, secondary can be manuals and tertiary artefacts (Wartofsky, 1979) enable aesthetic perception, planning, revising and new practices, institutional transitional events. The seven features are identified through investigating a kindergarten over time, following a series of transitional events, while encouraging and supporting a collaborative explorative practice.

The first feature of co-explorative practice is *institutional anchoring*. A premise for the project was that it was anchored in a leadership encouraging

Table 3.1 Seven features of collaborative explorative practice

	Features encouraging and supporting co-explorative practice	Transforming and expanding content; artefacts, symbols and methodology	Transitional events
1	**Institutional anchoring** of content that opens the way for exploration, transformation and expanding content	Leadership for change	Beginning to work with researchers and allowing staff to use personal knowledge and artefacts
2	**Personal engagement** By working with formative and bodily awareness and by valuing personal knowledge and story	Explore personal anchoring, their own experience, feelings, sensations and stories, e.g. photo, autobiographical narrative, and performative expression	Bringing the personal into the institutional context; the personal was added to the practice of professional development
3	**Local anchoring** of content By working with the local community, plan for and act upon cultural customs	Explore material objects like embroideries, *bunad*, glass pearls, beads, needle, thread etc.	Giving value to local art expressions and bringing in handicrafts items belonging to local customs and heritage; follow transitions in society and let it impact change of practice
4	**Imagination and creativity** Staff work in ways that include planning, new ideas and theorizing	Explore biographical narrative, poems, lyrics, signs and symbols, music, song, musical instruments, dance, movement, sensation, story, body, and performance	Thematic expansion: expeditions, new artefacts. Diversity issues embedded
5	**Initiations, responses and follow-ups** By inviting children and family into personal stories and local and global artefacts	Explore planning and practice with new artefacts, e.g. hijab, head cover	Opening for more histories and adding more varieties of artefacts and customs through the families. Reflecting upon the differences and similarities within and between cultures over time
6	**Collaborative investigation** Staff and children investigate questions deriving from the project	Explore excursions, museums, galleries and landscapes. Explore shared activities, creating new collaborate narratives	Follow-up on children's curiosity. Creating space for shared problem-solving and discovering
7	**Establishing a conversational genre for exploration** Dialogical and philosophical approaches in participatory space of action	Follow-up and explore talking of shared endeavours	Naming and renaming the world; artefacts, material objects, ideas and beliefs

change and a motivated staff. Beginning to work with researchers and allowed staff to use personal knowledge and artefacts, which the staff found motivating and inspiring, as illustrated by Susanne's narrative, her personal biography positioned in the photo and her imagination, suggesting that the kindergarten could use local heritage pattern in beads activity.

The second feature is *personal engagement*. The task created by the researchers, built on knowledge from previous research indicating that educational culture, could, in low-quality kindergartens, leave the children too much to themselves, ignoring that play exploration need nourishment to blossom and that teachers need to be involved in children's projects in order to make inclusive spaces over time. By creating an open-ended task encouraging staff to valuing personal knowledge and story through working with autobiographical narrative and performative expression, the staff chose artefact with personal meaning and value. Bringing the personal into the institutional context; seem to boost a personal engagement, discovering that personal resources and involvement are crucial in pedagogical practices and gave pleasure and meaning to work. This discovery eventually led to transitions of practice.

The third feature is *local anchoring of content*. By working with the local community and families, the kindergarten could deepen their exploration and learning into specific artefact. When the local anchoring followed diverse family backgrounds, they not only enhanced value to local art expressions, but they were then allowed to add more varieties both historically and internationally. This brought new knowledge and understanding to children, their families and themselves.

The fourth feature is *imagination and creativity*. The project design task included elements encouraging the staff to imagine how artefacts of high value to them, could be brought into kindergarten practices. This seemed to start off new ideas for the staff when planning and later the idea of imagination and creativity became a tool (tertiary artefact) for planning. They explored own biographical narratives at first, later this led to an interest of children and their families' biographical narrative and previous anchoring, allowing a co-exploration with children and families, starting with their resources like poems, lyrics, signs and symbols, music etc. Bringing more personal resources into the exploration led to thematic expansion, where a rich diversity was embedded.

The fifth feature is *initiations, responses and follow-ups*. When inviting children and their families to share personal stories and artefacts connected to a theme like folk costume, national celebrations, local food, architecture etc., collaborative exploration can occur when responses are given, and follow-ups are taken. In our case this is illustrated for example when they explore connections, similarities and differences between the local folk costume with head covers for married women and the cultural/religious custom with the hijab. Initiations can foreground co-exploration when responses are accepted and treated with new interest and respect.

The sixth feature is *collaborative investigation.* Here collaborative investigation entails a planned activity (as *didaktik,* as mentioned above) where staff and children explore in a systematic manner following an enquiry approach when visiting museums, galleries and landscapes. Collaborative exploration through investigation is a space for shared problem-solving and discovering, following up on children's curiosity in a critical and play-based manner.

The seventh feature is *establishing a conversational genre for exploration.* This feature is closely connected to the sixth feature. A premise for collaborative exploration and thereby also a central feature of a pedagogy that encourage and support co-exploration is the dialogical pedagogical manner, in early childhood education, this genre includes dialogues as when the staff names and renames the world as a response to children's interest and contributions; like naming and exploring the meaning and functions of artefacts, material objects, ideas and beliefs. The collaborative explorative genre follows up and explores talking of shared endeavours, but the genre also goes beyond the talking. Establishing a pedagogical genre for collaborative exploration entails the whole spectrum of bodily expressions, like song, dance and movements. This genre supports exploration when engaging in dialogical approaches to meet children and partners in a participatory space of action.

Reflecting the Case Analysis – Artefacts and Symbols in Society

In the first year, through Susanne's personal story, her performance, imagination and new initiatives, we came to understand how the research task encouraged the participants to use personal experiences and engagement, later provoking a series of transitional events.

In recent years, there has been an open discussion in Norwegian society on whether you can wear a hijab along with a Norwegian local folk costume (*bunad*). On a societal level, through mass media, there has been example where the folk costumes are being changed by adding a hijab to a folk costume variety that, traditionally, did not have any head covers. There was revolt against it in the media. To illustrate this debate, we use the example of a young politician, Sahfana M. Ali,[4] who embroidered the pattern of her local folk costume on a hijab so that the hijab would fit the folk costume. Sahfana Ali is a young woman born in Sri Lanka and, for some years now, a Norwegian citizen. Some became very upset and claimed that this violated the folk costume. Sahfana Ali said that she is proud to be a Norwegian and wants to wear a Norwegian folk costume, yet she is also the proud owner of a sari from Sri Lanka. 'I have mixed identities and want to show it,' she stated to the newspaper. The debate included racist hate comments on social media and utterances from owners and managers of *bunad* galleries such as (*Norske Husfliden*), a committee that regulates folk costumes in Norway. It was interesting to listen to the kind reminder from the *bunad* experts: they welcome change in traditions, with the argument that the Norwegian folk costume tradition is rich and has gone through many transitions over the years (Bjørnholt, 2005). In Norway today, at public events for Constitution Day, you can see hijabs and other head coverings combined with folk costumes.

These discussions and varieties of practices were also available to the staff and families of this kindergarten at the time (2016) because the village has galleries and a proud tradition of valuing their folk costume heritage and the handicrafts that follow this custom and industry. Anne reflects on the transformation in attitudes when taking part in the national debate. When Anne, her colleagues and the children noticed the head cover tradition, it opened a new understanding of the hijab tradition that was also present in the community. Anne focuses on how this project, when exploring new areas, materials and artefacts, opened for transitions in thinking and practices. New transitional events occurred through a common curiosity and exploration of head clothes in local and global contexts.

However, this is not the only reflection needed to understand the expansive use of folk costumes in Norway and its counterparts in the kindergarten thematic work. The institutionalization of handicrafts and the use of folk costumes in Norway were clearly ideological from the start. During the Norwegian Union conflict with Sweden, folk costumes and handicraft were an expression of a claim of Norwegian independence and later as an expression of the rural culture against the urban elite. One of the *bunad* pioneers, Hulda Garborg,[5] saw the folk costumes as a women-liberating alternative to the fashion industry at the turn of year 1900, and she pushed for the *bunad* to become a practical garment for everyday use, that they should be produced in Norway with home-made materials and that Norwegian production should contribute to both upgrading the cultural heritage and expressing national self-sufficiency (Bjørnholt, 2005).

Although *bunad* use was controversial and aroused aggression and contempt in the cities well into the 1900s, after the Second World War, the *bunad* became a more unifying national symbol and uncontroversial party clothing. The *bunad* gradually became part of a liberating and countercultural, national movement (as also seen in political counteractions today). Today, *bunad* use is common when receiving an audience from the King and Queen of Norway, and it is now a royal costume that the royalty use at official occasions and, along with the people of Norway, on Constitution Day. Eventually, an important alliance was established between the city and country when the *bunad* became a status symbol. What used to be connected to poor regions and opposition is now a highly regarded national heritage and is an area of constant debate around national identity and who is regarded Norwegian enough to wear it.

Norwegian national identity has historically been strongly linked to state power, democracy and autonomy. At the same time, Norwegian national identity has been – and still is – deeply rooted in the local. The revitalization of folk costumes, the recognition of the recreation of costumes, as seen with the examples of head coverings and hijabs being accepted as part of an official Norwegian *bunad*, go in parallel with a revitalization of folk dance. Today, we can find young dance assemblies taking up old folk dances and folk music and blending it with international new music and moves.

Taking an even more critical stance in this reflection, I point to the risk of bringing up a tradition so close to nationalistic values that it is not necessarily inclusive. So let us now reflect on the pedagogical resource for co-exploration that lies in the celebration of Norwegian Constitution Day and the preparations for it. We need to consider that nationalism here means the opposite of one strong nation; the Norwegian national ideal is that of celebrating a national community, one expressed in various national identities with a variety of national symbols and in various areas. The Constitution of 1814[6] gave the Norwegian national project and democracy a start, which was further strengthened by its independence from Sweden in 1905.

May 17 is now an inclusive event organized by local community committees and in schools by parents' committees. Not long ago, the May 17 parade was reserved for ethnic Norwegian children, and Swedish children, for example, were not allowed to participate. In the 1980s, threats were directed at schools with many immigrant children, but such threats were actively rebuffed, partly because politicians joined forces with these schools. Today, both the parade and the celebration are open and inclusive, and the day represents a low-key opening to the national community. Many have assumed that immigrants would feel excluded on this day, a time representing a peak of national romance and Norwegian nationalism, where the national is celebrated with a full range of national symbols, including the performance of wearing a *bunad* and waving a Norwegian flag. In a study of how people in Norway become Norwegians, the opposite became evident (Brottveit et al., 2004). This was a day when immigrants felt included: they participated in the public celebrations and thought that the Norwegians were much nicer than usual. The intensive – and in many ways pompous – celebration of the nation seems to be able to include new groups.

I will also add that in some occasions the borders between what can seem to be a content of local or national identity is part of historical international movements, as for example when the case kindergarten re-establish the historical local tradition of picking berries for making jam and connects it to calendar activities, it connects not only to the local. The tradition of using calendars with children was early a German didaktik, proposed by Fredrich Fröbel (1885).

In this way, the current case illustrates how a continuous enquiry and debate on a societal level can provoke exploration and transitions in the institutions. What is regarded as local is intertwined with global history and affects institutional practices (Birkeland, 2015; Ødegaard, 2015). Society and the persons in the institutions have had shifting ideas regarding how to introduce children to the cultures in which they live and how to regulate education.

Conclusion – Inclusive Practices through Collaborative Exploration

This chapter foregrounds how staff transitioned into increasingly new activities for exploration actualizing local culture and heritage, and thereby adding to our understandings of how kindergarten practice conditions the cultural formation of children in Norway going from monocultural to multicultural entities.

Moreover, the case study reveals how educational practice can be more inclusive by exploring on both a personal and societal level. Collaborative exploration can be a way into inclusive practices because it allows for the flow, waves and loops that come with opening for personal engagement and histories (Ødegaard, 2020), which always will be a potential change-maker. As I see it, exploration entails a dynamic process and captures the relational nature of exploration necessary to achieve quality early childhood education (Ødegaard, 2020).

This chapter clarifies and develops the notion of exploration in the context of early childhood education through a three-dimensional enquiry space.

a) *Exploration* is described as collaborative. Seven features were identified to encourage and support co-explorative practice: *Institutional anchoring, personal engagement, local anchoring of content, imagination and creativity, initiations, responses, and follow-ups, collaborative investigation, and establishing a conversational genre for exploration.* This analysis adds to the understanding of collaborative exploration as manifested in a complex matrix through body, movement, sensations, artefacts, materiality, symbols and discourses (Ødegaard, 2020). These loops provoke transitional events and can expand and develop kindergarten content and practice. More research is needed to validate the features. Other contexts and other epistemological approaches could lead to the identification of other features or more features of collaborative exploration.

b) *Transition* is described as micro-transition and adds a version to an analytic approach in studies of transition, identifying *Transitional events in practice* through case analysis. The analysis unfolded the processes of micro-transition in their relationship to the cultural artefacts made available for collaborative exploration over time. The analysis adds to our understanding of tertiary artefacts as imagination thinking tools enabling transitions. Along with Cole, this study explains how tertiary artefacts can support aesthetic perception, planning and revising of practice (Cole, 2019).

c) *The significance of artefacts* is enhanced in the analysis to add understandings and description that can explain the content dimension of early childhood education. Artefacts carry symbols and meaning and bring affordances and conditions for the curricular space. By adding focus to artefacts and the value and meaning they entails, this chapter adds understandings of how exploration is enacted and performed. Artefacts are here shown to be important thinking tools for transition and necessary to perform exploration.

Using a cultural-historical theoretical conceptualization, the current study depicts, through a detailed case description, how a participatory research project using explorative, performative and imaginative approaches provoked a personal engagement towards personal history; in Susanne's case, her story was interwoven with local and national history and set off a series of institutional transitional events, as further illustrated by Anne's stories.

Local and national forms of knowledge are disputed knowledge, as the reflections of the case illustrate. The practices and emotions that are embedded in a nation's history and society, when also embedded in institutional settings, create conditions for how children perceive, use and reconstruct the symbols, metaphors, songs and stories. If we are to understand how a child develops personal values and identity, one needs to conceptualize how values are developed historically in different institutional practices and realize that explorative practice will always entail content and value dimensions, what in education comprises the curricular space (Ødegaard & Krüger, 2012).

The study allowed me to draw attention to the ecology between early childhood educational institutions as symbolic spaces where cultural values are embedded and where teachers enact critical explorative engagement through institutional transitional events for the benefit of inclusive spaces for children. This current chapter supports the transition from a monocultural entity in national celebration rituals to a more multi-layered informed pedagogical practice that supports and reflects diversity. Establishing and continuing over the years, the shaping and reshaping of a locally anchored project for exploring the culture and handicrafts connected to a local folk costume creates an argument for how collaborative exploration, as with any pedagogical practice, will always be infused with the cultural values, ideals and beliefs embedded in teacher practices. When teachers engage in collaborative exploration with researchers and pick up on societal debates, this can expand and revise practices, content and institutional transitional events, and the conditions for children's exploration will be altered.

Notes

1 Co-exploration is an abbreviation for collaborative exploration and will be used interchangeably.
2 This project was funded by the Directorate of Education (2012–2014) and was embedded as an extra portfolio within a larger study founded by the Research Council Norway (2009–2014) called *Kindergarten as an Arena for Cultural Formation*.
3 Due to the Covid-19 situation, the interview was conducted as a telephone interview.
4 The newspaper feature interview and debate started in Stavanger Aftenblad 16 June 2016.
5 Hulda Garborg was born in 1862 and died in 1934. She was a renowned culture worker, an 'influencer' with a strong personal engagement in Norwegian theatre, where the New Norwegian language was spoken, in traditional Norwegian songs and especially in the revitalisation of the Norwegian folk costume. She urged it

being not a national costume but rather a folk costume valuing local handicrafts and female knowledge.
6   1814 was the year in Norwegian history when Norway was no longer ruled by the Danish King. A constitutional peace tractate (*Kiel tractate*) included a new union between Norway and Sweden with the Swedish King. On 17 May 1814, an independent Norwegian national law was officially signed.

References

Bakhtin, M. (1973). *Problems of Dostoevsky's Poetics* (R. W. Rotsel, Trans.; original work published 1929; 2nd ed.). Ardis.

Birkeland, Å. (2015). Cross cultural comparative education – Fortifying preconceptions or transformation of knowledge? *Policy Futures in Education, 14*(1), 77–91. https://doi.org/10.1177/1478210315612647

Birkeland, J., & Ødegaard, E.E. (2019). Hva er verdt å vite om observasjon i dagens barnehage? Metodologi i endring mellom tradisjon, ny vitenskap og personlig kunnskap [What is worth knowing about observation is todays kindergaten – methodology in transition between tradition, new science and personal knowledge]. *Norsk Pedagogisk Tidsskrift, 103*(2–3), 108–20.

Bjørnholt, M. (2005). Hvorfor er folkedrakt så viktig i Norge og marginalt i nabolandene? *Nordisk kulturpolitisk tidsskrift, (2)*, 34–50.

Bjørnestad, E. & Os, E. (2018). Quality in Norwegian childcare for toddlers using ITERS-R. *European Early Childhood Education Research Journal, 26*(1), 111–27. https://doi.org/10.1080/1350293X.2018.1412051

Boldermo, S., & Ødegaard, E. E. (2019). What about the migrant children? The state-of-the-art in research claiming social sustainability. *Sustainability, 11*(2), 459. https://doi.org/10.3390/su11020459

Brottveit, Å., Hovland, B. M., & Aagedal, O. (2004). *Slik blir nordmenn norske: bruk av nasjonale symbol i eit fleirkulturelt samfunn*. Unipax.

Cole, M. (2019). Re-covering the idea of a tertiary artifact. In A. Edwards, M. Fleer & L. Böttcher (Eds.), *Cultural-historical Approaches to Studying Learning and Development – Societal, Institutional and Personal Perspectives* (pp. 303–21). Springer Nature.

Davies, B. (2011), Open listening: Creative evolution in early childhood settings. *International Journal of Early Childhood, 43*(2), 119–32. https://doi.org/10/10007/s13158-011-0030-1

Degotardi, S., Page, J., & White, J. (2017). (Re)conceptualising relationships in infant-toddler pedagogy. *Contemporary Issues in Early Childhood, 18*(4), 355–61. https://doi.org/10.1177/1463949117742760

Eikset, A., & Ødegaard, E. E. (2020). Historical roots of exploration – Through a Fröbelian third space. In M. Hedegaard & E. E. Ødegaard (Eds.), *Children's*

Exploration and Cultural Formation: International Perspectives on Early Childhood Education and Development (Vol 29) (pp. 105–19). Springer.

Fleer, M. (2013). Attunements of knowledge forms: The relational agency of researchers, policy writers, and early childhood educators. In J. Duncan & L. Conner (Eds.), *Research Partnerships in Early Childhood Education – Teachers and Researchers in Collaboration* (pp. 27–47). Palgrave McMillan.

Fleer, M., Hedegaard, M., & Tudge, J. (2009). *Childhood Studies and the Impact of Globalization: Policies and Practices at Global and Local Levels.* Routledge.

Fröbel, F. W. A. (1885). *The Education of Man* (Jarvis, J. A Trans.). Lovell & Company.

Gradovski, M., Ødegaard, E. E., Rutanen, N., Sumsion, J., Mika, C., & White, E. J. (2019). *The First 1000 Days of Early Childhood: Policy and Pedagogy with under-three-year olds: Cross-disciplinary Insights and Innovations* (Vol 2). Springer.

Hedegaard, M. (2020). Children's exploration as a key in children's play and learning activity in social and cultural formation. In: M. Hedegaard & E. E. Odegaard (Eds), Children's Exploration and Cultural Formation (pp. 11–28). Springer Open.

Hedegaard, M. (2008). *Studying Children: A Cultural-historical Approach.* McGraw-Hill Education.

Hedegaard, M. (2011). *The Dynamic Aspects in Children's Learning and Development.* Cambridge University Press.

Hedegaard, M., & Munk, K. (2019). Play and life competencies as core in transition from kindergarten to school: Tension between values in early childhood education. In M. Hedegaard, & M. Fleer (Eds.), *Children's Transitions in Everyday* Life *and* Institutions (pp. 21–46). Bloomsbury Academic.

Hedegaard, M., & Ødegaard, E. E. (2020). *Children's Exploration and Cultural Formation.* Springer Nature.

Hu, A., & Ødegaard, E. E. (2019). Play and/or learning comparative analysis of dominant concepts in curriculum guidelines for ECE in Norway, Finland, China and Hong Kong. In A. Wiseman (Ed.), *Annual Review of Comparative and International Education 2018. International perspectives on education and society* (Vol 37) (pp. 207–24). Emerald Publishing.

Jensen, B. (2009). A Nordic approach to early childhood education (ECE) and socially endangered children. *European Early Childhood Education Research Journal, 17*(1), 14. https://doi.org/10.1080/13502930802688980

Kallestad, J. H., & Ødegaard, E. E. (2013). Children's activities in Norwegian kindergartens. Part 1: An overall picture. *Cultural-Historical Psychology, 9*(4), 74–82. https://doi.org/10.17759/chp

Kellogg, D., & Veresov, N. (2019). Setting the stage. In L. S. Vygotsky (Ed.), *L.S. Vygotsky's Pedological Works: Foundations of Pedagogy* (Vol 1) (pp. 5–19). Springer Nature

Khinkanina, A. (2014). The historic importance of L. S. Vygotsky's 'The Psychology of Art' and some problems of modern psychological and pedagogical field. *International Journal of Psychological Research, 7*(2), 85–91. https://doi/org/10.21500/20112084.661

Kjørholt, A. T. (2007). Childhood as a symbolic space: Searching for authentic voices in the era of globalisation. *Children's Geographies*, 5(1–2), 29–42. https//doi.org/10.1080/14733280601108148

Lawrence, C. (2010). Historical key words – Explore. *The Lancet*, 375(1).

Nilsson, M., Ferholt, B., & Lecussay, R. (2018). 'The playing-exploring child': Reconceptualizing the relationship between play and learning in early childhood education. *Contemporary Issues in Early Childhood*, 19(3), 231–45. https://doi.org/10.1177/1463949117710800

Ødegaard, E. E. (2007). *Meningsskaping i barnehagen: innhold og bruk av barns og voksnes samtalefortellinger*. Göteborgs Universitet.

Ødegaard, E. E. (2015). 'Glocality' in play: Efforts and dilemmas in changing the model of the teacher for the Norwegian national framework for kindergartens. *Policy Futures in Education*, 14(1), 42–59. https://doi.org/10.1177/1478210315612645

Ødegaard, E. E. (2020). Dialogical engagement and the co-creation of cultures of exploration. In M. Hedegaard & E. E. Ødegaard (Eds.), *Exploration and Cultural Formation* (pp. 83–104). Springer Open.

Ødegaard, E. E., & Krüger, T. (2012). Studier av barnehagen som danningsarena – sosialepistemologiske perspektiver [Studies of kindergarten as an arena for cultural formation – Socio-epistemological perspectives]. In *Barnehagen som danningsarena* [Kindergarten as arena for cultural formation] (pp. 19–49). Fagbokforlaget.

Ødegaard, E. E., & Pramling, N. (2013). Collaborative narrative as linguistic artifact and cultural tool for meaning-making and learning. *Cultural-Historical Psychology*, 8(2), 38–44.

Oliveira-Formoshino, J., & Formoshino, J. (2012). *Pedagogy-in-participation: Childhood Association Educational Perspective*. Porto Editora.

Paavola, S., Lipponen, L., & Hakkarainen, K. (2004). Models of innovative knowledge communities and three metaphors of learning. *Review of Educational Research*, 74(4), 557–76. https://doi.org/10.3102/00346543074004557

Pramling, N., Wallerstedt, C., Lagerlöf, P., Björklund, C., Kultti, A., Palmér, H., Magnusson, M., Thulin, S., Jonsson, A., & Pramling Samuelsson, I. (2019). Developing Play-responsive Didaktik – Mission Impossible? In N. Pramling, C. Wallerstedt, P. Lagerlof, C. Björklund, A. Kultti, H. Palmér, M. Magnusson, S. Thulin, A. Jonsson & I Pramling Samuelsson (Eds.), *Play-Responsive Teaching in Early Childhood Education* (pp. 3–16). Springer Nature.

Rogoff, B. (2003). *The Cultural Nature of Human Development* (1st edn.). Oxford University Press.

Schei, T. B., & Ødegaard, E. E. (2017). Stories of style: Exploring teachers' self-staging with musical artefacts. In S. Garvis & N. Pramling (Eds.), *Narratives in Early Childhood Education: Communication, Sense Making and Lived Experience* (1st edn.). (pp. 59–69). Routledge.

Schoggen, P., & Schoggen, M. (1985). Play, exploration and density. In J. Wolvet & W. Vliet (Eds.), *Habitats for Children – The Impact of Density* (pp. 77–95). Lawrence Erlbaum Associates.

Sutton-Smith, B. (1986). *Toys as Culture*. Gardner Press.

Tekin, A. K. & Kotaman, H. (2013). The epistemological perspectives on action research. *Journal of Educational and Social Research* (3), 81–91. https://doi.org/10.5901/jesr.2013.v3n1p81

Vygotsky, L. S. (1978). *Mind in Society: The Development of Higher Psychological Processes*. Harvard University Press.

Vygotsky, L. S. (1997). *The Collected Works of L. S. Vygotsky* (Vol 4). Plenum Press.

Vygotsky, L. S. (2004). Imagination and creativity in childhood. *Journal of Russian & East European Psychology, 42*(1), 7–97. https://doi.org/10.1080/10610405.2004.11059210

Wartofsky, M. W. (1979). *Models – Representations and the Scientific Understandings*. D. Reidel.

Wartofsky, M. W., Gould, C. C., & Cohen, R. S. (1994). *Artifacts, Representations, and Social Practice: Essays for Marx Wartofsky*. Kluwer Academic Publishers.

White, E. J. (2016). *Introducing Dialogic Pedagogy: Provocations for the Early Years*. Routledge.

Zipes, J. (1997). *Happily Ever After: Fairy Tales, Children, and the Culture Industry*. Routledge.

4

Play Exploration and Active Learning in a Chinese Kindergarten: An Educational Experiment into How Teachers Meet the New Societal Demands of the Educational Reform and Transition into New Play Practices

Marilyn Fleer and Liang Li

Introduction

In the Asia-Pacific region many Governments have legislated for play-based programmes through the release of new curricula (Rao & Li, 2009). The new societal expectation for playful learning has created new pedagogical demands upon teachers when responding to Government requirements. The curriculum reform in China has seen the emergence of two separated play-based teaching approaches in kindergarten education (Vong, 2012). At the institutional level, child-initiated free play activities and teacher-directed play-oriented learning activities have emerged as the dominant institutional practices (Vong, 2012). These two types of activities within the institutional practices of the Chinese Kindergarten have been reported by Pan et al. (2018) to be acting in parallel and this bifurcation has created tension for teachers.

We know from research that China has imported Western educational ideas valuing play-based teaching and learning (Fleer & Li, 2018). One of the goals of the educational reform is to change the teacher-directed group instruction to play-based and child-centred teaching and learning (Lin et al., 2019; Liu & Feng, 2005; Pan et al., 2018; Tobin et al., 2009). However, the local literature suggests that the imported educational theories and models from Western contexts are incompatible with Chinese tradition (Pan et al., 2018), which values collective orientation, spirituality and high levels of self-discipline of its people (Lin et al.,

2019; Zhu, 2006). Local scholars are worried about the philosophical differences between cultures when developing new practices to support child-centred play-based programmes (Yang & Li, 2019), as well as the concerns for an emerging cultural fusion that is not empirically based (Rao, Nig et al., 2009). Very little research has been undertaken in China at the institutional level, and therefore little is known about the impact of cultural fusion on the activity settings.

Confucianism value of the group, rather than the individual, is highlighted as a goal by Government through its reforms and early childhood curriculum guidelines (Zhu & Zhang, 2008). Confucianism values the collectivist orientation which promotes teaching oriented to the group (Choy, 2017). A collective orientation appears to create the pedagogical conditions for high levels of child self-regulation that are oriented towards group goals and actions (Fleer & Li, 2020). Confucius culture is ethics-based, in which individual identity is not defined by his/her capabilities and rights, but by his/her responsibilities and obligations for others, and importantly, individual's rights are not claimed by an individual, but are imbued by others (Liang, 1987). Therefore, the roots of early childhood education are greatly influenced by the ideological and philosophical foundations of Chinese culture, and these values frame how the child is conceptualized, the beliefs about learning and teaching, and the relationship between children and teachers (Zhu, 2006). This requires a new practice tradition on the one hand, to meet the societal demands for play-based active learning to support the development of the whole child (Minster of Education, China, 2012), and on the other hand to be culturally situated (Pan et al. 2018). Furthermore, what is missing, as argued by Pan et al. (2018), is introducing curriculum with the main goals of ensuring that it is 'congruent with the needs of society' (p. 617) and can support the cultural formation of children within a context of achievement and modernization as a goal of social construction. But what kind of teaching and learning can best support the cultural formation of the child for becoming creative, where play-based active learning, respecting how children approach learning, rather than group instruction, become increasingly important?

In this chapter, we report on the outcomes of an educational experiment with teachers from Mainland China in Chengdu where we sought to develop new institutional practices that were sensitive to children's exploration in play, while maintaining the important cultural value for group teaching and children's self-regulation that is directed to the group. As researchers, we worked in collaboration with the teachers to support their transition into new practices within the kindergarten that were oriented to exploration in play. Our goal was to study the collective exploration of play and learning as teachers transitioned into using the *Guidelines for Kindergarten Education Practice-Trial Version* (Ministry of Education, 2001) and *Early Learning and Development Guidelines for Children Aged 3–6* (Ministry of Education, 2012) which formulate to strengthen the implementation of the *Guidelines*.

To achieve the goal of this chapter, we begin by introducing the central problem, followed by a theoretical discussion and details of the educational experiment (Hedegaard, 2008) that was used to design this cultural-historical study. Next, we present the findings through examples from two periods of data collection, where exploration and transition into new play and learning practices are featured. We conclude with a model of teaching that showcases the new institutional practices that resulted from this in-depth educational experiment with one kindergarten located within the societal context of educational reform in China.

The Central Problem

The early childhood educational reform in China has seen the development of Regulations for Kindergarten Education Practice-Trial Version (National Education Commission, 1989), emphasizing the government-directed top-down reform (Pan et al., 2018) and the development of the *Guidelines for Kindergarten Education Practices-Trial Version* (Ministry of Education, 2001). Pan et al. (2018) have shown that one of the core values advocated by the Reform is active learning and play-based integrated curriculum. It has been reported by scholars in China that there is a need for 'developing theories appropriate to the Chinese context and the conduct of theoretically motivated research' (Yu, 2017, p. 108) that will support new directions for teachers who introduce play-based programmes.

The Western models of play available in the literature cannot be transplanted into the pedagogical practices of China because of different societal values (Fleer & Li, 2020). Rather they appear to set up a dualism between play and learning that is unhelpful for solving the theoretical problem faced by scholars and teachers in China. In our conceptualization of the problem, we draw upon Hedegaard's (2012) wholistic approach in order to widen the theoretical frame of the problem context to include play and learning exploration within the activity setting of the practice traditions of Chinese Kindergartens. Here we draw upon the analytical concepts of *transition* and *exploration*, as is the focus of this volume, and use these for examining the changing institutional practices and what this means for the lives of both children and teachers who are entering into new practice traditions.

We study the societal conditions, institutional practices, activity settings and personal perspectives by taking each into account in our research. First, the societal conditions foreground the values and goals that a country has for its citizens and in China this is realized through the hybrid of Confucianism traditional values, Communist culture and Western culture that shape the different aspects of Chinese early childhood education and support the best developmental conditions for children (Zhu & Zhang, 2008). China started to implement the 'reform and opening-up' policy in 1978, which has led the whole country into rapid social and economic development, which also influences the fundamental change in contemporary early childhood education in China. Active learning and playfulness are represented in the kindergarten curriculum reform of the Government, but how these are realized in practice has not been empirically driven. Government has left it to the teachers in kindergartens to realize these new goals for transitioning into new practices. The Government guidelines for play-based programmes support active learning as embedded across the curriculum and this creates new demands upon teachers because new kinds of institutional practices are needed to support the activity setting of play-based learning.

Second, the institutional practice for the cultural age of the 3–6-year-old child in China sees learning as the traditional focus for this age period. Consequently, the practice traditions centre on learning as the leading activity of the preschool child. Teachers focus on whole group teaching in support of the value of learning in kindergartens, while also recognizing high levels of self-regulation as part of the group orientation that has been the practice tradition of the kindergarten (Fleer & Li, 2020). But with new guidelines to promote play-based activities, new demands are made upon the teachers to change the practices and to be oriented to new social situations that promote play. Therefore, a new model of exploration in play is needed. Our educational experiment sought to support teachers transitioning into these new practices for introducing play-based activity settings.

Third, the personal perspective focuses on the motive orientation of the children and their intentions within the activity settings. The child's social situation has to be considered in relation to how s/he enters into the activity setting, as well as how s/he contributes to, is shaped by and shapes the activity setting. Therefore, the possibility for a child to play or to learn, as well as how teachers are orientating children to play or learning, is expressed in the activity setting through collective exploration. This theoretical reading of the societal conditions, institutional practices, the activity settings and personal perspective draws from Vygotsky's (1998) revolutionary theory of development and Hedegaard's (2012) model of child development.

Central to Vygotsky's revolutionary view of child development are the cultural age periods that are tied directly to the institutions that children attend and the dominating practices of those institutions. The wholeness approach to child development was developed from research in schools (Hedegaard, 2014) in Denmark where the social situation is for play and the personal motive orientation of the child is also play. However, in China children's social situations in the practice traditions of the kindergarten have been oriented to learning when taking a Confucian perspective. The change in societal conditions for new activity settings for play in kindergartens has created new demands upon teachers and has left open the question of children's motive orientation for play exploration. A new problem situation has arisen, not just for transitioning into new practice traditions, but also in relation to the cultural age of the child in China where both learning and play are now seen as the leading activities of the preschool children. Therefore, our key research question in this chapter is about how teachers meet the new societal demands for active learning and play-based curriculum in a Chinese kindergarten and create new conditions for exploration in play. We specifically undertake an educational experiment in order to address a two-part problem of *How do teachers transition into the new practices that meet the demands of the Reform for active learning and play-based integrated curriculum and what conditions do they create to support children's exploration in play in collective learning contexts?*

In line with the chapters in this volume, the interrelated research questions will be answered by drawing upon the analytical concepts of *transition* and *exploration* in order to distil the characterizes of exploration in the Chinese institutional context where both play and learning are being re-worked pedagogically.

Importantly, the conception of cultural age periods as a theoretical foundation for determining the conditions for children's exploration is also being re-theorized within a dynamic and changing web of activities in the activity settings of the kindergarten. The results reported in this chapter contribute empirically, but also theoretically in relation to the construct of how to use *exploration* as a concept in pedagogy for transitioning into new kindergarten practices in China.

An Educational Experiment

In light of the research needed and the central problem discussed above, we drew upon the method of an educational experiment to study the transition in teacher pedagogical practices over time. The idea was to determine what might be a model of exploration in play for supporting the goals of the reform, at the same time as foregrounding Chinese values, beliefs and ways of teaching in kindergartens. We selected this method because '[t]he experiment implies a cooperation between researchers and educators' (Hedegaard, 2008, p. 200) and this framed how we undertook the research over time. This cooperation in research features two characteristics that we adapted to be more relevant for creating new practices in China. This also echoes Fleer's (2013) argument that the successful partnership building between the researchers and teachers 'pay simultaneous attention to societal goals and values, institutional discourse and practice, and individual motives and demands, in the creation of new knowledge and practice' (p. 42).

First, in order to determine a model that develops localized exploration in play in activity settings in kindergartens, the researchers and teachers began by interrogating existing practices, beliefs and values in relation to the traditional puppet and drama activities in the kindergarten practice. The common focus was on examining the activities that foregrounded play and which could develop a motive for learning concepts in the context of those values important for the cultural formation of the child in China. As will be shown later, Period 1 of the data collection included the process of documenting institutional practices that support puppet theatre performances in kindergarten settings.

Second, in an educational experiment both the planned activities of the teacher and the children's actual activities were conceptualized as part of the intervention. Specifically, the formulation and revision of the planned activities are seen as a *dialectical process* (Vygotsky, 1997) between the teacher's pedagogy and the theoretical knowledge that is the content of the teaching (Hedegaard, 2008). That is, an educational experiment in the context of our study had to be based on a *theoretical-dialectical methodology* (Hedegaard, 2008) where the researchers and the teachers seek to study three interrelated dimensions:

1. Teaching practice as concrete implementation of a playful curriculum.
2. The group and individual exploration of children and how the teaching conditions contribute to the development of motives for play and for learning.

3. Children's appropriation of knowledge and thinking as a key for Chinese values.

These interrelated dimensions follow Hedegaard (2008) but expand her educational experiment to be more relevant for the cultural formation of children in China, where learning concepts is seen as a valued collective practice of the kindergarten. With the new reforms, play has become the new pedagogical activity being foregrounded in kindergarten practice in China. The central problem of our study is similar to Hedegaard (2008), where the Danish primary teacher sought to build children's theoretical knowledge in school. However, in our study the children are much younger, and we were therefore interested to determine how to draw upon children's motive for play in the context of families and community valuing learning in kindergarten settings. We therefore included the additional dimension associated explicitly with play:

4. Imaginary play practices that open up possibilities for children's explorations and theoretical thinking.

The educational experiment had to also capture how teachers could work with children's motives for play and develop much needed pedagogical practices for supporting a theoretical model of exploration in play for collective, rather than individual cultural formation of children. We knew from practice and from the general literature into Chinese cultural values that high levels of self-regulation in group settings are a core value of educational settings (Fleer & Li, 2020; Liang, 1987). Here the allegiance with the group outweighs individual interest as is what is shown in much of the Western literature on play, and the models of play being considered in China as part of the fusion discussed in the Introduction. We wanted to ensure that the development of theoretical knowledge as a core societal value was maintained as an important educational practice in kindergartens. Therefore, we further expanded Hedegaard's conception of an educational experiment to include this dimension:

5. Cultural formation of Chinese cultural values for self-regulation within group settings.

The idea in Hedegaard's educational experiment in schools is to develop a motive for learning in which core content is determined and children build their understandings through expanding the relational model. However, because our study involved the Chinese learner within a kindergarten rather than a school context, and because teachers and Government wanted a more playful curriculum, new practices were needed to capture what mattered in society and in kindergartens as part of the educational experiment. The central focus was on working with children's motive orientation for play in ways that allowed children to build core concepts through embodied play practices in support of the cultural formation of children in China as active learners.

In our expanded theorization of an educational experiment, the essence or core model of practice also meant determining not only what might be the essence or core model in learning content, but also what were the core values inherent in Chinese society that needed to be maintained and developed during the process of teaching and learning within newly introduced play-based settings in kindergartens. That is, we had to determine in our educational experiment what were core values and practices and examine how they could still be realized within the educational experiment for new practices of the Chinese preschool. We did this by building upon Hedegaard's (2008, 2012) educational experiment and model of child development, the relational core values of motive development of self-regulation to the group, and a collective orientation as the dominating institutional practices, in order to reveal the tension that teachers in China appear to be grappling with. In cooperation with the teachers we posed the problem of what might be the new form of exploration in play that teachers could develop in relation to their existing everyday activities of puppet theatre performances. In Figure 4.1 we show the model that we conceptualized to understand the development of new activities for exploration in play that took account of collective teaching while expanding towards new practice traditions introduced by the Chinese government for play-based programmes. The approaches advocated are designed to positively support active learning, such as exploring, imagining and creating (MOE, 2012, p. 2).

The model has to be read as dynamic dialectic where children in collective contexts realize personal meaning through social relations, and at the same time everyday activities create conditions for thinking with concepts, which simultaneously give pathways for understanding the content of the concrete activities. This is always in motion because children in kindergartens enter into activities and meet new demands, but also create new demands and shape the activities as part of the process of exploration in play.

In our educational experiment, the planned discussions between researchers and teachers generated a productive zone for exploration of new play activities, but also a meeting point for discussion of teachers transitioning into new institutional practices in kindergartens in China. We drew upon the relational dimensions shown in Figure 4.1 rather than a bifurcation when studying how

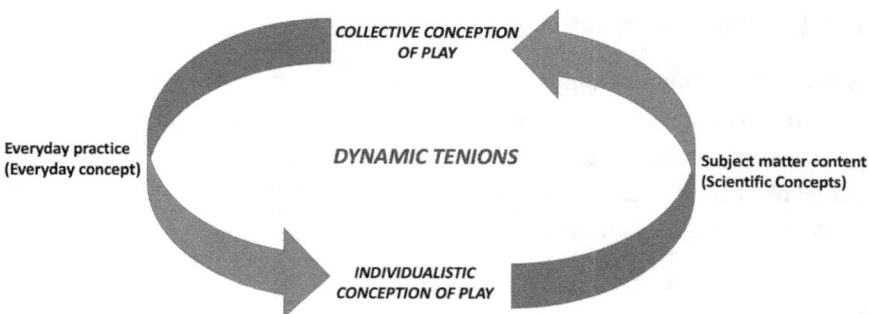

Figure 4.1 Model for conceptualizing new institutional practices for introducing activity setting for exploration in play.

exploration in play can be realized as new activities as part of the institutional practices of Chinese kindergartens.

Overview of Research Context for the Educational Experiment

The educational experiment took place within a public kindergarten setting in Chengdu, Southwest of China. Participating in our educational experiment were two researchers and two teachers. In the first year there were thirty-five children (senior class who graduated; mean 5.6 years at the start of the study). In the second year there were thirty children aged between four and five years (mean 4.3 at the start of the study). Both teachers had a Bachelor of early childhood education. The educational leader, Teacher Jing, had seven years of experience in the field and the other was a new graduate at the beginning of the study. In Chinese kindergartens normally two classroom teachers take turns to work with children between the morning and afternoon. In this chapter, we follow Teacher Jing's teaching activities within two research periods. The children were from middle-class families and were all Chinese.

Workshop

A two-hour workshop with the focus teachers was organized as part of the discussion of the concept of play and learning. The core model shown in Figure 4.1 guided the workshop process and resulted in a new model of exploration in play (Figure 4.4). The workshops were digitally video recorded.

Digital Video Observations

A total of 53 hours of digital video observations over ten weeks to capture the daily activities in the kindergarten were collected by the researchers and participating teachers. Each data collection visit lasted 5–8.5 hours. In Period 1 a total of 21 hours was gathered and in Period 2 of the educational experiment (six visits) a further 32 hours were collected.

Researcher-teacher Dialogue

In addition to the researcher generated digital video and photographs, the teachers also captured the activities of the kindergarten during the educational experiment when the researchers were not there. These data were used as the basis for the ongoing cooperation between the researchers and the teachers through the medium of WeChat. The researchers responded to questions and discussed activities that teachers had video recorded and sent through WeChat platform. The researcher-teacher dialogue has been generated as part of data collection. This cooperation was daily/weekly and lasted over the duration of the educational experiment. The educational experiment developed the ideas of teaching methodologies related to the new practice traditions focusing on the play exploration and active learning.

Pair Group Interviews

Pre- and post-group interviews are made with the participating teachers. An interview with both teachers was conducted before the group workshop and after the first video observation at the kindergarten lasting 1.5 hours. Post-group interviews lasting 1.5 hours were conducted after the video observation of the planned implementation of their play-based programme, in order to capture teachers' views of their experience of what became known as a Chinese PlayWorld. A total of 6 hours of interview data were collected.

Digital Data Analysis Process

In line with an educational experiment, we drew upon Hedegaard's wholeness approach for data analysis (societal, institutional and personal) when studying the transitioning into new activity settings for exploration in play. Activity settings for exploration in play were an important part of the educational experiment, and we were interested to see how activities developed over time in relation to the cultural formation of children in China. Data of activity settings were imported into an iMovie project and were digitally edited into smaller video clips related to exploration in play. These clips from the folders of activity settings were transcribed and translated from Chinese to English. In line with an educational experiment, these processes were ongoing. We tagged particular points in time in relation to the goals of the research, as well as teacher-initiated activities in practices and researcher dialogue, as part of our analysis. We iteratively studied the data. This is in keeping with Vygotsky's (1997) metaphor of *skipping* because the cultural formation process is dynamic (p. 223) and exploration in play takes place within the living laboratory of the kindergarten as part of the educational experiment. Skipping captures the idea of viewing the raw data many times and copying extracts of data (as vignettes) on each cycle of viewing of the raw data set.

Findings

In line with our two research questions, we present two periods (made up a series of episodes) from our educational experiment as a 'dialectical unit' (Vygotsky, 1997, p. 22) to show (1) how through the educational experiment, the teachers transitioned into new practices for exploration in play, and (2) supported new developmental possibilities for exploration in play that were aligned with cultural values and new societal demands for play-based programmes in China.

To answer these questions, we sought to examine the existing activities for play exploration in the kindergarten. We were interested to know how the bifurcation of play and learning reported by Chinese scholars existed in practice. This constituted Period 1. The educational experiment constituted Period 2 of our data collection where we followed two focus teachers from the same setting developing new activities as they explored how play could be organized to support children's active learning in their kindergarten. We pay close attention to how the teachers transitioned into a new practice tradition.

Period 1

Before beginning our educational experiment, we wanted to understand the existing practice tradition of the kindergarten that was related to group teaching and children's play as presented in Period 1. It could also act as a benchmark for studying the transitioning of the teachers' new practices as they sought to introduce exploration in play into their kindergarten. We were particularly interested to know more about the culturally valued activities that were part of children's everyday routines and activity settings relevant in their community and which were central for the cultural formation of the children in China. Consequently, the teachers and researchers chose to focus on puppet theatre play because of its importance in the kindergarten programme and in the community.

In Period 1 we found that the dominant institutional practices focus on group instruction and group reflection, individual work at tables or desks, and play at tables and in learning corners. As expected, puppet theatre was important cultural practice. But what was new for the researchers was that this activity was considered a form of play by the teachers. A common activity was for children to collectively reflect on their shared play experience together after each theatre play session. Teacher Jing during interviews said that '[r]eflection helps children understand how they cooperate with each other and how the play performance can be acted in a better way' (Teacher Interview, Period 1).

We begin by presenting a Vignette of Activity Setting 1, followed by an analytical discussion of personal, institutional and societal perspectives of the example.

Activity Setting 1: Group Reflection

After each performance a group reflection is organized by the teacher through a yellow reflection sheet with happy and sad faces. The teacher invites the whole group to talk about how the children's play performance goes and what they need to improve next time. The teacher asks the questions first, and the whole group of children respond in turn. What follows is a typical example of this activity setting.

T:		What are the problems during the theatre play performance? For example, come onto the stage. Did you see? The leading role. Who are the leading roles in this theatre play?
Lili:		Little princess.
T:		The little princess and the frog prince, right? Which part of the screen were they on during the play?
Yi:		Below.
Beibei:		They were on the one side of the stage.
T:		They were on the one side of the stage, right? Where should they be?
Lili:		In the middle.

T:	And they held their shadow puppets too low.
Lan:	Stand up to watch.
T:	We write down the problem of 'on the one side of the stage'. Think about how to solve it
T:	I describe it objectively. When the princess Lan was playing, Lan was the leading role and when she was talking, other actors did not show up.
Lili:	It's because, that, when Duoduo was moving (the sticks), the sticks were not tightly connected and became loose. Then he looked at his shadow puppet moving here and there, and he did not show up.
Duoduo:	Tong (the group leader) took my shadow puppet and played my role.
Tong:	Duoduo was too slow and he didn't show up when it was his turn.
T:	That is to say that during the whole play, was he serious or not?
Children:	Not serious.
T:	Yes, this is the problem today. I did not say that it is a fault … So, the problem we have today is not the problem of acting, but the problem of what?
	Then, the teacher answers herself to emphasise the issue
T:	Cooperation.
	Duoduo hangs his head down.

The practices of teacher questioning during whole group sessions are relatively common practice tradition in many countries (Alexander, 2001). However, what is different for this kindergarten in China is that the whole group questioning is deepened as the teacher supports a group reflection that is more like an overall performance evaluation. This group reflection has supported the children to be aware of the importance of being oriented to the group when performing puppet theatre play – which the teacher names to the children as 'cooperation'. In alignment with traditional cultural values, such as collectiveness, children become oriented to the group and this value has a long history in China. The practice tradition reported here is a common part of the cultural formation of the child (Choy, 2017; Hammer & He, 2016; Zhu & Zhang, 2008). In order to have a wholistic understanding of this group reflection activity, the interpretation is first taken from the personal perspective, then the societal and the institutional perspectives.

Personal Perspective

How a child enters into the activity setting of the puppet theatre play and becomes oriented towards the group goals can be seen in the example of Duoduo. In Activity Setting 1 the teacher acted as an outsider and gave suggestions to

Duoduo to think about how to cooperate with others in the puppet theatre performance. The moral concept of cooperation was offered by the teacher as the imperative for solving the problem that arose during the theatre play. Solovieva and Gonzale-Moreno (2017) argued, '[T]he child learns to regulate his/her own behaviour by hearing the external speech of other participants (parents, teacher or other children). Later on … the child begins to regulate independently' (p. 101). In considering Duoduo's perspective, we could argue that the process of *internalized conscious regulation* is not simple or easy for children. Duoduo was being oriented towards self-regulation of his own behaviours but in ways that were oriented towards the group's goals for the successful performance of theatre play. The moral value that the teacher was seeking to orient Duoduo towards was cooperation. Through the group evaluation and public reflection on the success or not of the performance, children were being oriented towards cooperation when in the group and towards the group goals. It was not just Duoduo who was being oriented in this way, but it was all of the children through their need to regulate towards the group and towards the goals of the activity setting for a successful theatre performance. Exploration in play appeared in line with the script of group instruction and achieving the goal for a collective theatre production using shadow puppets. There appeared to be very little room for exploration in play for the children and particularly for Duoduo.

Societal and Institutional Perspectives

The practice traditions of the kindergarten are closely tied to the cultural values of that society and this needs to be understood when following the perspective of the child within an activity setting. During Period 1 we observed the dynamics between valued cultural practices for self-regulation as part of a motive orientation to the group and the goals of the group. The teacher was focused on a cultivation of self in relation to the group. This 'Cultivation of self in the community' is reported by Choy (2017) as 'one of the purposes of education' in China (Choy, 2017, p. 33). Understanding this self-community dynamic has to be seen from within the cultural traditions and Chinese values, by doing so, we are able to grasp the core values of a collectivist orientation towards promoting group teaching (Choy, 2017). Consequently, in Period 2 the researchers and teachers engaged in an educational experiment which sought to take account of the new goals of Government for active learning and play-based integrated curriculum (Pan et al., 2018) but with cultural values in mind. Here the transitioning of teachers and children into exploration in play became the new goal.

Period 2

In Period 2 we followed the teachers and children as they progressively transitioned into new activities. After the researchers examined the existing activities in the kindergarten, the teachers and researchers discussed how to introduce play practices into their programme. During this process, Teacher Jing commented her own teaching that,

> I found that I almost continued teaching the same things years by years. I have never jumped out the traditional ways of approaching theme-based teaching to the whole group. I found that I don't feel happy to continue doing the similar things every year.
>
> (Teacher Interview, Period 1)

The teachers discussed the different play practices from Western contexts (Figure 4.1) with the researchers to formulate a core model of play practice and then worked together with the second named author to create new practice traditions that drew upon storytelling (Conceptual PlayWorlds) and puppet theatre activity setting to create new play practices in the kindergarten.

We introduce an example of the new activity setting below. We begin with a short orientation to the activity setting of *Rescuing the Snake*, followed by the vignette, and then an analysis of the activity setting where a personal and institutional perspective is given. The societal analysis is woven into the discussion and conclusion where we discuss both examples from the two periods.

As is shown through the Activity Setting that follows, the teacher began by reading the storybook of Gruffalo (Donaldson, 1999). After exploring Gruffalo's world through puppet play and role play, children were invited to join the *Gruffalo* playworld by role-playing a character from the story. As shown below, Teacher Jing's new practice is to be a play partner, and to introduce a problem situation that is to be solved within the story line. This constitutes a new form of exploration in play for children in this kindergarten as children and the teacher collectively entered the collective imaginary situation to solve the conceptual problem.

Activity Setting 2: Rescuing the Snake

By taking children's interests, Teacher Jing starts the new storyline by borrowing the character roles of Snake and mice from storybook of *Gruffalo*. Teacher Jing, being a magic *Little Flower* in the forest, enters the playworld with children. 'In the forest ... In the forest, I have lived for a long time. But, I have seen a lot of animals in the forest. Not just snakes, but mice. But, during this time'

The teacher introduces a problem:

> One day, I notice that the snake family are going to catch mice. But the little mice are very smart! I see him running, running, running, Suddenly, now, he sees a pile of hay. He moves the hay onto a hole. The snake doesn't see it, and falls into it. Then in the evening, I hear that Master Snake asks Follower Snake to find the Third Snake. But I have never seen the Third Snake come out.

The teacher then asks, 'What do we do? How can he be saved? How do we save him?'

The teacher in role as a magic flower in the woodland asks this dramatic question to invite the children to think and imagine collectively about how to rescue the snake from a deep hole. Feng responds and says, 'Snake can climb a tree, right?' The teacher encourages Feng by saying, 'Tell us! Tell us!' Feng continues, 'Snakes can climb a tree, right? We can take a stick, and put it here.' He points to the front, and gestures as he says, 'Put it in the hole, and it will climb out!' The teacher positively reinforces his ideas and extends by offering a suggestion, 'Ah! That's a good idea! It means that we can find a twig or a stick, right?' A range of suggestions are put forward and then the children begin to try out their ideas (Figure 4.2 and 4.3). Yu gestures and says, 'A log ... Here is a log, and on the two sides there are two little logs. It is held on top!' Feng adds, 'Hold it on top and it wouldn't fall, would it?'

Figure 4.2 Whole group role-play.

Figure 4.3 Collectively solving the problem in the play.

Wen selects a long log from the 'forest'. Feng lifts up the log and shouts, 'I build it with this, Little Flower!' Getting no reply from the teacher, he continues, 'Little Flower! Little Flower! The hole is so big!' A girl picks up a cylinder and comes back to the group (Figure 4.3).

Personal Perspective

According to Teacher Jing,

> Children are very active in the playworld environment compared to the normal classroom. One girl who is very quiet in the class normally, however, in the playworld environment, she is very active and contributes her ideas and supports the group's problem solving.
>
> (Teacher interview, Period 2)

We can see that children have the motive orientation towards solving the problem in their play through their actions in rescuing their friend in the woodlands play. Teacher Jing has been aware of children's motive orientation to play and motivates them to rescue their friend, another snake who dropped in a big hole. As Hedegaard (2012) suggests, 'In an educational situation it is important to be aware of the child's motive orientation as well as directing the introduced activities toward supporting new motives' (p. 135). Teacher Jing dramatized a problem in how to rescue snake from a big hole. The problem was integrated into the play by the teacher and this opened up an active space for children to offer and try out solutions. The focus of the children's actions was in relation to the play narrative and the problem situation in the woodlands. Although the teacher supported the play narrative through her dialogue and had initiated the problem situation, the children were equal partners in the imaginary play, acting together with the teacher as a collective to solve the problem. The activity setting related to Gruffalo's world gave more opportunities for all of the children's play exploration of the storyline and role-play actions, than was evident in Period 1. Exploration in play was not a reproduction of the shadow puppet with the goal of being oriented to the collective actions for reproducing the original storyline and action within the activity setting, but rather it was a group production of finding the ways to help snake, where there were many possibilities for different actions and new story plots that could be collectively played, such as rescuing the snake.

Societal and Institutional Perspectives

The Gruffalo playworld activity also draws upon the cultural traditions of the society by valuing collectivism. The teacher and children collectively entered the playworld activity setting and the group teaching and learning was thereby transformed. Furthermore, the teacher's role changed in Period 2. The teacher was a character in the imaginary play situation and this positioned her as a play partner, even though she initiated the problem situation. The children referred to her as the magic flower and this suggests they responded to her as a play partner, rather than in her real role as the teacher. As commented by Teacher Jing,

'Our role is very important to play with children in playworld to support children to learn, and children like to see our role as a play partner. I feel I am very close to children too' (Teacher interview, Period 2).

Consequently, the teacher was able to dramatize the everyday mathematical and scientific conceptual problem in the context of imaginary play situation, as we saw when she used prepositional language as part of story of helping snake to meet the pedagogical goal in this activity setting. The teacher through her actions opened up possibilities for the children's exploration in play as a stimulating motive for learning content, but by realizing new activities in the kindergarten which were in line with the children's motive to play.

The children appeared to actively engage with spatial knowledge and embodied physics as everyday concepts in order to find solutions to solve the increasing complex problems introduced through the problem situation when rescuing their friend who fell down to the big hole. The emerging exploration in play was deepened because the teacher was an active play partner in the new activity setting where new institutional practices were being formulated. The children appeared to be cooperating and acting collectively in support of the common problem introduced through the imaginary play – a social goal for cooperating that was identified in Period 1 as important for the teacher. When some children questioned the action of putting only two logs together, another child (Yu) brought another log to help stabilize the standing logs. The exploratory approach of the children suggests that the children were using their collective imagining to visualize the effect of the shapes of the logs in relation to each other, and the problem of how to effectively stabilize them. This collective visualization supported the educational goals of the teacher but also the value of the collective orientation, and in ways that gave space to children to initiate and to add to the personally meaningful problem situation within the story. As noted by Teacher Jing in Period 2:

> I also found that the story has a lot of directions we could go into deeper in the playworld. Children also can think about their own questions. Because children can have richer imagination than the adults. I think we really need to learn from our children and let them initiate the playworld. We need to connect to our everyday activity/concepts in play now. Also, while they play, they start more collective way instead of playing individually during the free play time. Listening, cooperation, and negotiation are all embedded in the learning process in playworld.
>
> (Teacher interview, Period 2)

Discussion

Traditionally, the Confucian values emphasized, 'diligence, the endurance of hardship, perseverance, concentration, and respect for teaching authority were valued as Chinese learning virtues' (Lin et al., 2019, p. 84). Until the reform, play has not been valued as a practice for achieving the goals of early childhood education. We know from the literature (Pan et al., 2018; Rao, Ng et al., 2009;

Yu, 2017), and from our previous research (Fleer & Li, 2020), that the guidelines have set up a tension between traditional Chinese values and the need for models of practice that can support play-based teaching. This is within a context where Chinese parents demand that kindergartens primarily support the teaching of academic skills as early as possible, due to the contemporary exam-oriented educational system (Lin et al., 2019).

In taking a *societal perspective*, government demands and cultural values and traditions related to child education need to be considered in research. Teacher Jing understood the importance of shadow puppet play to Sichuan people. The shadow puppet play-based curriculum was used by the kindergarten as a specialty curriculum that is foundational to the cultural formation of children.

The educational experiment showed how the Chinese cultural values for group teaching and collectivist orientations in everyday teaching were an important value of kindergarten education. The activity settings as shown in Period 1 (group reflection) and Period 2 (rescuing the snake) exemplified this, but in different ways. In both activity settings, the dynamics were collective. All the children and teachers were together discussing and engaged in theatre play in Period 1. Through the educational experiment, the teacher shifted her role by entering the playworld activity setting with children collectively. Her role was no longer central to the activity setting, but rather she took on the role of a play partner and explorer to support children's explorations in play. The play explorations were distributed across the activity settings as an interaction between the children and teachers. Period 2 showed a very different activity setting to Period 1. The positioning of the teachers was different, and this showed an important characteristic in successfully transitioning into a new practice tradition in support of the Government reforms.

In considering *the perspective of the institution of the kindergarten*, our study found that teachers became increasingly aware of the significant role they hold in developing a motive orientation for learning through introducing problem situations in children's imaginary collective play. In both periods, the children and teachers were explorers and problem solvers. Yet the problem scenario was introduced, explored and solved in quite different ways in the two periods. In Period 1 the teacher aimed to teach the child Duoduo how to cooperate with others in theatre play during reflection time and support all the children's understanding of the concept of cooperation in play. The teacher had taken a central and dominant role in solving the conceptual problem of cooperation. The group reflection had not considered Duoduo's perspective or understood his expectations of what he could do best in the play show. What can be learned from this is that the teacher's intervention and group reflection need to align with children's motive orientation in play. Duoduo was engaged in active exploration of the puppet materials, which was an individual rather than collective action and this did not fit with the goal for cooperation and whole group puppet performance. The teacher tried to make suggestions and explain the conceptual problem, however, her attempt was not responsive to the Duoduo's orientation, and she could not build a motivational situation to allow Duoduo to be active in problem-solving and understanding cooperation in theatre play.

During the pre-interview (Teacher Interview, Period 1), Teacher Jing expressed her willingness to change her teaching approach (See Teacher Interview, Period 1) and suggested she would like to try something new. Through the workshop and ongoing discussion during the educational experiment, Teacher Jing realized the important role of the teacher in play for supporting children's play exploration. Therefore, in Period 2 she entered into the activity setting together with the children, not as the leader but as a play-partner, and the children were able to actively explore and problem-solve in ways that allowed them to try out different ideas in the activity setting. The problem-solving event was distributed across the group rather than centred directly on the teacher. Teacher Jing dramatized the conceptual problem by taking a role in the imaginary play as a magic *Little Flower*, and this changed her relationship with the children from being the teacher to being a play partner. This change in relations oriented the children towards trying out different ideas for solving the problem situation as part of the collective imaginary play situation.

In Period 2, children's motive orientation to play was sustained and extended to develop a new motive in addressing the conceptual problem. Children were supported in their play explorations in ways that extended their imaginary play in the woodlands. They explored concepts in solving the problem to rescue their friend. The play exploration activities effectively met the new demands of implementing a play-based curriculum that supports active learning of children at the everyday level. In Period 2 demands were made on the play of the children, but in ways that aligned with a collective orientation that is usually demonstrated through group teaching as was shown in Period 1. The new play activities in Period 2 foregrounded exploration and supported the children's conceptual learning in mathematics as well as physics, as a learning goal at the everyday level and this echoes the importance noted in previous research of teachers thinking carefully about the concepts to be embedded in children's play, so that the concepts can act in the service of children's play (Fleer, 2018). The double subjectivity in play allows the teachers to take an active role in children's play and children in turn take an active role in learning concepts. In this way, the new exploratory play activities being developed by the teacher through the educational experiment in this kindergarten (Period 2) are in service of children's play (Fleer, 2018) and aligned with everyday practices in that community. This means children can explore and imagine in play and borrow concepts to solve problems in their play. As commented by Teacher Jing, 'I am so surprised to see that children have a lot of ideas in playworld, and I have to learn from them' (Teacher Interview, Period 2). A familiarity with role-playing stories through theatre play meant that the teachers were comfortable to bring to the collective imaginary play characters not just from the theatre, but from well-known storybooks.

From a *personal perspective*, we found through the educational experiment of Period 2, children's motives for learning were developed when the play was organized in response to their everyday knowledge and was open for their active exploration. As shown in Period 1, the shadow puppet play was organized in response to children's everyday knowledge of theatre performances and shadow puppets. The woodlands play in Period 2 was initiated by the children based on their understanding of the characters in the storybook. The children's motive to play as well as to learn was noted by the teacher as being different between Period 1 and 2. The principal reflected on the transition between the activity settings for children's explorations in play:

> I feel that Teacher Jing's image of child has been changed. She starts focusing on children's voices and her role and positioning in the interactions between children and teachers. That is the reason I see her as excellent teacher. We don't see the excellent teacher is good at controlling and organising the children. I think the best teacher should be good at playing with children and guiding them in learning.
>
> (Period 2, Principal)

In summary, the teachers transitioned from being at the centre of the activity setting to de-centring and becoming play partners in the collective play, thereby opening up explorations in play in Period 2. This in turn created more space for the children to become producers and creator of the play through their explorations, rather than acting as reproducers of the original storyline. The new activity setting in the kindergarten created a new practice tradition for explorations in play, while continuing to support societal values towards a collective orientation. This means each child regulates in relation to the collective, but does so through the teacher being together with the children as a play partner guiding learning

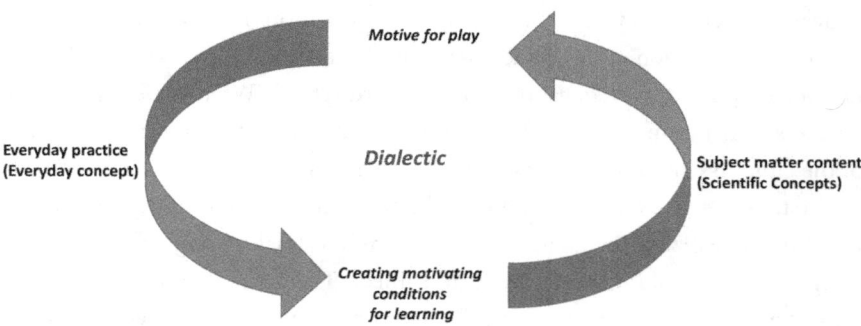

Figure 4.4 Model of play and learning for the Chinese Kindergarten.

and cooperation from within the storyline, rather than being in the position of whole group instructor.

The transitioning of the teachers took place through their active participation in practice supported by our educational experiment. What was developed was a new practice tradition in the kindergartens, captured in a new model of practice that we show in Figure 4.4. This model shows the valued societal outcomes for learning (everyday and scientific concepts; Vygotsky, 1987), while at the same time draws upon children's motive for play and gives more room for children's initiatives in producing rather than reproducing the storyline. The teachers created the motivating conditions for children's play exploration through collectively and cooperatively playing with them in support of meeting problems that need to be solved using concepts. The new kindergarten practice for exploratory play and active learning became the new tradition in the kindergarten for meeting the goals of the educational reform.

Conclusion

The educational experiment reported in this chapter sought to show how teachers transitioned into new practices for exploration in play, while supporting new developmental possibilities for children that were aligned with cultural values and new societal demands for play-based programmes in China. We presented examples to show how teachers transitioned from Period 1 into Period 2. In Period 1 we discussed the existing practice traditions in the kindergarten in relation to the cultural formation of the child in China, and in Period 2 the teachers transitioned into a new practice tradition for realizing the goals for educational reform in China. The result was explorations in play as a new activity within the institution of the kindergarten in China. Our findings align with what has been reported in Hedegaard and Odegaard (2020). What we learned about teachers transitioning into exploration in play as part of the cultural formation of the child in China centred around four key ideas.

First, through examining valued practices in the community, important insights for realizing the goals of the Government for learning and play-based integrated curriculum could be determined. The local community valued puppetry and theatre performance. These community practices acted as a source for recognizing existing story narratives and playfulness, which the teachers could draw upon for creating imaginary play situations together with the children. The story gave a collective narrative and supported play exploration possibilities, as well as the context for the imaginary play, and this changed the teacher's position in the kindergarten. The teacher was no longer at the centre demonstrating or instructing, but rather acted as a play partner orchestrating problems related to everyday learning, but in ways that were personally meaningful and motivating for children – how to save their friend snake. The teachers noted how engaged the children had become, and this in turn affirmed the new activities they were developing as part of the educational experiment.

Second, a genuine development of institutional practices to support exploration in play activities had to be seen as being located within societal values and beliefs. Institutions in China cannot appropriate models of practice developed in different societies because this leads to bifurcation of practices and holds no personal meaning for teachers. As argued by Hedegaard and Lyberth (this volume), the preschool teachers need to develop collective activities drawing upon local tradition. The transitioning into new practices by the teachers were focused on the children's motive orientation for play in ways that allowed for the building of core concepts at the everyday level through personally meaningful problem situations that supported the cultural formation of children in China as active learners.

Third, the educational experiment put centre stage the relations between the Hedegaardian concepts of motives and motivation within her wholistic approach to research. Without examining the personal perspectives of how teachers and children enter into the activity settings within Period 1 and 2, and studying the social situation (motive orientation) and the social situation of development of the children (motives), it would have been difficult to understand the relation between self-discipline and a collective orientation (Lin et al., 2019; Zhu, 2006) (societal values) that underpins the cultural formation of children in China. The latter could be seen through the practices of group teaching and collective play (institutional practices). Under the umbrella of the key principle of *learning in the service of play* (Fleer, 2018) the educational experiment revealed new play exploration activities for kindergarten settings that were in tune with the dynamic tensions between the individual and the collective. This tension acted as a productive force for realizing the significance surrounding the need for group teaching where the teacher is at the centre of the children-teacher dynamic for cultivating the learning of discipline concepts, such as mathematics. Understanding that self-regulation is more than just individualistic, but is a relation between self and the group, meant that as researchers we could work cooperatively with teachers with this knowledge when consciously considering how group teaching could be realized through the narrative and problem solving in collective play. Valued practices of being oriented to the group could be maintained in collective play because play explorations opened up new possibilities for children and teachers alike to problem solve as part of the play. This represented a significant transition in the practice tradition of the kindergarten.

Finally, our study identified how teachers transitioned into new activities. The focus teacher positively responded to the new demands to change the institutional practice to be in line with the educational reforms. The process of the educational experiment supported teachers to realize play exploration activities and allowed for the realization of new practice traditions in the kindergarten. As teachers realized new practices, they appeared to build both competence in designing activity settings for play exploration, but also, they were positively predisposed to developing a new practice tradition because of the high engagement of the children. It was through giving more space for children's initiatives that they noticed how children become active producers of play, and this was different to how their previous practices positioned children. Play explorations were seen as a production of new storylines and actions and not as reproduction of original storylines and content knowledge. This study has realised new play and learning activities for the cultural formation of the kindergarten child in China which is different to other societal contexts (Hedegaard & Ødegaard, 2020), and shown how teachers successfully transition into new institutional practices within the cultural context and values of the educational reforms in kindergarten settings in China.

References

Alexander, R. J. (2001). *Culture and Pedagogy: International Comparisons in Primary Education*. Blackwell.

Choy, G. (2017). Chinese culture in early educational environments in Shanghi, Guizhou, and Ningshan. In N. Rao, J. Zhou & J. Sun (Eds.), *Early Childhood Education in Chinese Societies* (pp. 31–4). Springer.

Donaldson, J. (1999). *The Gruffalo*. Macmillan Publishers.

Fleer, M. (2013) Attunement of knowledge forms: The relational Agency of researchers, policy writers, and early childhood educators. In J. Duncan & L. Conner (Eds.), *Research Partnerships in Early Childhood Education: Teachers and Researchers in Collaboratio*n (pp. 27–48). Palgrave Macmillan.

Fleer, M. (2018). Conceptual Playworlds: The role of imagination in play and learning. *Early Years*. Online publication. https://doi-org.ezproxy.lib.monash.edu.au/10.1080/09575146.2018.1549024

Fleer, M., & Li, L. (2020). Curriculum reforms as a productive force of the development of new play practices in rural Chinese kindergartens. *International Journal of Early Years Education*. Online publication. https://doi.org/10.1080/09669760.2020.1778447

Hammer, A. S. E., & He, M. (2016). Preschool teachers' approaches to science: A comparison of a Chinese and A Norwegian Kindergarten. *European Early Childhood Education Research Journal, 24*(3), 450–64. https://doi.org/10.1080/1350293X.2014.970850

Hedegaard, M. (2008). The educational experiment. In M. Hedegaard & M. Fleer (Eds.), *Studying Children: A Cultural Historical Perspective* (pp. 181–201). Open University Press.

Hedegaard, M. (2012). Analysing children's learning and development in everyday settings from a cultural-historical wholeness approach. *Mind, Culture, and Activity, 19*(2), 127–38. https://doi-org.ezproxy.lib.monash.edu.au/10.1080/10749039.2012.665560

Hedegaard, M. (2014). The significance of demands and motives across practices in children's learning and development: An analysis of learning in home and school. *Learning, Culture and Social Interaction, 3*(3), 188–94. https://doi.org/10.1016/j.lcsi.2014.02.008

Hedegaard, M., & Ødegaard, E. E. (2020). *Children's Exploration and Cultural Formation*. Springer Nature.

Liang, S. M. (1987). *Gist of Chinese Culture (in Chinese)*. Xue Lin Press.

Lin, X., Li, H., & Zu, W. (2019). Bridging a cultural divide between play and learning: parental ethnotheories of young children's play and their instantiation in contemporary China. *Early Education and Development, 30*(1), 82–97. https://doi-org.ezproxy.lib.monash.edu.au/10.1080/10409289.2018.1514846

Liu, Y., & Feng, X. (2005). Kindergarten educational reform during the past two decades in mainland China: Achievements and problems. *International Journal of Early Years Education, 13*(2), 93–9. https://doi.org/10.1080/09669760500170933

Ministry of Education (2001). 幼儿园教育指导纲要 *[Guidelines for Kindergarten Education Practice-trial Version]*. Ministry of Education.

Ministry of Education (2012). 3-6岁儿童学习与发展指南 *[Early Learning and Development Guidelines for Children Aged 3-6]*. Ministry of Education.

National Education Commission (1989). *Regulations on Kindergarten Education Practice- Trial Version (in Chinese)*. National Education Commission.

Pan, Y., Wang, X., & Li, L. (2018). Early childhood education and development in China. In M. Fleer & B. Van Oers (Eds.), *International Handbook of Early Childhood Education* (Vol 1) (pp. 599–622). Springer.

Rao, N., & Li, H. (2009). 'Eduplay': Beliefs and practices related to play and learning in Chinese kindergartens. In I. Pramling Samuelsson & M. Fleer (Eds.), *Play and Learning in Early Childhood Settings: International Perspectives* (pp. 97–116). Springer.

Rao, N., Ng, S. S. N., & Pearson, E. (2009). Preschool pedagogy: A fusion of traditional Chinese beliefs and contemporary notions of appropriate practice. In C. K. K. Chan & N. Rao (Eds.), *Revising the Chinese Learner: Changing Contexts, Changing Education* (pp. 255–80). Springer.

Solovieva, Y., & Gonzale-Moreno, C. X. (2017). Introducing social role-play to Colombian children 5-6 years. In T. Bruce, P. Hakkarainen & M. Bredikyte (Eds.), *The Routledge International Handbook of Early Childhood Play* (pp. 108–24). Routledge.

Tobin, J., Hsueh, Y., & Karasawa, M. (2009). *Preschool in Three Cultures Revisited: China, Japan, and the United States*. University of Chicago Press.

Vong, K. P. (2012). Play – a multi-modal manifestation in kindergarten education in China. *Early Years*, *32*(1), 35–48. https://doi.org/10.1080/09575146.2011.635339

Vygotsky, L. S. (1987). *The Collected Works of L.S. Vygotsky: Problems of General Psychology* (Vol 1). Kluwer Academic and Plenum Publishers.

Vygotsky, L. S. (1997). *The Collected Works of L.S. Vygotsky: The History of the Development of Higher Mental Functions* (Vol 4). Kluwer Academic and Plenum Publishers.

Vygotsky, L. S. (1998). *The Collected Works of L.S. Vygotsky, Child Psychology* (Vol 5). Kluwer Academic and Plenum Publishers.

Yang, W., & Li, H. (2019). Changing culture, changing curriculum: A case study of early childhood curriculum innovations in two Chinese kindergartens. *The Curriculum Journal*, *30*(3), 279–97. https://doi.org/10.1080/09585176.2019.1568269

Yu, Y. (2017). Early childhood curriculum development in China. In N. Rao, J. Zhou & J. Sun (Eds.), *Early Childhood Education in Chinese Societies* (pp. 101–10). Springer Nature.

Zhu, J. X. (2006). 幼儿园课程 *[Kindergarten-based Curriculum]*. 五南图书出版公司 [Wunan Tushu Publisher].

Zhu, J. X., & Zhang, J. (2008). Contemporary trends and developments in early childhood education in China. *Early Years*, *28*(2), 173–82. https://doi.org/10.1080/09575140802163584

5

Children with Disabilities Growing Up and Exploring Life as Adults – Sociocultural Challenges around the Transition to Adulthood

Louise Bøttcher

> Interviewer: I think this conversation is becoming derailed.
> Sarah: Welcome to my life!

The transition from childhood to adulthood is an important developmental period during which a child explores what it means to be an adult and what kind of adult he/she can and wants to be. While this is true for all children, such a transition poses particular challenges for those children with a severe disability. In Denmark, societal support diminishes at the time when a child finishes compulsory school and needs to find his or her path among adult demands and obligations, which are usually based on what the typical person on the verge of adulthood can do. Young people with disabilities might begin to explore their possibilities for an adult life and develop a motive for becoming an adult. However, as expressed in the quotation from Sarah above, the search for a meaningful adult life might present challenges. This chapter will explore how impairments and social opportunities are intertwined by analysing eight young people's transition to adult life in a Nordic welfare context at the beginning of the twenty-first century.

Development and Disability

Previous research on disability and transitions to adulthood has mainly been positioned within the social model of disability. The social model accentuates the central role of legal, societal and social factors and how these factors act as barriers to equal social participation for children and adults with disabilities, both within and across social institutions (Shakespeare, 2006). Social model-informed research has highlighted that, when young adults with a disability finish compulsory school, the opportunities available to them are limited and the institutional support offered for the transition into adulthood is characterized by uncertainties and flaws (Pallisera et al., 2016; Winn & Hay, 2009). Social barriers around the transition to adulthood include the organization and structure of the educational system and a lack of training options (Pallisera et al., 2016).

It is important that we acknowledge these social barriers; however, the cultural-historical approach to disability argues that, rather than focusing on social barriers alone, we should instead focus on the dialectical relation between the young adult with a disability and the environment. How do impairments and social barriers affect the psychology of young people with a disability as they explore the transitional developmental period between childhood and adulthood?

In his approach to disability, labelled 'Defectology', Vygotsky proceeded from his analytical distinction between the individual and biologically based development of the child (the natural line of development) and the social and cultural development of the child, which is conditioned by the institutional practices in, for example, families and schools (the cultural line of development) (Vygotsky, 1993). Under normal circumstances, the natural and the cultural line of child development support each other. In their everyday settings, children and young people encounter and participate in activity settings organized according to the cultural expectations of what children, adolescents or young adults are able to do – or able to do given the support that is also part of the activity setting. The expectations and support are built into the organization of the activity settings as aged-graded zones of proximal development, and they are apparent as typically taken-for-granted ways of organizing children's and young people's everyday life within a particular cultural-historical setting. This *dialectic* intertwining is central to the developmental thinking within cultural-historical theory and means that analysing child development – for children with or without disabilities – involves analysing how the biological/individual and cultural lines of development condition each other and create future developmental possibilities by offering solutions for present conflicts and challenges (Bøttcher & Dammeyer, 2016). From the cultural-historical tradition perspective, disability arises and develops dialectically from an *incongruence* between the natural line and the cultural line of development (Vygotsky, 1993). The often problematic development of children with disabilities is not only based in the different psycho-physical endowments, but just as much because many age- and context-typical activities are less relevant and supportive for children with disabilities. The developmental potential of activities with more competent others and the mediation with tools and procedures in mainstream activity settings imply that the participating children have particular motor, cognitive, perceptual and communicational capacities. Thus, for children with disabilities, any primary biological impairments (such as sensory, organic or neurological impairments) will affect the ability of the child to participate in social activities, including learning activities, since these activities may fall beyond the child's zone of proximal development. The cultural-historical institutionalized mediation in mainstream settings does not support and accommodate the development of children with atypical psychophysical constitutions in the same way as it supports and accommodates children without impairments. Alternative mediation or alternative ways to organize education will often be called for, especially in situations in which children have more severe impairments.

The aim of this chapter is to further examine and elaborate how the concept of incongruence can shed light on how young people with severe disabilities explore and strive for positions in the adult world. While social marginalization and other problems of social participation are often considered as either a consequence of individual impairments or of a lack of social opportunities, this chapter will seek to untangle individual and social challenges during the transition from childhood to adulthood for young people with disabilities living in a twenty-first-century Nordic welfare society.

Transition to Adult Life and Exploration of How to Be an Adult

Transitions are changes from one practice to another, each consisting of several activity settings (Hedegaard & Edwards, 2014). To analyse exploration in the transitional process as changes in the developmental relation between person and environment, I will draw on Hedegaard (2012, 2014), who, as part of her wholeness approach, assigns a pivotal role to the concepts of value positions, demands and motives. Beginning with value positions, different institutional settings endorse particular ideas about what constitutes a good life. The activity settings are organized according to the institutional goals about a good life for the participants under the conditions of the institution as set by the societal objective (Hedegaard, 2012). The institutional value positions are expressed in the dominating activity or activities associated with particular institutions.

Transitions will thus involve changes from often well-known activities, demands and institutional motives to unknown or lesser-known activities, demands and institutional motives. As suggested by Winther-Lindqvist (2019), new demands and motives might be anticipated before the transition, but they still need to be concretized and actively adopted by the person in the new setting. Within the institutional setting, the institutional motives are experienced by the individuals as demands (Hedegaard, 2014). Participating in new and different institutional practices can thus also be an exploration of how one experiences the demands and the values about a good life path endorsed by the practice.

From a cultural-historical perspective, transitions hold potential to spark exploration because they interrupt established relations between the child (or adult) and its social settings and create opportunities for new forms of social relations (Hedegaard & Fleer, 2019). When the young adult anticipates or is confronted with tasks that challenge his or her existing ways of thinking and acting, new demands are placed on the person's way of participating and this stimulates the development of new motives. Children and adults develop their motive orientations from the wholeness of their social situation, the demands of the social situation and their engagement in activities within the setting. Elkonin proposes that, in a general sense, the transition to adulthood is associated with the development of the motive to be accepted by one's peers and to be recognized as competent by others (Hedegaard, 2002). In the present Danish society, adult demands will often include gaining a professional position and being able to sustain oneself economically and practically. However, the current society offers many different ways to meet this demand and an important developmental task on the verge of adulthood is orient oneself among the many opportunities and decide for oneself which that are considered attractive and possible. Young people on the verge of adult life explore this motive through activities in which they consider and experiment with ways of being an adult and being accepted as an adult by others. Naturally, such an exploration will vary depending on which peer group one wishes to be recognized by and what kind of competence one is seeking.

The cultural-historical approach to the transition to adulthood thus stresses the active nature of the transition. Both the age periods and the transition from one to the next are related to the social situation of development rather than age per se as suggested in more classic theories of development as universal stages. Furthermore, the transition from childhood to adulthood has become rather protracted in twenty-first-century Western heritage countries as the social situation of development for most young adults includes prolonged schooling rather than earlier times' abrupt transition at the end of compulsory school into wage-labour especially among people from rural areas and the working class. The current prolonged transition period and the more open range of possibilities may allow for more explorative activity. As expressed in Fleer (2014), the strength of the cultural-historical approach is its ability to bring out the dynamic motions of development rather than mechanic temporality. In this chapter, the cultural-historical approach will be used to analyse the transition from childhood to adulthood as a motive-driven process of exploration.

Research suggests that having a disability potentially affects this exploration. Societally embedded prejudices might shape how young people with disabilities perceive and employ social opportunities. For example, a recent study found that young people with autism spectrum disorders chose to hide their disability when seeking employment to avoid potential stigmatization, yet, as a result, they forfeited their access to tailored support (Nolan & Gleeson, 2017). Niemi and Mietola (2017) found that being a young adult with a disability in the twenty-first century implies negotiating two competing cultural narratives of disability: the first (and older) narrative sees disability as lack of ability and the second narrative, which originates in the disability rights discourse and forms a counter-position to the first narrative, highlights the social nature of barriers and the personal competences of people with disabilities despite impairments (Niemi & Mietola, 2017). Having a disability potentially affects both which demands the young adult recognizes and how the young adult can relate to the different demands within an activity setting. Furthermore, opportunities for participation will be related to how the institution values diversity among its different participants and prospective participants (Ebersold, 2008). If inclusion is endorsed and enacted as a value, demands may be adapted and support may be tailored to diverse participants, including participants with different types of disabilities.

Taken together, the concept of exploration is in this chapter understood as a socially embedded activity that includes experimentation of both what one can do and what one would like to do based in one's motive orientation. Motives are developed via a protracted process and cultivated through activity (Leontjev, 1978). Thus, motive development and explorative activity are dialectically related: As the child or adult develops his motives, the person engages and participates differently in his or her current activity settings or begins to consider other activity settings, and, as he or she participates in old or new activity settings, he or she may redefine existing or create new motives. Engaged participation is a prerequisite for the development of personal motive orientations that corresponds to institutional motives (Hedegaard, 2014). The development of motives in activity thus seems a key part of further developing the concept of exploration (see also Fleer & Li, Chapter 4 about the relation between motives and exploration).

Presentation of the Study

In the study presented here, explorative activity around the transition to adulthood was investigated by following eight young people with severe disabilities on the verge of adulthood. All of these young people had severe physical impairments and were dependent on others for their basic needs. In addition, all of them had communicational impairments and either used alternative communicative means (such as books or voice-output computers) or were dependent on helpers to translate their dysarthric language. The young people in the study were between fifteen and twenty-five years of age, which matches the prolonged transition period from childhood to adulthood in present-day Denmark. The study used a combination of interviews with the young participants and interviews with their parents. The interviews were individually tailored to accommodate the communicational preferences of each participant. All participants were interviewed twice. The first set of interviews focused on the life history of the young participant and his or her family. The second set of interviews, which took place one year later, were follow-up interviews that explored the events of the previous year regarding the transitional challenges identified in the first interviews. This chapter will focus on the young people's perspectives as they expressed them. For the analysis, all participants and interviews were included in the initial search for relevant themes in relation to exploration. However, in the final write-up I have chosen more in-depth analysis of the exploration of four of the participants whose interviews were most rich in relation to the chosen themes (for analyses including other participants, see e.g. Bøttcher, 2018, 2019).

References in parentheses refer to statement numbers in the interview material. Sarah and William communicated with their dysarthric natural (verbal) language, which was decoded by their teacher or helper. In quotations from Sarah and William, the back-and-forth mediation of the helper (e.g. spelling of words the helper had difficulty decoding) has been omitted and only the condensed meaning stated.

The study is set in a Danish context. Societal value positions about people with disabilities are informed by the UN convention about equal rights for people with disabilities (https://humanrights.dk/our-work/our-work-denmark/disability). The welfare system is guided by the obligation to ensure people with disabilities have equal opportunities to social participation (e.g. legislation on social service no. 369 from 18 April 2017 https://www.retsinformation.dk/Forms/R0710.aspx?id=191895) and to counteract the discrimination of people with disabilities. Suitable education, relevant equipment (such as wheelchairs, communication devices and other necessary aids) and professional support are all provided as part of the free welfare system, according to the person's needs. The legalization for individuals under eighteen typically offers more support, for example, closer health-care follow-up and educational support, than the legalization for people at eighteen or above. For adults with disabilities, the Danish (and Nordic) welfare system offers user-managed assistants. Those adults with disabilities who are able to plan and direct their own life may apply for around-the-clock user-managed helpers. Those who are unable to live independently with user-managed assistants (from the perspective of the municipality) are offered accommodation at an institutionalized living unit.

Exploring Capabilities for Independent Life

For the young people in the study, the exploration related to the transition to adult life began more concretely as an exploration of their capabilities for life away from their parents. Most of them had been enrolled in adapted classes, although Emilia and Freya had been enrolled in mainstream classes all along, with practical help and continued adaptations of everyday activities. Thus all participants had substantial experience with how their impairments affected their opportunities for participation and were aware of the need for ongoing negotiations to be able to do what they would like to do. At the verge of adult life, their substantial physical impairments hindered a mainstream trajectory of simply moving out of home into a flat or student accommodation when they wished. To live independently, they needed to make themselves eligible for user-managed assistants or accept an institutionalized living unit. Most did not view institutionalized living as an attractive option, and several of the participating young people expressed strong motives to become eligible for user-managed personal assistance:

> Jonathan [With Tobii, a gaze-controlled voice-output computer]: I would like to live independently
>
> (Jonathan2, 54).

This more general motive, expressed here by Jonathan but shared by several of the other young participants (Emilia2, 5-6; Sarah2, 77-82; William1, 739-760), needed to be further developed in relation to the kind of life they wished to live aided by their assistants and what this would require of the young people themselves. Jonathan had tried institutionalized living at a boarding school, where he had attended the first part of his adapted young people's education. Among other things, he had been annoyed about his activities being decided by the institutional time structure and availability of staff rather than his own preference for when to do what, for example, go to bed at night. Jonathan chose to complete the final part of his adapted young people's education at Egmont Højskolen. Egmont Højskolen (https://www.egmont-hs.dk) is a unique folk high school founded in 1956 with the aim of creating more life opportunities for people with disabilities. Egmont welcomes students with and without disabilities and offers subject teaching in 'life with user-managed personal assistants' and 'my life- my responsibility'. While at Egmont, students with disabilities hire personal assistants among the students without disabilities who have a wish to work as assistants during their stay at Egmont. As all students pay for their stay at Egmont, getting a job as assistant is a way for students without disability to finance their stay while also getting relevant work experience. According to the rules at Egmont, the students with disabilities who have personal assistants are responsible for conducting job interviews, describing work tasks for their assistants, instructing their new assistants and much more, in cooperation with their primary teacher (https://www.egmont-hs.dk). Thus, the young people were supported in exploring their capabilities to live independently by participating in institutional practices that helped to develop their independence through demands and tailored support (see also Fleer, Chapter 9 for further elaboration on how institutional settings structure development). To master these tasks will be necessary for the young people with disabilities who wish to be eligible for independent living with user-managed personal assistants afterwards. The educational environment at Egmont created a demanding situation for Jonathan that required him to explore his own capabilities in relation to concrete tasks with user-managed assistants. Jonathan described the experience in the following way:

Interviewer:	How was it moving to Egmont?
Jonathan [with Tobii]:	I think it is great, but a little tough.
Interviewer:	Why is it tough?
Jonathan [Tobii]:	I am completely new and employer and school.
[...]	
Interviewer:	What is it you need to be able to do to be an employer?

| Jonathan [Tobii]: | Responsibility and meetings and laundry and other things (Jonathan2, 10-13, 38-40). |

The activity settings at Egmont placed new, high demands on Jonathan that exceeded his initial capabilities. However, the presence of supportive teachers and tailored practices enabled him to explore his own capabilities in relation to his future responsibilities and to gradually acquire new skills and competences, thereby becoming able to participate in new and more advanced ways and refine his motive for how to live with user-managed assistants. After a few months at Egmont, Jonathan began to go on individual trips with his assistants on his own accord (Jonathan father2, 56-58).

Sarah, who was twenty-two, had also spent time at Egmont. She stated that '[i]t was a good thing to be at Egmont. Because they made a lot of demands on you' (Sarah1, 145-157). Sarah described how her time before Egmont was difficult because she had realized and felt depressed about the fact she was disabled. During this time, her communication had been dependent on a very small set of people who were able to understand her dysarthric language and she became socially withdrawn (Sarah1, 937-976). The incongruence between Sarah's biologically based communicational impairments and the available support in her environment had hampered her exploration of her own capabilities. Sarah's main teacher recommended Egmont, because she had prior knowledge of how the practices at Egmont supported development of self-determination in young people with disabilities, including those with communicational disability. Sarah went there at her recommendation. The demanding learning environment at Egmont changed Sarah's tendency to withdrawal. At Egmont, she became part of a youth social life environment and quickly experienced that she could communicate successfully with her new teachers and assistants (Sarah1, 1183-1195). Thus, the unique adapted learning environment at Egmont supported both Sarah and Jonathan in exploring their capabilities as active social participants and furthermore contributed to Sarah's emotional acceptance of her situation. Sarah herself felt Egmont had helped her 'grow up' and become ready to apply for independent living with user-managed assistants (Sarah1, 656-673).

Exploring One's Own Motives and Ideas about Oneself as an Adult Person

For the young people in the study, the motive to develop their capability for independent life with user-managed assistants was part of a broader motive of building a desirable adult life. In current Western heritage societies, education functions as preparation for finding an occupation, acquiring professional skills and becoming someone with socially accepted capabilities. For the young people in the study, participation in compulsory school and different types of youth education with institutional motives informed by inclusion provided similar motives for finding an occupation and a socially accepted professional position:

One example is William, twenty-one years of age. William had graduated from a three-year course in music sound editing at a local youth education institution for people with disabilities who were unable to attend mainstream youth education. He had sought out this school in particular because it allowed him to pursue his interest in music sound editing (William1, 601–666). William was able to edit music using eye-tracking technology together with computer software for sound editing. Because of his severe level of impairments, he was deemed unable to support himself financially through paid work and was assigned disability allowance and user-managed assistants. However, William wanted to employ his competences as a professional sound editor. He wished to be recognized for his professional skills and to be given the opportunity to use the knowledge and competences he had acquired through his education (William2, 63–65). He wished to pursue further opportunities to apply and develop his skills as a music producer through commercial commissions, but this was difficult, both because his status as a disability allowance recipient did not allow him to engage in paid work and because his physical and communicational impairments made it difficult for him to actively advertise his professional services. Not all music production studios would be wheelchair accessible, and not everybody would have the patience and the open mind to recognize William's competence when expressed in his dysarthric speech (it could take a long time, even for a helper familiar with William's pronunciation, to decode his meaning).

Sarah felt thwarted too. Similar to William, she was living independently in her own flat on disability allowance and managing her daily life with user-managed assistants. However, as she had come to realize the motive of being eligible for user-managed assistants, she found that just sitting at home managing her helpers was lonely (Sarah2, 19–20, 84–87). She wanted to involve herself in society outside of home, but was unsure how to do it. She was currently exploring what to do with her life. She was keen to do something with occupational therapy (Sarah2, 152–153), but Sarah had severe learning impairments and had finished compulsory school without qualifications. Thus, the educational pathway to become an occupational therapist would require her to pass both lower secondary and upper secondary examinations at an adult education centre. Only then would she be in a position to apply to a university college to become an occupational therapist. This long-term plan seemed even longer for Sarah, given that learning had been difficult and time-consuming for her in the past. She would only be able to manage a few subjects at any given time. Sarah had started to enquire at local adult education centres, but, for her, the conventional educational trajectory seemed too protracted. Like William, Sarah felt restricted by a lack of available opportunities in her exploration of how to move forward, as she expressed in the introductory quotation to this chapter.

William and Sarah and most of the other young participants in the study (Emilia1, 52–53; Magnus2, 375–406; Freya1, 77–80; Jonathan2, 140–141) had adopted the societal value position about education as the way forward into a meaningful adult life. However, they experienced the transition towards further education or employment as an encounter with very high and inflexible demands, which created a sudden increase in the incongruence between their capabilities and the demands within desired activity settings. Some of them felt hampered either, like William, by the transition from education to occupation or, like Sarah, by the substantive incongruence between her personal capabilities and the organization of educational trajectories. In their exploration of how to be adults, the conflict between their motives for adult life and their present social opportunities forced them to explore what kind of positions, given their impairments, were actually possible for them in the twenty-first-century welfare society.

Exploring Alternative Pathways for Adult Life

Since their motive to become an adult with a recognized professional position was challenged by a lack of opportunities in the mainstream trajectory for secondary education or on the labour market, the young people in the study were forced to consider, negotiate and explore alternatives. Sarah's original motive to become an occupational therapist was based in two motives: to escape loneliness and to employ her extensive experience as a user of different aids to develop and adapt aids for people with physical disabilities (Sarah2, 153–154). If this was not possible as an occupational therapist, Sarah wished to revisit her original motives and consider how else she could engage in society and share her experiences and contribute meaningfully to practices associated with improving life for people with disabilities. No existing trajectory or social position of this kind was apparent to her and, thus, there was no established activity setting she could apply to be a part of. In a self-initiated activity, Sarah had written an article for the cerebral palsy organization magazine about her treatment experiences, especially with chiropractic. In the process of getting her article accepted, the editor had changed Sarah's wording in several places. Sarah wrote and objected to his editing, stating that her original, very explicit wording appealed better to the article's intended target audience – young people with cerebral palsy (Sarah2, 243–251). In this activity, she explored her idea that, as a young user of physical therapies, she had something unique to offer other people in similar situations.

As described above, William found it difficult to explore his skills as a professional sound producer that musicians would value (William2, 63–65). William's father had managed to negotiate a novel position for William at his former youth education institution. One day a week, William assisted other students to record music by editing their sound and, in doing so, he applied and further developed his skills (William2, 93–135). His disability allowance was put on hold to allow him to try out this tailored job opportunity. In addition, one of William's personal assistants was a professional musician and William had offered to master his new album free of charge. In both instances, William's unique position as a person with a disability and music production skills created alternative and novel adult positions that William could explore. For William, the important motive was still 'in that way, to be able to feel as an ordinary person' (William2, 152–158) but he was exploring alternative ways to pursue this motive. Furthermore, William's ability to use the sound editing software on his gazed-controlled computer had attracted the attention of the company that sold the gaze-control hardware. William was asked to be their ambassador and to participate in sale promotions to demonstrate the product's potentials for other people with similar disabilities (William2, 217–236). While this was not the type of professional career for which William was originally motivated, the assignment as an ambassador for a professional company offered William an alternative opportunity to become recognized as a competent adult.

The most ambitious of all the young participants was Emilia. She was seventeen years old and a student at a mainstream upper secondary school. She had similar ambitions to – if not higher ambitions than – her friends without disabilities regarding her future education and occupation; since she started upper secondary school, she had wanted to become a physicist and a researcher. However, in her exploration of how to fulfil her ambitions, she was well aware that working hard in school might not be sufficient:

Emilia (1, 54–57) [email interview with Tobii]: What it takes to reach my dreams is actually a very interesting question. I think this area is where I experience most extensive discrimination. I feel like, because I have a disability, I have to perform 110 per cent to gain legitimacy in upper secondary school. This impression is based on the fact that the first upper secondary school I applied for declined my application even though I had the required grades. I don't know if you will be able to understand what I mean, but it [is like] I always have to do perfectly to legitimize my presence. Another key to reaching my dreams is also that I retain my spirits, my health and my happy disposition. And that I am granted yet another flexible arrangement to be able to go through university.

Like William and Sarah, Emilia explored possibilities for alternative pathways. Unlike Sarah, Emilia's ability to learn was similar to her peers'. She had attended mainstream school and followed a mainstream curriculum throughout her compulsory education. She faced a different kind of challenge when moving onto upper secondary school, as Emilia's mother elaborated in her narrative of why Emilia was rejected by the first upper secondary school she applied for:

Emilia's mother (1, 95): They wanted her to study for her upper secondary exams at an adult education centre, because that's what most people with cerebral palsy do, one subject at a time and then it takes them twenty years to finish.

Emilia therefore had to negotiate her way into mainstream upper secondary school. First, she had to get accepted. Second, she had to be allowed to take five years, instead of the usual three, to finish. Emilia's need for an adapted schedule in upper secondary school originated mainly from her motor impairments. Writing the extensive amount of assignments required in upper secondary school would take much longer for Emilia, who had to write by gaze control, joystick control or lengthy communication with her assistants, who would operate the computer at Emilia's command. However, her need to negotiate extended beyond practical educational arrangements. Emilia explained that her *having ambitions* was in conflict with societal expectations about people with a disability. Because of this experience, Emilia chose to explore a new social role:

Emilia (2, 11): I am active on social media in that way that I regularly post photos of my daily life and what I do. [...] My target group is the general population, but especially people in relation to disability; for instance, people with disabilities who need to see that someone else with a disability can accomplish a lot and thus be motivated not to give up, but I also want to reach people who don't know anybody with a disability.

Thus, in response to the different conflicts she had experienced between her motives and existing societal expectations and opportunities, Emilia had chosen to explore how to be a role model for other people with disabilities, showing that disability and ambition were not mutually exclusive. Emilia's two types of exploration – being a mainstream upper secondary school student and a role model on social media – were related, since Emilia had a role model herself, and she underlined the importance she attached to this role model. Emilia did not doubt her ability to become a physicist researcher, but she felt uncertain whether society, and more specifically a university, would accept someone like her as a student and later as a member of academic staff:

Emilia (1, 52–53): In the future, I dream about going to university. Actually, I think it is more than a dream, it is beginning to look more and more realistic. [...] I have got a new good friend who has infused me with an extra zest for life, because he is an associate professor at [name] university, uses Tobii [the gaze-controlled computer] and at the same time, he is a really nice and sympatric person, who, despite his ALS [Amyotrophic lateral sclerosis], can function in this position.

The fact that she and her good friend were in similar situations, that is, that they both have severe physical impairments and communicate with a gaze-controlled voice-output computer, helped Emilia to believe that her ambitions would not be thwarted by lack of social opportunities, as she had thought when she first applied for upper secondary school.

Discussion: Exploration, Incongruence and Development of Motives

This chapter set out to explicate exploration as a socially embedded activity closely connected to a person's motive development. For the young people in this study, who had severe disabilities and were in transition to adult life, two things were changing. Firstly, the young people with disabilities started to develop new motives that were largely similar to the motives of those without disabilities, as they regarded independent living, the acquisition of secondary education and professional skills as the means of finding a social position as adult. Secondly, although the young people in the study initially shared motives and values about a desirable adult life with their non-disabled peers, as people with severe disabilities, they were eventually instigated to modify their motives. Previous studies have also identified social barriers in the transition to adulthood for young people with disabilities (Nolan & Gleeson, 2017; Pallisera et al., 2016; Winn & Hay, 2009), but the cultural-historical conceptualization of disability used in the present study further reveals how specific impairments can also give rise to challenges to participation, because some impairments are difficult to fully compensate for. For example, a lack of verbal speech can only be partly compensated for, even with assistants or well-developed alternative communication means and practices. Slow and difficult learning can be compensated for with tailored learning support and extra time, but the extra time involved cannot be regained by the affected person. Severe physical impairments can be compensated for with user-managed assistants, but this arrangement results in an alternative, rather than a mainstream, life path. These different types of incongruence affected the types of activities the young participants could explore. Such a persistent incongruence was apparent for Sarah, for whom a mainstream educational path was incongruent with her style and speed of learning, for William, whose lack of fluent verbal language limited his ability to present himself as a professional sound producer in music studios (even if they were assessable), and for Emilia, who needed a less intensive schedule in upper secondary school and at university. Thus, while the personal motives of young people with severe disabilities mirrored the broad societal value position about inclusion – endorsed in compulsory school and youth education institutions – these young people were forced to explore the nature of the incongruence between their biologically based impairments and societal conditions in order to develop their motives and carve out alternative life paths for themselves.

At the psychological level, the original motives of the young adults related to adult life were transformed and further refined through different experiences of conflict and increasing incongruence. For the two young adults William and Sarah, life in their twenties did not seem to offer the way forward promised by the inclusion value position. Rather than following a mainstream educational path to an adult position in society, they were instigated to explore what kind of position was actually possible, given the incongruence between their impairments and their societal opportunities. Contrary to the young people in the study by Nolan and Gleeson (2017), who could choose to hide their autism spectrum disorder, Sarah and William and the other young people in this study had both noticeable and severe impairments. They were forced to move beyond general inclusion-informed motives and explore how to negotiate alternative life paths that balanced personal motives with societal opportunities. Their exploration of their own capabilities became intertwined with an exploration of what kind of life was actually possible as an adult with a severe disability. As they grew into adulthood, their earlier motives for adult positions, which were similar to those of the young people without disabilities, contributed to an activist mindset and refinement of motives dialectically connected to incongruence challenges encountered in different practices. They explored and created alternative pathways, not by ignoring their impairments but by accepting them as particular limitations while recognizing their personal assets. They explored ways to find a position as an adult given both their limitations and assets. Revisiting the two competing cultural narratives about disability – disability as lack of ability or as an activist stance of rights to societal participation (Niemi & Mietola, 2017) – the young people expressed themselves as people exploring their unique abilities within the conditions of social barriers and their biologically based impairments.

Conclusion

Exploration for young people with disabilities on the verge of adult life is socially embedded as an exploration of how particular impairments transform social opportunities. As revealed by previous research, social barriers to participation are widespread for people with disabilities. Productive exploration by people with disabilities hinges on institutions with value positions that endorse the inclusion and accommodation of demands. A lack of opportunities and the necessity of carving out an alternative path for oneself arise from the dialectic interaction between impairments and societal practices. However, at the psychological level, the value position of inclusion and the rights of people with a disability not to be hindered in social participation has advanced an activist mindset and individual exploration of activities that create alternative life paths, sometimes even in response to social barriers. Emilia is the most salient example of how concrete activities related to the following of one motive – to pursue education – had given rise to a new activity aimed at changing societal prejudices about the level of ambition in people with severe disabilities. The motivated striving to find or create social positions for themselves also created small changes to society that could potentially remove social barriers and improve future life opportunities for people with similar disabilities.

References

Bøttcher, L. (2018). Creating relevant and supportive developmental conditions for children and youth with disabilities. *Learning, Culture and Social Interaction, 26*(1), 1–164. https://doi.org/10.1016/j.lcsi.2018.04.007

Bøttcher, L. (2019). Children with disabilities growing up and becoming adults: Sociocultural challenges around the transition to adulthood. In M. Hedegaard & A. Edwards (Eds.), *Supporting Difficult Transitions: Children, Young People and Their Carers* (pp. 241–62). Bloomsbury Academic.

Bøttcher, L., & Dammeyer, J. (2016). *Development and Learning of Young Children with Disabilities: A Vygotskian perspective*. Springer.

Ebersold, S. (2008). Adapting higher education to the needs of disabled students: Developments, challenges and prospects. In OECD, *Higher Education to 2030: Demography* (Vol 1) (pp. 221–41). OECD publishing.

Fleer, M. (2014). Beyond developmental geology: A cultural-historical theorization of digital visual technologies for studying young children's development. In Fleer & Ridgeway (Eds.), *Visual Methodologies and Digital Tools for Researching with Young Children. Transforming Visuality* (pp. 15–34). Springer Press.

Hedegaard, M. (2002). *Learning and Child Development: A Cultural-historical Study*. Aarhus University Press.

Hedegaard, M. (2012). Analyzing children's learning and development in everyday settings from a cultural-historical wholeness approach. *Mind, Culture and Activity*, 19(2), 127–38. https://doi.org/10.1080/10749039.2012.665560

Hedegaard, M. (2014). The significance of demands and motives across practices in children's learning and development: An analysis of learning in home and school. *Learning, Culture and Social Interaction*, 3, 188–94. https://doi.org/10.1016/j.lcsi.2014.02.008

Hedegaard, M., & Edwards, A. (2014). Transitions and children's learning. *Learning, Culture and Social Interaction*, 3, 185–7. https://doi.org/10.1016/j.lcsi.2014.02.007

Hedegaard, M., & Fleer, M. (2019). Children's transitions in everyday life and institutions: New conceptions and understanding of transitions. In M. Hedegaard & M. Fleer (Eds.), *Children's Transitions in Everyday Life and Institutions* (pp. 1–18). Bloomsbury.

Leontjev, A. N. (1978). *Activity, Consciousness, and Personality*. Prentice Hall.

Niemi, A., & Mietola, R. (2017). Between hopes and possibilities: (Special) educational paths, agency and subjectivities. *Scandinavian Journal of Disability Research*, 19(3), 218–29. http://doi.org/10.1080/15017419.2016.1239588

Nolan, C., & Gleeson, C. I. (2017). The transition to employment: The perspectives of students and graduates with disabilities. *Scandinavian Journal of Disability Studies*, 19(3), 230–44. https://doi.org/10.1080/15017419.2016.1240102

Pallisera, M., Fullana, J., Puyaltó, C., & Vilà, M. (2016). Changes and challenges in the transition to adulthood: Views and experiences of young people with learning disabilities and their families. *European Journal of Special Needs Education*, 31(3), 391–406. https://doi.org/10.1080/08856257.2016.1163014

Shakespeare, T. (2006). *Disability Rights and Wrongs*. Routledge.

Vygotsky, L. S. (1993). The fundamentals of Defectology. In R. W. Rieber & A.S. Carton (Eds.), *The Collected Works of L.S. Vygotsky* (Vol 2). Plenum Press.

Winn, S., & Hay, I. (2009). Transition from school for youth with a disability: Issues and challenges. *Disability & Society*, *24*(1), 103–15. https://doi.org/10.1080/09687590802535725

Winther-Lindqvist, D. (2019). Becoming a schoolchild – a positive developmental crisis. In M. Hedegaard & M. Fleer (Eds.), *Children's Transitions in Everyday Life and Institutions* (pp. 47–70). Bloomsbury.

Part Two

Children's Explorations during Microgenetic Transitions within Activity Settings

6

Crisis as Microgenetic Developmental Transitions: Using Explorative Activities in Micro-transitions to Recognize Opportunities for Development between Young Children and Their Fathers – A Cross-national Study

Rita Chawla-Duggan and Rajani Konantambigi

Introduction

Internationally, the social context of parenting is changing, so what men do as fathers is also changing (Adler & Lenz, 2017; Henz, 2019; Sriram, 2019a; United Nations, 2011) and this will be increasingly important to children's well-being (OECD, 2016) in the future. In this chapter we shed light on fathers and child development in families across national contexts, focusing on how explorative activities in moments of crisis helped us to recognize opportunities for development. The chapter draws from a study of families in England, Hong Kong, Norway and Mumbai, India. Here we present data from families in England and Mumbai, India. Ours' is an example of a study that engaged in the microgenetic analysis (Vygotsky, 1998b) of instructional relationships within family practices.

We use a Vygotskian approach to *crisis* (a variation of the concept of conflict), to draw attention to important developmental moments. Moments are understood to occur when disruptions in the lines of development (Vygotsky, 1978) prompt qualitative change. They are developmental transitions. In our study we use Hedegaard's (2008, 2009) model of learning and development to examine how transition happens through moments of crisis from the child's social situations of development during father-child interactions. The model makes it possible to make visible moments of crisis occurring between a dominant motive, the other motive as the child sees it, and the subsequent micro-transition. In the chapter we characterize children's exploration through its relationship with the fathers' instructional strategies in micro-transitions. Taking the position that exploration occurs within a regulative structure of pedagogic communication (Bernstein, 1971) (relating to adult-child power relations), the study also traces how the *framing* (Bernstein, 1971) of instructional strategies (Bugrimenko & El'konin, 2001) in father-child interactions, limits developmental possibilities. This is important because we assume that *framing* can facilitate or limit the mobile characteristic of the object-motive relationship in exploration. The study raises theoretical questions about connections between institutional regulation, opportunities for individual development through children's explorative activities and societal values about childhood and fatherhood, constituted through the demographic make-up of the fathers in this study.

The chapter divides into five parts. Part one presents the problem of father involvement and our rationale for the research. Part two discusses our research design in terms of theory, method and analysis. In part three we present data from a family in Mumbai and in England to analyse exploration in micro-transitions. Part four discusses the analysis and makes connections with wider instructional strategies (Bugrimenko & El'konin, 2001), framing (Bernstein, 1971) and developmental possibilities. We argue that exploration in micro-transitions occurs through a series of moments, demonstrating the mobile characteristic of the object-motive relationship, but this mobility is limited or facilitated by the framing in the pedagogic relationship. In this respect young children's opportunities for development occur with children being both a producer and product of wider institutional and societal values about fathering and childhood.

Background and Rationale

The last two decades demonstrate increasing international interest in father involvement, at both policy and research level (Adler & Lenz, 2017; Burgess & Davies, 2017; Chawla-Duggan & Milner, 2016; Hook & Wolfe, 2012; Kwok & Li, 2015; Sriram, 2019a; United Nations, 2011; Williams, 2008). Our study examined father engagement in England, Hong Kong, India and Norway; countries which are increasingly interested in father involvement and child socialization, but who are at different stages of their own histories and cultural practices in terms of gender regimes, family policies and work-based cultures

(Adler & Lenz, 2017). In this chapter we refer to data from families living in Mumbai, India and in England.

In India, although fathers are invisible in policy (Sriram & Sandhu, 2013), traditionally they do play an important role in their children's family lives (Sriram, 2019b; Sriram & Sandhu, 2013). Fathering is part of the duties of a *family householder*. A father is expected to perform his *swadharma* (duty in life) for the family's welfare, and to fulfil roles of provider, guide, mentor, and nurturer and pass on *sanskar* (social/moral conduct) (Kapoor, 2000; Seymour, 1999). With more middle-class women entering the workforce, parenting in India is in transition (Kumar, 2019). Men, for example, are increasingly required to share co-parenting responsibilities (Saraff & Srivastava, 2008), and urban Indian fathers are becoming more conscious of sharing the parenting role (Kumar, 2019). In fact, an increasing number of blogs and WhatsApp groups in urban India involve exchanges about father involvement (Sriram, 2019a), suggesting the desire by younger, educated, middle class, urban men, to develop their fathering role beyond the traditional duties.

In England, while a changing landscape about child well-being and gender equality generally forms the background for changes in ideas about father involvement (Henz, 2019), recent trends still demonstrate socio-economic status as the key driver in many aspects of British society. Father involvement is no exception, but Henz's survey reveals that the problem is compounded by the fact that the father's education now plays a key role in shaping involvement. When compared with other European countries in the millennium, Britain exhibited clear differences in father involvement between socio-economic groups (Henz, 2019), and this existed despite the emergence of policies such as shared parental leave introduced by the UK government in 2015.

Our choice of countries was strategic, in that despite differences in cultural positions of fathering in Europe (including England) and Asia, we assumed that changing family structures or policies may or may not actually change the way men think about their roles, because there are cultural values that may continue to exert a strong influence on paternal engagement. Tulviste (1999) argued there are various ways of describing societies and cultures within psychology. We draw upon a *cultural-psychological* approach which is compatible with the cultural-historical (C-H) perspective we adopt, because of its ability to trace connections between the psychological and the social. Furthermore, since cultures are grounded in histories, and change over time, analyses of what people do at any point in time has to be viewed in relation to the historical trajectories in which their actions take place. In this respect we assume 'a culture's values, beliefs and practices are examined from an insider's point of view' (Berry 1999, cited in Freitas et al., 2008, p. 162), so that:

> When two or more cultures are compared the intention is not to use a single measuring stick (LeVine, 1989), or means of ranking, but rather to show how each cultural group, as it developed over historical time, is both the evolving producer and the evolving product of cultural values, beliefs, practices, and policies relevant to prevailing material conditions. (Ibid.)

Despite changes to father involvement cross nationally over the last twenty years, we remain limited in knowing about *how* fathers actually engage in the psychological work of a child's development; and we know even less about the connections between the psychological, the institutional practices and their relation to wider societal values. We do know from longitudinal data in the United States (Sarkadi et al., 2008) and England (Flouri, 2005) that correlations exist between father involvement and children's developmental outcomes, even when controlling for mother involvement (Flouri, 2005) and socio-economic status (Lamb & Lewis, 2013). Early father involvement is particularly associated with a protective factor in counteracting risk conditions that might lead to later low educational attainment levels (Cabrera & Tamis-LeMonda, 2013). Having said that, nothing in the developmental literature actually suggests that children need something vastly different from fathers than from mothers; but it may be that *how they get it* could be different (Roggmann et al., 2013), and this might be related to wider societal and cultural practices associated with the experiences and expectations of being men in families. In this chapter we examine *how* opportunities for development are created in micro-transitions by focusing on children's explorative activities in father-child interactions. Accordingly, the problem we address, asks:

How does an examination of children's explorative activities in micro-transitions, from the child's perspective, help us recognize opportunities for development through father-child relations, in families in Mumbai and in England?

Theory, Method and Analysis

A Cultural-historical Model (C-H) of Learning and Development through Family Interactions

We adopt a C-H perspective of development because dominant conceptions of development tend to be one dimensional (Hedegaard, 2009), dependent on time and focus on developing different psychological functions and competencies. For us, a more fruitful perspective understands the child's development as a person, developing in relation to the institutions in which s/he participates. This means understanding how conditions lead children through their crisis of development. From a C-H perspective those conditions are dialectical; they contribute to children's development of competencies and motives and are part of the activities in which they participate (Hedegaard, 2009). A C-H perspective of development therefore allows us as researchers to ask questions about how social and material conditions support or inhibit children's exploration in micro-transitions. Hedegaard's model (2008, 2009) uses three contexts to examine child development – society, institution and persons. An institutional perspective helps us to understand different practices within the family; and a person perspective tells us about the child's motive as an indication of their perspective. In this study we examine each child's motives in their everyday family interactions with their fathers; the similarities and differences in family practices; and we identify connections between patterns of interactions and beliefs and values about fathers and childhood in wider society.

Children's Exploration within a C-H Approach to Learning and Development

The concept of exploration can refer to play or curiosity related actions; essentially any social situation that affects what and how objects and relationships are explored (Ødegaard & Hedegaard, 2020; Ødegaard, 2020). Exploration in pedagogy not only occurs through the verbal (Bakhtin, 1986), but also through the non-verbal, the body (Linnell, 2009); for example, through silent practices, driven by body, performance and doings (Ødegaard, 2020). Ødegaard (2020) characterizes exploration and subsequently clarifies how we might recognize whether a pedagogic practice is supporting exploration or not. She contrasts monologic cultures with dialogic cultures. In the former, the teacher is a judge or referential organizer and, in the latter, a guide and participant; the latter being more aligned with exploration. In reality, the two cultural orientations are a hybrid in complex communication. In the chapter we consider how characteristics of exploration activities as they occur through micro-transitions, helped us to recognize opportunities for development in father-child interactions.

The Families and Their Activity Settings in England and Mumbai

We studied a total of seven families in Mumbai (three) and England (four).[1] The families were heterosexual and middle class, living in the same household with at least two children, one of preschool age (up to six), and the other of early years' school age (four to eight). We selected middle-class fathers because their employment is generally more flexible and so they can accommodate fathers' parenting roles (Williams, 2008), because they have more control over their hours of work (Kossek & Lautsch, 2017).

Each country level investigator (from a team of four) identified families as middle class using the criteria of private housing, employment and/or degree level education. The fathers in England and in Mumbai were from cluster samples. In England they all lived in the same village in the South West of England. Their children attended the same village preschool and primary school. In Mumbai, the families all lived in the same housing colony, towards the north east end of the Mumbai Metropolitan Region; more specifically, Navi Mumbai. Their children did not attend the same schools or preschool. Tables 6.1 and 6.2 provide an overview of the cluster families in England and Mumbai.

Table 6.1 Families in England

Family	Father/mother employment	Age/nos of children	[2] Target child/ children
Family 2 Mr & Mrs Corbett	Father FT self-employed – researcher Mother – PT administrator	3 children: Fleur (F) 9 Lance (M) 8 Bea (F) 4	Lance (M) 8 Bea (F) 4
Family 3 Mr & Mrs Major	Father FT self-employed – maths educational software designer with mathematics tutoring business Mother – works with father in the business	3 children: Hugh (M) 8 Bell (F) 7 Dicky (M) 3	Bell (F) 7 Dicky (M) 3
Family 4 Mr & Mrs James	Father FT – employed in engineering/design company Mother – PT health/ fitness instructor	3 children: Mary (F) 8 Charles (M) 7 Simone (F) 4	Charles (M) 7 Simone (F) 4

Table 6.2 Families in Mumbai, India

Family	Father/mother employment	Age/nos of children	³ Target child/children
Family 1 Mr & Mrs Mohan	Father FT self-employed private banker Mother – housewife	3 children: Shruti (F) 9 Dev (M) 5 Arush (M) 11 months	Dev (M) 5 Arush (M) 11 months
Family 2 Mr & Mrs Sharma	Father FT employed – in an electrical engineering company Mother – housewife	2 children: Pushpa (F) 5.5 Sonia (F) 2.5	Pushpa (F) 5.5 Sonia (F) 2.5
Family 3 Mr & Mrs Mahal (middle brother) Joint family structure of 12 members in one household; 3 brothers, 3 wives, 2 children per brother	Father FT self-employed – the family business with the 3 brothers; Recently moved from rural community Mother – housewife	2 children Deepika (F) 9 Anuj (M) 4	Anuj (M) 4

Data Collection Methods

We collected five data sets:

1. Participant generated videos. Participants (children or with their parents) chose and recorded up to ten routine activities of father-child interactions over two weeks.
2. Telephone interviews with fathers (for feedback on evolving technical methodological issues, e.g. camera positioning).
3. Film elicitation interviews with children/fathers (two per family).
4. Video recordings of film elicitation interviews (we refer to this as researcher generated videos).
5. Face to face, semi-structured interviews with fathers.

Overall, we collected between 5 and 10 hours of combined participant and researcher generated video material from each family. We theoretically sampled activity settings and each child's social situation of development for moments of crisis.

Data Analysis: Analysing Explorative Activities in Micro-transitions

Identifying Moments of Crisis

Conflict of motives is central to our understanding of crisis as micro-developmental transitions; and a child's intention can be explicated through studying conflict of motives. In moments of crisis within a particular social situation 'the child can become relatively difficult due to the fact that ... the pedagogical system applied to the child does not keep up with the rapid changes in their personality' (Vygotsky, 1998a, pp. 193–194). In other words, there is a clash between the personal and the social; a crisis point between what they want, and what they see is demanded of them. Through interaction with others, for example, fathers, they can begin to envisage things a new way. This is a dialectic mechanism. Looking at conditions dialectically makes it possible to explicate a child's intention.

Sign Mediation, Explorative Activities and Development

Tools and signs orient human behaviour differently; 'the tool's function is to serve as the conductor of human influence on the object of activity ... it must lead to changes in objects ... aimed at mastering and triumphing' (Vygotsky, 1978, p. 55); and sign mediation is internally oriented 'aimed at mastering oneself' (ibid). Bugrimenko and El'konin (2001) propose that researchers examine the mediational function of sign itself; for example, how does language in crisis build a mental operation? Accordingly, after identifying the moments of crisis, we examined the mediating function of the tool/sign – object relationship, because we view signs as a universal means of learning that lead development (involving both object and tool). From this position, learning happens in development because a child builds mental operations with objects as they form concepts (Bugrimenko & El'konin, 2001). The process involves passing on an action to a child gradually via external props such as language, for them to form meaning. We examine the characteristics of this process because we assume *moments* that form meaning could be missed in child socialization. Maturational views of development using *assimilation* rather than internalization assume an evolutionary path to development, so that action leads to organizing meaning via external objects which in turn lead to an ideal understanding (ibid). As a result, they miss *moments*. Moments might involve a moment of mutual orientation, or of searching together and or even testing. In our analysis we honed into these meaningful missed moments because they are part of a process showing what happens in crisis that serves to build up mental operations, within the child's social situation of development.

Power in Pedagogic Communication and Exploration

As part of examining the internal mechanisms of development, we also examine the external framing of communication (verbal and visual), and how it might differentially regulate opportunities for development. For this we drew on Bernstein (1971) and his concept of framing, because we believe explorative activities occur within a structure of pedagogic communication. This sociological construct allows us to consider *authority* when we analyse explorative activities in adult-child interactions. Framing is a concept used to describe social and hierarchical relations in pedagogic communication and 'refers to the locus of control' (Daniels, 1989, p. 125), which can be applied to any encounter considered involving relationships, communication and power:

> It can refer to the relations between parents and children, between teachers and pupils and between teachers and parents. Strong framing is where the transmitter has explicit control over the communication; weak framing gives the acquirer more apparent control over the communication.
> (Power & Whitty, 2008, p. 4)

Ethics

We obtained ethical approval from the lead university institution and followed ethical guidelines from the British Educational Research Association. The project's Principal Investigator sought ethical approval from the overseas research collaborators, who in turn with the Principal Investigator, followed the ethical guidelines in eliciting participation from the families. We addressed general issues of data storage related to confidentiality, anonymity and availability in an initial meeting with parents and children when signing consent forms. As the project continued, we managed certain ethical issues which were confidentiality and anonymity of visual data, informing participants of research outcomes and dissemination.[4]

Findings

Activity Settings and Moments of Crisis

This section begins by providing an overview of the most regular activity settings created through father-child interaction in the families. We then hone in on two families, from England and Mumbai, respectively, to analyse a regular activity setting. The analysis focuses on the child's social situation of development and the explorative activities in micro-transitions. Our selection of activity settings in the analysis aims to show differences in ideas about *exploration* in micro-transitions, and demonstrates how the mobile character of the object-tool relationship is limited or facilitated by the framing in the pedagogic relationship between father and child.

The cluster of families in England was similar in their kinds of activity settings. Table 6.3 shows mealtimes with all fathers involved eating and talking at the dining table, invariably doing homework with him, for example, spellings and reading, particularly at breakfast time; bedtime stories characterized the end of the day. All the fathers were involved in organized sports with their children. We think one reason for the close variation of activity settings in this cluster is because there is a common object of preschool/school demands.

Table 6.3 Father-child activity settings in the cluster families in England

Family 2 Mr Corbett	Family 3 Mr Major	Family 4 Mr James
Mealtimes – eating and talking together with family at a dining table		
Doing homework around family members at mealtimes (esp. At breakfast)		Homework (esp. Saturday lunch or suppertime)
Bedtime routines personal hygiene; bedtime stories		Bedtime stories
Dong homework 1:1		
Travel to preschool/school together in the car	Travel to preschool/school together (3 children and father) on cycles	Travel to weekend sports activities in the car
Playing computer games/using digital technology together		
Walking the dog		
Cooking together 1:1		
	Family TV night; playing family games (e.g. Twister)	
Playing organized sports with father observing or participating		
Having lunch with pre-school child		

Where we did see variation in activity settings of families in England, it related to whether the father's employment enabled him to make himself available. For example, in Family 2, Mr Corbett was a self-employed, freelance professional researcher who worked from home for much of the time. He chose flexible working to make himself more available to Bea, his four-year-old preschool child. In Family 3 both parents were self-employed and spent much time together as a family unit. They had changed the way they developed their business, so they could be more available for family time. Consequently, most of Mr Major's interactions were with the family as a group. In Family 4 the demands of Mr James' employment meant that he was only available at the weekend and in the evenings, when he was tired.

Most of the father-child interactions in the Mumbai cluster were at home. There was variation within the home space as Table 6.4 indicates. This may partly be because of differences in employment and family structures. In our Mumbai family cluster, the relationship between employment and availability was the reverse of families in England. That is, self-employment in the Mumbai cluster meant less available time with children.

Table 6.4 Father-child activity settings in the cluster families in Mumbai

Family 1 Mr Mohan	Family 2 Mr Sharma	Family 3 Mr Mahal
Eating and watching TV together (with extended family in Family 3)		
	Playing sports outside – ball games (basketball)	Playing sports outside – cricket
	Playing games/craft activities inside	
Using technology for information gathering/leisure		
		Talking with little one – about the dog on the colony 1:1
	Reading with papa	
	Family trips – zoo	
In the car – on family trips to relatives: weekends		
Eating out as a family: weekends		

Explorative Activities in Moments of Crisis as Micro-transitions

Case Study Example: *The Corbett Family in England; Activity Setting – Bedtime Routines*

It is a weekday bedtime. There are three children in the family and a dog. The children are Bea (4), Lance (8) and Fleur (9). Together with father they create the activity setting of reading bedtime stories. After cleaning teeth and bathing, father reads to each child in their respective bedrooms. Mother and father take turns to do this in the family. In the following scene father is lying in bed with the youngest child, Bea, reading a story about swimming and a dog. Bea interrupts his reading and brings Minnie (their dog) into their conversation.

(Field notes)

Table 6.5 F2 England: Participant video data: Activity setting/social situation: Bedtime routines

Verbal interaction/action	Non-verbal interaction/action
Bea: I can do doggy paddles as well Father: yes you can Bea: I can do doggy paddles with my arm bands; so can Minnie do doggy paddles Father: is that because you're a dog? Bea: (shrieks): no I'm not a dog, Minnie's a dog so she can do doggy paddles Father: oh we should take you both together	Bea interrupts the reading ... She kicks her legs out of the bed and father turns his head towards her so they are both looking at each other as they speak She kicks her legs Father looks at her, both lying down She shrieks at the teasing; kicks her legs and waves her arm as she talks
Bea: yeh ... cos we can both do doggy paddles Father: you can both do doggy paddles together Bea: yeh ... so ... we can both do doggy paddles together in the sea can't we Father; yes you can, can't you? Bea: cos Minnie has to go in the sea, and I have to go in the sea as well cos Minnie's joining in with me Father: when are we gonnna go to the seaside next? Are we gonna go in the winter? Bea: no ... ooooh we're not going in the winter, we're going in the summer Father: okay (continues reading and looks back at the book); *now let me see you swim dog paddle said mummy, Topsy ...*	... dad returns to looking at the book as he speaks ... looks at Bea and returns to looking at book. They look as though they are enjoying the book together (Figure 6.1)  **Figure 6.1** Bea and her father enjoying the book together.

Bea: ... and then I'll be able to go and sleep in the sun ...
Father: that'll be nice, going to sleep in the sun
Bea: with Minny, with Minny
Father: yeh she loves the beach doesn't she?
Bea: yeh

Now Bea decides to sit up in bed as she speaks again and looks at her father as she holds her cuddly toy. They both look interested in their talk.
Father looks at her (Figure 6.2), Bea is leaning forward still holding her soft toy.

Figure 6.2 Father looks at Bea.

Bea leans on her father holding onto her toy and looks at the book as father reads it and as she initiates the next part of the conversation.

Father: *Topsy paddled like a puppy, her armbands helped her to float. Tim paddled hard ...*
Bea: she is a little girl
Father: she is, she's actually a dog
Bea: I *know*
Father; *she splashed (reading)*
Bea: she's a doggy girl that's a bit little ... she's only zero but she's nearly one
Father: yes, she's nearly one yes ...
... he splashed more than Topsy but his legs kept sinking. The end

F continues to read the story
Bea sits up again
looks at Bea briefly before returning to the story
dad looks at her
(continues reading)
Bea interrupts
Father finished story

Bea: daddy
Father: yes
Bea: daddy
Father: yes
Bea: (whispers) can people actually go in the pool with glasses on?
Father: can people go into the pool with glasses on? yes they can as long as they don't lose their glasses in the water ... but yes they can
Bea: well people without glasses can definitely
Father: people without glasses can go swimming, but people with glasses can also go swimming too. Swimming is for everyone isn't it Bea?
Bea: yeh
Father: yes
Bea: even dogs?

She sidles up to father
sidles up a bit more
(looks at Bea)
She whispers in his ear to ask the question
Father repeats the question ... then answers it, looks at Bea and she nods

Father: even dogs even for Minnie
Bea: yes, even for Minnie and even for penguins
Father: even for penguins and even for giraffes
Bea: no not giraffes and even for hippos
Father; definitely for hippos and don't forget ...
Bea: they drink the water, so does Minnie
Father: don't forget polar bears, they like to swim
Bea: (shouts) yeh!

Bea starts to get back under the covers and lie down
Father helps to put covers over her
Bea lies down and rolls over to go to sleep
Father gives her a sign of affection ... a good night kiss (Figure 6.3)

Figure 6.3 Father gives Bea a good night kiss.

she shouts out 'yeah' as she holds her cuddly toy up in the air and then over her face, before closing her eyes to go to sleep.

In this activity setting the father reads a bedtime story to his youngest daughter Bea. Bea wants to talk to her father and the content of their talk is stimulated by the story which is about a dog swimming. First, she refers to a swimming stroke (doggy paddles) in the story; she relates the swimming stroke to her own past experiences with the family dog, Minnie. They talk about their dog and make plans. Father asks what time of year they might plan to take their dog to the seaside and Bea plans for summer when Minnie can do 'doggy paddles' with her in the sea. Enquiry characterizes their communication as dialogue, and it is one which illustrates how Minnie their dog is very much part of the family. Although the story is the stimulus, it is Bea who initiates the conversation through reflections, questions and physical movement; she moves towards father with her soft toy, leans on him, looks at him and frequently kicks her legs in the air shrieking with excitement.

In this social situation of development Bea's object related motive was to talk with her father, despite the demands of the activity setting (to listen to the story); her motive is demonstrated through her constant interruptions. The father allows this object-related motive to proceed, because he values one to one conversation during bedtime stories:

> We just talk about it, you know … create a moment where, you may go up to their bedroom or just get them one on one and then have a chat. … To tell me stuff, but I think that does, that does open up good conversations.
>
> (Father interview)

It is a process-oriented dialogue. The leading activity is the bedtime story, but it is used by the young child to have a talk with her father. It is communication as dialogue, one where she can start and stop the conversations, and decide on its content, sequence and pace (Bernstein, 1971). In this respect, the structure of the pedagogic communication is weakly framed. While the talk itself displays characteristics of the explorative as *dialogic* (Ødegaard, 2020), it is also underpinned by a kind of ironic humour which seems to function as an *invisible mediation* (Hasan, 2002a) where the emphasis is upon the affective referent behind the talk; which is humour (Bea knows he is joking evidenced in her excitable shrieks). The explorative in this microtransition is therefore both an affective and cognitive experience for the child.

Case Study Examples

The Sharma Family in Mumbai, India; Activity Setting – Playing Board Games with Pushpa and Sonia

> It is a weekday in mid-December at home. There are two children in the family, Pushpa (5.5) and Sonia (2.5). They decide to play board games with their father whilst sitting on the bed in their parents' bedroom. The two children have their respective games in front of them. Pushpa has a chess board in front of her with four chess pieces laid out on it. Sonia removes coloured cubes from a box and is piling them on the bed in front of her. Their father comes into the room and sits cross legged on the bed to join them. Together they create the activity setting of playing games. The mother records the setting by locating a camera on a tripod in the corner of the room.
>
> The situation begins with the father approaching the bed while Pushpa is placing chess pieces on her chess board. He tells her where pieces should be placed, every so often asking her to pass him different pieces so that he can also place them on the board. Meanwhile Sonia is busy pushing her coloured cubes together in a pile. She glances over to see what Pushpa and daddy are doing. Then daddy redirects his attention to Sonia (Field notes).

Table 6.6 F2 Mumbai-India: Participant video data: Activity setting/social situation: playing games – Scene 1

Verbal interaction/action	Non-verbal interaction/action
F: … teach me how to count. Count all these here. … tell me how many are there here? teach me 1, 2, 3,4 … Sonia: NO. Colour F: colours, okay tell me all the colours and count them too. Sonia: White F: See … (points to cubes) One, Two, Three, Sonia: White F: Four, Five (points to cubes) Sonia: Blue F: (pointing to cubes) Six, Seven, eight, nine, ten … … … Now … count these … count them Sonia: Blue	F: points to cubes F: points to cubes F: points to cubes F: He looks at her quizzically as she responds incorrectly to the questions. F: points to cubes At this point Pushpa, the elder sibling, who is now watching the two of them having moved her chess piece, stretches out her arm and joins their conversation moving some cubes.

Scene 1

Father and Siblings

The actions in Scene 1 can be characterized as non-compliance (both direct and indirect), a show and tell approach, with an emphasis on performance and outcomes. In Sonia's social situation of development (Scene 1) Sonia wants to name the colours of the cubes, but she knows father wants her to count the cubes. At first, she refuses directly, saying 'no'. Herein lies the emergence of a micro-crisis between the father's object-oriented motive as Sonia sees it, and her own motive in her social situation of development. The father attempts to resolve what Sonia wants, into his own expectations, by expanding the task, so that it includes both motives (colours and counting). However, Sonia persistently provides intentionally incorrect responses to her father's questions by naming colours. It is an indirect act of non-compliance; given her direct refusal could not give her what she wanted. It is at this point that the micro-crisis begins to unfold as a transition (a deconstruction); so that Sonia's motives are still achieved but through the attunement and intervention of the elder sibling in Scene 2, as follows (Table 6.7).

Table 6.7 F2 Mumbai-India: Participant video data: Activity setting/social situation: playing Games – Scene 2

Verbal interaction/action	Non-verbal interaction/action
Pushpa (looking at father): Idea! Sonia will tell you through this way. F: You were playing chess? (said rhetorically). This game (referring to the cubes) is for younger children. You're older. Pushpa: Look … like this (looks at father). See explain it to Sonia like this F: okay Pushpa: Which colour is this? Tell me different colours. Teach Sonia like this. F: okay; fine you teach this to Sonia	Pushpa takes over and moves the cubes differently as her sister watches. P and S: Pushpa's attention turns back to her younger sister and they both lean in towards each other to play with the cubes. Dad watches them, still sitting on the bed next to them. F: Points to Sonia and then the chess boards; but Pushpa continues playing cubes with her younger sister. He watches them as Pushpa seems to organize the cubes into colour groups for her sister. Her younger sister watches her. P and S: What we see is Pushpa the older sister moving the younger sister's hand away from touching the cubes which she has organized into different colour groups on the bed – blue, green, white and red. Pushpa moves any cubes that are not in the right colour groupings and her sister Sonia watches.
Pushpa: Sonia, tell me different colours. Like, look here …. Which colour is this? This! Take this. Take this (points to cubes). (Sonia moves the colours)	Dad leaves the bed and Pushpa continues to organize the cubes as her sister watches her. At this point the camera is moved so that the focus is on the two sisters interacting.
Pushpa: Hey, what are you doing? Sonia. Don't put it there. Look, which colour is this? Sonia: White Pushpa: Very good (applauds). She told this one is white. Now this. What's this? Sonia: Green Pushpa: No. This one is green. Which colour is this? Sonia: White Pushpa: This one is White. Not this Sonia: Green Pushpa: this one is green	S: Sonia throws the blue ones in the air to land back on the bed as a group. P: Pushpa points to the white group and when her sister responds correctly, she applauds, turning to the camera. Her sister watches her. Then Pushpa points to the pile of red cubes; Sonia responds, and Pushpa then points to green and red groups in turn. F: Meanwhile F returns to watch them on the bed. P and S: The older sister continues to point to the different coloured groups of cubes and the younger sister watches and responds to the questions.

Scene 2

The Elder Sibling Intervenes

In Scene 2 the elder sibling Pushpa sees the interaction around the cubes between her father and younger sister is not working, and knowing her sibling very well, Pushpa wants to *show and tell* another way, for a better interaction. Although this may not initially sound like an explorative activity, it is indicative of potential because it moves away from a *one size fits all* attitude to interacting with the cubes (the leading activity), in order to accommodate her younger sister's motive to proceed. By scene 3 (below) however, although the father revises the activity so that it is about naming colours, his orientation towards a *show and tell* approach remains. That is, the emphasis remains on performance, outcome and certainty (Table 6.8).

Table 6.8 F2 Mumbai-India: Participant video data: Activity setting/social situation: playing Games – Scene 3

Verbal interaction/action	Non-verbal interaction/action
F: NO. Not like this. Let's do this. These many colours are confusing her. We will teach her 2 colours at a time. Okay? Let's hide these (father removes some cubes of different colours). Lets take this colour and this (holds up blue and green cubes). Now … look … Sonia. Look carefully. Come give me everything else. LOOK. This one blue and this is green. Okay?	F: F decides to intervene and points to one of the groups now. He moves the groups so that there are just two coloured groups in front of Sonia (blue and green). He holds out his hand for her to give him the blue cube she is grasping in the palm of her hand and he places it on the blue pile. Dad touches the blue and green piles respectively and looks at Sonia asking her a question to which she responds. Her elder sister Sonia watches the two of them.
Now, tell me, which one is blue? Sonia: This is blue (and points) F: very good (applauds). And which is green? Sonia: This (Sonia points to the green cube) F: Very Good. Now look. This is red colour (introduces a new colour) Sonia: Red (and points to the red cube) F: okay? Red blue green (points to each colour)	Sonia pauses after her dad's question and then points to the blue group (Figure 6.4).Figure 6.4 Sonia points to the blue group.

Now Sonia tell me which one is green?
Sonia: this is green (points to the green cube)
F: Wow! Look this is also green (points to her green shorts). This is also green and she is also wearing green (points to elder sibling's T shirt). Which other colours are here? Tell me ... Is there red around here somewhere? Look

Both Dad and her elder sister applaud. Dad repeats the process with the green group.
Then he takes the white group of cubes. He places them in a group on the bed next to the other groups and points to the red, blue and green respectively as he speaks. Sonia and her elder sister watch him. He asks Sonia a question and she points to the blue (Pushpa also points to it); and dad applauds. He turns to Pushpa and they both smile at one another for a moment before he returns his attention to Sonia.
He repeats the process with the green pile. Then he points to her green shorts and then to her elder sister's T shirt which is also green. He looks around the room. Sonia and her sister look at each other.
Her elder sister looks around the room, looks up and points to a corner of the room towards the ceiling.

Pushpa: Look there (elder sibling points to the opposite wall) Red colour
F: Look, look at this flower. this one is red (father points to the poppy on the pillow case)

F looks in that direction and then so does Sonia.
Dad picks up the pillow and points to the red flower ... And then picks up a red cube (Figure 6.5)

Figure 6.5 Dad picks up the pillow and points to the red flower, and then picks up a red cube.

Scene 3

Father Intervenes

In Scene 3 the father reduces the number of cube colours to two (blue and green) and *imitates* the elder sibling's earlier demonstration, once again applauding each time Sonia provides the correct answer, demonstrating she has understood colours. He then expands Sonia's understanding of colours by choosing different articles in the room, which correspond to the colours of the cubes (such as the red poppies on the pillow as the image shows). This is a glimpse of a slight orientation to explorative activities in that the *show and tell* becomes oriented to a new element. Nonetheless, the overwhelming approach is non-explorative. What is interesting in the analysis of the interaction is how playing with the cubes changes alongside the father's instructional strategy, as the interaction progresses. In this respect it is an example of the transformative movement of the object related motive occurring during micro-crisis. In Sonia's social situation of development, there is a reconstruction of the social situation in Scene 3, in which her motive for development was allowed to proceed, albeit through non-explorative activities. In the discussion that follows we explain how we see the connections between our analysis of exploratory activities in micro-transitions, with opportunities for development at the institutional level, and its relationships to wider cultural formations.

Discussion

Opportunities for Development, Explorative Activities, and Micro-transitions in the Family in England

The opportunities for development emerging from the micro-crisis in the Corbett family were essentially created through two instructional strategies. The first strategy was of mutual orientation (Bugrimenko & El'konin, 2001) by which we mean there is an attention with the child. In the example it was orientated to ideas from the bedtime story. However, the object of their attention and associated motive moved as the shared reading experience unfolded. An ease and curiosity characterized the encounter, indicating the mobility of the object of the child's thinking and its associated motive, is very much dependent on how the interaction progresses with the father. While the father focused his attention with the child on the book and ideas from the book, he responded to each of her interruptions in ways that were open to possibilities (the father, e.g. expanded on the subject in a creative way, he connected and compared, and he combined this with humour). They talked together and therefore shared the experience together. It was an example of exploration as a dialogic occurring through a micro-transition. This was largely possible because it was a loosely regulated routine; bedtimes are for this family, a time to open conversations. Control in terms of the structural conditions of the pedagogic communication was weakly framed (Bernstein, 1971), and therefore created a space for discursive activities to occur.

Ødegaard (2020) expands on the idea of exploration as dialogic engagement in that 'engagement is an interest in children's exploration and meaning making processes – in how children shape themselves and are being shaped in a dynamic wave, where personal, structural and discursive conditions operate in a flux' (Ødegaard, 2020, p. 95). The conversation unfolded, and the book combined with an instructional strategy of mutual orientation (an explorative characteristic), was the tool shaping the content in which opportunities for development emerged. With explorative activities beginning through the talk and the book 'a participatory space is opened' (Ødegaard, 2020, p. 97) which facilitates collaborative meaning making.

Sign and Invisible Mediation as a Habit of Mind the Family in England

While the instructional strategy in the story time example was *mutual orientation* which involved explorative activities as a dialogic; our analysis of the Corbett family also found examples of a *testing* strategy in regular activity settings (e.g. testing the extent to which Bea complied to expected social conduct at mealtimes). What was interesting about the father-child interactions in the Corbett family was how his *ironic* humour appeared in all the activity settings we analysed; and indeed his older children adopted the same expressive *ironic banter* in their conversations. At an internal level then, we believe the father's use of *ironic* humour behind dialogue across all activity settings in the Corbett family, functioned as a trigger to Bea's affective state in her interactions with her father. It was an example of internal sign mediation; where the child's object-related motive is related to an affective state or need. In this respect, it is the quality of feeling 'behind' Bea's behaviour that becomes the internal mechanism for change; and her overt behaviour is one of several possible expressions of the referent.

In discussing Vygotsky's notion of semiotic mediation, Hasan (2002a) refers to this kind of communication as invisible sign mediation. It is an *assumed habit of mind* (Hasan, 2002a), because the children in the Corbett family know he is joking. In terms of opportunities for development, invisible mediation happens in early childhood in a range of contexts but it will influence the visible because 'the habits of mind they create are crucial to an individual's ways of engaging in visible semiotic mediation; therefore, visible mediation is not entirely independent of invisible mediation' (Hasan, 2002a, p. 114). Hasan (2002a) demonstrated this through analysing natural dialogues between mother and child (aged 3–4) in different cultural activities. She argued that invisible everyday mediation embedded in everyday cultural activities is effective precisely because it is ordinary. Also, because it starts in early childhood 'it becomes the ruler of attention and interest, of motivation and relevance' (Hasan, 2002a: 120). Furthermore, 'engaging in discourse of this kind produces in the children, a particular kind of orientation to meanings … in ways that are qualitatively different from those of children whose mental habit and experience of everyday discourse is different' (Hasan, 2002a, p. 118).

For Hasan (2002a, 2002b) variation is underpinned by social positioning. This raises questions about how cultures of exploration are formed at the institutional level. Recent trends in England demonstrate how socio-economic status continues to be a driver of father involvement (Henz, 2019), where the father's education is a factor shaping involvement. So when we specifically refer to engagement as an aspect of father involvement (Lamb et al., 1985), we might raise questions about the *habits of mind* middle-class fathers bring with them through the language they use with their children, and the extent to which they afford better opportunities for cultures of exploration, to shape engagement with their children.

Opportunities for Development, Explorative Activities and Micro-transitions in the Family in Mumbai

In the family in Mumbai our analysis demonstrated how the activities in the instructional strategy were mainly characterized as non-explorative, but there were glimpses of a co-creation of creative spaces through a collective strategy formed by the sibling alliance. In the three scenes we presented of the Sharma family, crisis emerged through moments of testing (Bugrimenko & El'konin, 2001) where the father, for example, tried to test the younger child's recall of numbers; but the object of their attention and associated thinking moved when the older sibling supported the younger child's motive. The father allowed this kind of intervention from the older sibling to proceed; and in doing so, it opened possibilities for the father's instructional strategy to change. There was a shared attention to working on grouping colours followed by expanding their application to objects in the immediate environment, therefore showing indications of exploration, and a glimpse of a mutual orientation as a strategy to learning colours (Bugrimenko & El'konin, 2001). However, the *testing* strategy which dominated most interactions may be partly explained through Sriram and Sandhu's (2013) understanding of fathers in the Indian tradition.

Cultural Formations and Institutional Level Interaction: The Indian Urban Parenting Ethos and Fathers

Cultural formations are an ever present and continuous process and a way of conceptualizing humans in relation to their culture (Ødegaard, 2020). According to Sriram and Sandhu (2013) Hindu culture recognizes that one's conduct is shaped in accordance with the demands of the changing era/time (referred to as Kala) and place (referred to as Desa). These prescriptions also state that efforts (explained as Shrama) required for achieving a goal vary according to the situation and the innate characteristics (explained as Guna) of people involved. In studies of urban middle-class fathers in India they found some elements of Hindu culture at play in fathers' inputs. First, they align to roles prescribed by Hindu culture (Chaturvedi, 2003; Kapoor, 2000; Madan, 2010) such as provider, guide, mentor, protector and teacher, with fathers displaying highest involvement in planning and providing, followed by guiding, mentoring and practical and emotional support. Second, fathers' conduct is shaped by the demands of a changing context (Kala [time] and Desa [place]), as they wish to help the child attain a good future and career to survive a competitive global environment. Beyond fulfilling necessities, they provide a comfortable study environment, entertainment, sports, and learning materials, save money through insurance policies, and some plan to migrate to enhance their children's life chances. These fathers also make efforts (*Shrama*) according to the child's age to help in school and college admissions and career choices, and ensure that children can access the right opportunities. Fathers' reasons for involvement highlight an emphasis on cognitive and affective aspects of children's development that will enable them to secure better marks and grades and, provide opportunities, new experiences, sustained motivation, and help to relieve children's stress (Sriram & Sandhu, 2013). We maintain these are all indications of future-oriented object-related motives, helping the child to *become* in order to produce a future life of certainty, stability and security.

However, Sriram and Sandhu (2013) also state that when examining their findings from the perspective of *Guna* (father's or child's innate characteristics), only a few fathers acknowledged the need to understand their children's strengths, weaknesses and limitations. The findings taken together reaffirm that middle-class Indian fathers provide a variety of inputs in the nurture of their children. However, they 'focus on child's becoming' rather than 'the child as a being', providing a glimpse of the 'Indian urban parenting ethos' that has become more child-centred vis-à-vis competition (ibid). In fact, Sriram (2019b) suggests that fathers in urban India often fall in the category of conflicted parents being caught between tradition and modernity (Sriram, 2019b). Certainly Saraff's (2010) study on 350 fathers of children below ten years in Mumbai city revealed conflict between what fathers perceive and practice. We found evidence of conflicts and its connections with wider societal issues in our Mumbai cluster, as the following quotes indicate:

> Work is key in the family. People will respect you only when you are working, stable, good with family values

> Indian values nowadays, it is difficult to follow in Bombay. ... Because I didn't have time, we will not be able to follow old family culture. Nowadays, demand is too much. I will stay with my family. I will not give so much time to other relatives. ... I must see that discipline is kept ... grow in your home environment.
>
> (Mr Mohan)

> I get to enjoy my family ... So, there is a good work life balance. Yes, career growth is slow, but family life is also important.
>
> (Mr Sharma)

> No, daddy does not stay at home even on Sundays, he will be busy (working).
>
> (Mr Mahal's youngest child)

Conclusion

This chapter referred to data from a cluster sample of families living in Mumbai, India and in England, and examined the relationship between fathers and child development. We drew on the Hedegaard's (2009) model of learning and development, to identify connections between the individual interactions, the family as an institution and societal values. At the individual level, we analysed opportunities for development in moments of crisis (micro-developmental transitions) by looking more deeply at the mediation activity within the tool/sign – object relationship; and the extent to which the mediation displayed characteristics of exploration.

The opportunities for development emerging from the micro-crisis of the family in England were essentially created through two instructional strategies associated with dialogic characteristics and weak framing (Bernstein, 1971), underpinned by invisible everyday mediation. Invisible mediation as a habit of mind is potentially very powerful, because it is ordinary (Hasan, 2002a) but most importantly, it is linguistically associated with social position (Hasan, 2002b), and this raises questions about current trends of father involvement in England (Henz, 2019) which are correlated with the educated middle classes, and the opportunities for cultures of exploration they afford for their children.

The opportunities for development emerging from the micro-crisis situations in the family in Mumbai were essentially created through moments of testing as an instructional strategy, with fewer explorative activities, and therefore fewer opportunities for development. There were glimpses of moments of mutual orientation through sibling intervention. The orientation remained however, on the child's 'becoming' rather than 'the child as a being'. Indian fathers in our sample considered, *kala* (era, time), as important. They focused on enhancing the cognitive capacities of the children (though not necessarily the affective), to accommodate competition in the context of education and future career opportunities. This element is akin to the prescribed traditional role. But it raises questions about how traditional ideas of fathering and the Hindu concept of *guna* associated with potential in the individual, may pave a way to realize exploration for some children in families in India.

We maintain that explorative activities in micro-transitions occur through a series of moments demonstrating the mobile characteristic of the object-motive relationship, but that the mobility can be limited or facilitated by the framing of the instructional strategy employed in the pedagogic communication, and the institutional and societal values about fathering and childhood. In this respect young children's opportunities for development through exploration in micro-transitions occur with children being both a producer and product.

This study draws attention to fathers and child development; in which development is no longer dependent on time, but on relationships and conditions for exploration. A cultural-historical perspective which foregrounds the child's social situation of development (Vygotsky, 1998a) within a dialectical framework, the family's perspective and societal perspective (Hedegaard, 2008, 2009), offers a genuine step forward (Fleer & Hedegaard, 2010) for examining exploration in father-child interactions. We recommend further cross-national studies about fathers and child development from this perspective.

Notes

1   Family 1 was part of a pilot study, so it is not included in this chapter.

2   We collected data on one or two target children in each family, depending on the activity settings filmed.
3   We collected data on one or two target children in each family, depending on the activity settings filmed.
4   Parents granted permission to show faces in this chapter because the data is not sensitive.

References

Adler, M. A., & Lenz, K. (2017). *Father Involvement in the Early Years: An International Comparison of Policy and Practice*. Policy Press.

Bakhtin, M. M. (1986). The problem of the speech genre (T. V. W. McGee, Trans.). In M. M. Bakhtin (Ed.), *Speech Genres and Other Late Essays* (pp. 60–102). University of Texas Press.

Bernstein, B. (1971). On the classification and framing of educational knowledge. In M. Young (Ed.), *Knowledge and Control* (pp. 47–69). Collier-Macmillan.

Bugrimenko, E. A., & El'konin, B. D. (2001). Sign mediation in processes of formation and development. *Journal of Russian and East European psychology*, *39*(4), 20–33. https://doi.org/10.2753/RPO1061-0405390420

Burgess, A., & Davies, J. (2017). *Cash or Carry? Fathers Combining Work and Care in the UK*. (Full Report) (Contemporary Fathers in the UK series). Fatherhood Institute.

Cabrera, N. J., & Tamis-lemonda, C. S. E. (Eds.). (2013). *Handbook of Father Involvement: Multidisciplinary Perspectives* (2nd edn.). Routledge/Taylor & Francis Group.

Chaturvedi, B. (2003). The householder, grihastha in the Mahabharata. In M. Pernau, I. Ahmad & H. Reifeld (Eds.), *Family and Gender: Changing Values in Germany and India* (pp. 113–39). Sage.

Chawla-Duggan, R., & Milner, S. (2016). Father involvement in young children's care and education: Exploring boundaries and starting conversations [Article]. *Cambridge Journal of Education*, *46*(4), 473–89. https://doi.org/10.1080/0305764X.2015.1069792

Daniels, H. (1989). Visual displays as tacit relays of the structure of pedagogic practice. *British Journal of the Sociology of Education*, *10*(2), 123–40. https://doi.org/10.1080/0142569890100201

Fleer, M., & Hedegaard, M. (2010). Children's development as participation in everyday practices across different institutions. *Mind, Culture and Activity*, *17*(2), 149–78. https://doi.org/10.1080/10749030903222760

Flouri, E. (2005). *Fathering and Child Outcomes*. Wiley.

Freitas, L., T., Shelton, T., & Tudge, J. (2008). Conceptions of US and Brazilian early childhood care and education: A historical and comparative analysis.

International Journal of Behavioral Development, 32(2), 161–70. https://doi.org/10.1177/0165025407087216

Hasan, R. (2002a). Semiotic mediation and mental development in pluralistic societies: Some implications for tomorrow's schooling. In G. Wells & G. Claxton (Eds.), *Learning for Life in the 21st Century: Sociocultural Perspectives on the Future of Education* (pp. 112–126). Blackwell.

Hasan, R. (2002b). Ways of meaning, ways of learning: Code as an explanatory concept. *British Journal of Sociology of Education, 23*(4), 537–548 https://doi.org/10.1080/0142569022000038396

Hedegaard, M. (2008). A cultural-historical theory of children's development. In M. Hedegaard & M. Fleer (Eds.), *Studying Children: A Cultural-historical Approach* (pp. 10–29). Open University Press.

Hedegaard, M. (2009). Children's development from a cultural–historical approach: Children's activity in everyday local settings as foundation for their development. *Mind, Culture, and Activity, 16*(1), 64–82. https://doi.org/10.1080/10749030802477374.

Henz, U. (2019). Fathers' involvement with their children in the United Kingdom: Recent trends and class differences. *Demographic Research, 40*(30), 865–96. https://doi.org/10.4054/DemRes.2019.40.30

Hook, J. L., & Wolfe, C. M. (2012). New fathers? Residential fathers' time with children in four countries. *Journal of Family Issues, 33*(4), 415–550. https://doi.org/10.1177/0192513X11425779

Kapoor, S. (2000). *The Hindus: Encyclopedia of Hinduism* (Vol 2). Cosmo Publications.

Kossek, E. E., & Lautsch, B. A. (2017). Work-life flexibility for whom? Occupational status and work-life inequality in upper, middle, and lower level jobs. *The Academy of Management Annals, 12*(1), 5–36. https://doi.org/10.5465/annals.2016.0059

Kumar, N. (2019). Flavours of fathering in the Indian capital: Insights from a qualitative study. In R. Sriram (Ed.), *Fathering in India: Images and Realities* (pp. 83–95). Springer.

Kwok, S. Y. C. L., & Li, B. K. K. (2015). A mediation model of father involvement with preschool children in Hong Kong. *Social Indicators Research, 122*(3), 905–23. https://doi.org/10.1007/s11205-014-0708-5

Lamb, M. E., & Lewis, C. (2013). Father-child relationships. In N. J. Cabrera & C. S. Tamis-lemonda (Eds.), *Handbook of Father Involvement: Multidisciplinary Perspectives* (pp. 119–34). Routledge/Taylor & Francis Group.

Lamb, M. E., Pleck, J. H., Charnov, E. L., & Levine, J. A. (1985). Paternal behavior in humans. *American Zoologist, 25*(883–94). https://www.jstor.org/stable/3883043

LeVine, R. A. (1989). Cultural environments in child development. In W. Damon (Ed.), *Child Development Today and Tomorrow* (pp. 52–68). San Francisco: Jossey-Bass.

Linnell, P. (2009). *Rethinking Language, Mind and World, Dialogically: Interaction and Contextual of Theories of Human Sense Making*. Information Age Publishing.

Madan, T. (2010). *Family and Kinship: A Study of Pundits of Rural Kashmir* (2nd edn.). Oxford University Press.

Ødegaard, E. E. (2020). Dialogical engagement and the co-creation of cultures of exploration. In M. Hedegaard & E. E. Ødegaard (Eds.), *Children's Exploration and Cultural Formation – International Perspectives on Early Childhood Education and Development* (Vol 29) (pp. 83–104). Springer.

Ødegaard, E. E., & Hedegaard, M. (2020). Introduction to children's exploration and cultural formation. In M. Hedegaard & E. E. Ødegaard (Eds.), *Children's Exploration and Cultural Formation – International Perspectives on Early Childhood Education and Development* (Vol 29) (pp. 1–10). Springer.

OECD. (2016). *Enhancing Child Well-Being To Promote Inclusive Growth (Note By The Secretary-General) Meeting Of The Council At Ministerial Level*. OECD.

Power, S., & Whitty, G. (2008). *A Bernsteinian Analysis of Compensatory Education* (5th Basil Bernstein Symposium). Cardiff University.

Roggmann, L. A., Bradley, R. H., & Raikes, H. H. (2013). Fathers in family contexts. In C. S. Tamis-lemonda & N. J. Cabrera (Eds.), *Handbook of Father Involvement: Multidisciplinary Perspectives* (pp. 186–201). Routledge.

Saraff, A. (2010). *Culture and Conduct of Fatherhood in India: Are They in Synchrony*. International Conference on Fatherhood in the 21st Century Asia: Research, Interventions, and Policies, Asia Research Institute, National University of Singapore, Singapore.

Saraff, A., & Srivastava, H. C. (2008). Envisioning fatherhood: Indian fathers' perceptions of an ideal father. *Population Review*, *47*(1), 41–55. https://doi.org/10.1353/prv.0.0002

Sarkadi, A., Kristiansson, R., Oberklaid, F., & Bremberg, S. (2008). Fathers' involvement and children's developmental outcomes: A systematic review of longitudinal studies. *Acta Paediatrica*, *97*, 153–8. https://doi.org/10.1111/j.1651-2227.2007.00572.x.

Seymour, S. C. (1999). *Women, Family, and Child Care in India: A World in Transition*. Cambridge University Press.

Sriram, R. (2019a). Men as Fathers: An Indian perspective. In R. Sriram (Ed.), *Fathering in India: Images and Realities* (pp. 35–60). Springer.

Sriram, R. (2019b). Summing up the evidence: Final reflections. In R. Sriram (Ed.), *Fathering in India: Images and Realities* (pp. 331–54). Springer.

Sriram, R., & Sandhu, G. (2013). Fathering to ensure child's success: What urban Indian fathers do? *Journal of Family Issues*, *34*(2), 159–81. https://doi.org/10.1177/0192513X12461136

Tulviste, P. (1999). Activity as an explanatory principle in cultural psychology. In S. Chaiklin & M. Hedegaard (Eds.), *Activity Theory and Social Practice* (pp. 66–78). Aarhus University Press.

United Nations. (2011). *Men in Families and Family Policy in a Changing World*. Department of Economic and Social Affairs.

Vygotsky, L. S. (1978). *Mind in Society: The Psychology of Higher Mental Functions*. Harvard University Press.

Vygotsky, L. S. (1998a). Early childhood. In R. W. Rieber (Ed.), *The Collected Works of L.S. Vygotsky: Child Psychology* (Vol 5) (pp. 261–83). Plenum.

Vygotsky, L. S. (1998b). Part 2: Problems of child (developmental) psychology. In R. W. Rieber (Ed.), *The Collected Works of L.S. Vygotsky: Child Psychology*. (Vol 5) (pp. 187–296). Plenum.

Williams, S. (2008). What is fatherhood? Searching for the reflexive father. *Sociology*, *42*(3), 487–502. https://doi.org/10.1177/0038038508088837

7

Babies in Motion within Daycare Transition: (Co)construction of Locomotor Exploration in a Brazilian Case Study

Natália Meireles Santos Da Costa and Katia De Souza Amorim

Babies Who Explore and Move: A Historical Overview

Babies have high brain plasticity combined with a complex perceptual apparatus (Bussab & Ribeiro, 1998) that allows broad engagement with the world and people around them. Babies are also substantially curious and explorers of the world and others, whose dialogical relationship (Rossetti-Ferreira et al., 2007) leads them to attribute meanings to the world, others and themselves, while being interpreted and signified by others. Nonetheless, grasping the here-and-now dynamics of how infants perceive and explore their naturalistic surroundings through movement and locomotor action is a more recent development that still requires further understanding and empirical data (Adolph, 2019; Franchak, 2020).

According to the ethologist Cesar Ades (Ades, 2018) it wasn't until the 1950s that experimental psychology – a pioneer groundbreaking field of infants' studies and developmental concepts – singled out and matured the notion of exploratory behaviour. A pivotal understanding emerged when studies shifted focus from schemes of *selection of response* to *selection of stimulus*, hence directing attention towards curiosity, motivation or even desire regarding novel stimulation (Ades, 2018).

Drawing upon infants' relation to the new and unknown, a significant coupling of exploratory action and attachment was put forward by Ainsworth and Bell (1970) arguing that affectionate ties to the mother, or a significant other, modulate babies' spatial displacement in a less familiar environment. Seeking proximity with an attachment figure is a hallmark behaviour in learning to discriminate between the familiar and the strange, the stable and the changing, so locomotion operates as a modulator of exploratory behaviour, constituting the baby's sense of security to explore. As a contemporary unfolding of this theory, the concept of *safe exploration* argues that realistic and cautious recognition of challenges represents a positive exploratory pattern supported by secure infant-parent relationships (Grossman et al., 1999).

Though not short of criticism (Keller, 2018), attachment studies set the stage for a new line of research for motor studies. Infants' relationship with the novel and the familiar provoked curiosity on how the baby ventures into a lesser-known world and engages in a broader exploration of the environment through locomotion described as *self-initiated* (Gibson, 1988; Rheingold & Eckerman, 1969). However, in a different investigative turn, rather than overemphasizing socio-emotional elements, studies focused on babies' urge and strength to explore new territories and learnt about the world through their actions. Alongside, a paradigm shift started around the 1970s, as multidisciplinary works among some fields – notably perceptual psychology, neurosciences, movement science and systems theory – began to emphasize the fluid, contextual and self-organizing nature of exploration and developmental change (Thelen, 1995). In this scenario, studies of exploratory and motor development acquired a processual and ecological orientation in which we highlight authors such as James and Eleanor Gibson.

James Gibson's (1966) theory describes exploration as a dynamic interaction between an evolutionarily constituted organism and a complex multisensorial-array context in which, through the articulation of the several perceptual systems, a person obtains detailed and specific environmental information that impacts subsequent actions, and, in a looping manner, perceived feedback impacts the upcoming activity. Defined as the perception-action cycle, such mechanism assists the acquisition of knowledge and instrumentalizes infants' action and further development. The concept of *affordance* derives from this notion, and is described as an environmental array (e.g. space and objects), according to what a person can perceive and execute, that guides the perception/action process in grasping opportunities or impediments for particular actions (Gibson, 1977; Liempd et al., 2018).

Building on James Gibson's research, Eleanor Gibson's addresses exploratory processes that develop over infancy, and draws attention to locomotor-based exploration and development (Franchak, 2020; Gibson, 1988). From this perspective, she argues that acquiring locomotor abilities affords infants new forms of exploration and apprehension of the environment, as integrated bodily and cognitive skills support overall developmental processes.

According to E. Gibson (1988), becoming mobile is a highly complex challenge for the baby, requiring both exploratory and performative actions, and causing a series of bodily and cognitive transformations that inform them about the broader world in an unprecedented manner. Perception, especially within the visual and haptic systems, guides locomotor movement as babies learn to (re)distribute their body weight throughout their limbs, to maintain the firmness of the neck and head in the quadruped position, and to (re)direct gaze and (re)configure their visual field, among other perceptual processes. Learning to identify obstacles or openings in space, steering through them, seeking and detecting information about surfaces and layouts are some highlighted tasks of this complex integration between visual and haptic systems. Babies plan actions within a temporal and spatial sequence and key acquisitions reconfigure other developmental areas, whilst perceptual errors, falls and increased performative costs are expected significant elements of this process (Adolph, 2019; Franchak, 2020). This way, a more robust conceptualization of locomotor exploration has been elaborated considering infants' here-and-now dynamics and changing use of visual and haptic strategies throughout development.

Though investigations have progressed conceptually, the field still lacks empirical research about how infants, in their everyday lives (Franchak, 2020), learn to move and explore their surroundings and settings, which are immersed in a relational and cultural-historical reality (Sumsion et al., 2014). Hence, we questioned how these processes occur and transform when collective educational settings become a significant part of infants' everyday life, outside of the home.

Locomotor Exploration in Everyday Settings: Transition to ECEC Contexts

The daily life of babies is varied, in different societies, and generally receives the influence of women's role in society and related labour/public policies. In the Brazilian context, babies used to be predominantly cared for by their mothers at home. However, with the rise of working women, several policies have been adopted since the 1988 National Constitution, such as four-to-six-month maternity leave, financial assistance for private day care or availability of public and free early childhood education network. As a result, there is increasing demand and enrolment of babies in ECEC settings on the national scene, who start attending these institutions at an early age (six months or less) and very often on a full-time period (Brazil, MEC/INEP, 2013).

Enrolling a baby in ECEC institutions entails transition processes. Historically, literature, mainly that based on attachment theory (Bowlby, 1969), describes the home-day care transition as a rupture and discontinuity of modes and places of living more adequate condition to the child's mental health, supposedly, setting a tone of opposition. Hence, when the baby is settling in ECEC institutions, much of the focus lies on assessing the baby's risk and emotional loss due to the mother's daily separation.

We argue, however, that the transition experience is more complex, and is not limited to the baby individually. According to White et al. (2020), transition also involves family members, teachers and others within the educational context who, in one way or another, are also learning to navigate their way in a new environment, starting to (co)build a new routine gradually, relating to unfamiliar people, and engaging in new interactive arrangements. Moreover, babies and their families start dealing with belonging issues, as they all must master other modes of communication and even exploration within an unfamiliar context.

In this sense, we endorse that exploration in ECEC settings must be analysed considering the various partners and the multiple relational interchanges taking place on different levels. Exploration and transition take form in babies' embodied experience, which is constrained by the physical and spatial organization, the types of furniture and objects, their affordances and cultural meanings. Moreover, conceptions of family members and educators may constrain the child's participation in institutional space and their access to artefacts and other children in the everyday routine (Rossetti-Ferreira et al., 2007).

Therefore, grasping exploration throughout the transition process would not be limited to the child's entry to ECEC, as a larger time range of analysis reveals a complex process that transforms continually from the dialectic and dialogic succession of interrelated events. Thus, we carried out an investigation to follow up the locomotor exploration development when the baby enters the service, during the first two months of the child's attendance at ECEC. Also, we aimed to search the transformations through acquisition of new exploratory actions, through the babies' engagement and reactions to institutional routines, which lead to the emergence of new meanings and practices thereof (Rossetti-Ferreira et al., 2007). In this chapter, we will present the analysis of one case study (Yin, 2009) to highlight the interplay between locomotor exploration and transition experience as a relational activity within a contextual and cultural flow (Costa & Amorim, 2018).

Methodology and Ethical Issues

Among other children, we followed Isabela (all names are fictional) who started attending a Brazilian ECEC institution when she was six months old. Data was collected over a year, through observations and video recordings of her participation in daily institutional life. In this chapter, we will highlight two observed dates along the first two months of her attendance: the first day and a day in the second month. We obtained authorization from the Ethics Committee of FFCLRP – USP, as well as consent from family members to carry out the study. However, as we are required to not expose the original photo images from this centre in publications, the analysed episodes will be presented in drawing illustrations. The empirical material is part of a database linked to the International Project 'Infant's transition – Social and emotional experiences in the first year of transition from home to early years setting for infants' (Amorim, 2016).

We will discuss here some episodes of locomotor exploration in light of the transition process. We define *episode* as a clear and conspicuous sequence of selected actions coordinated within an interactive field that illustrates the phenomenon of interest (Carvalho et al., 1998). In our case, it is the occurrence of locomotor exploration unfolding from haptic and visual strategies/actions due to locomotor challenges or accentuated interest towards specific stimulation in a relational setting. The episode includes one of the three forms of displacement: postural progression, autonomous locomotion and falls/locomotor failures. We view these elements within a frame of existing affordances in the institutional practices of organized occupation of time and space, and here-and-now interactive mediation by partners, whether adults or peer-age infants.

Episodes undergo microgenetic analysis (Goes, 2000), specifying intertwined bodily, interactive, contextual and social details/elements that constituted Isabela's experience and locomotor exploration in her transition process. The episodes compose a microhistory of transforming processes and flow of actions that we interpret through a cultural-historical perspective (Rossetti-Ferreira et al., 2007; Vygotsky, 2000, 2010) based on a semiotic approach.

Isabela's entrance age (six months) coincides with initial locomotor development, so the selected episodes also highlight mobile acquisition. In this sense, a locomotor transition unfolds as a means of learning to navigate in a new concrete, relational and semiotic space (Pol, 1996), while experiencing and appropriating a changing body and changing affordances thereof. To indicate the intertwining of these elements, we present a brief description of Isabela's background and start from her first day in day care.

A Case Study of Transition and Locomotor Exploration

Isabela lived at home with her mother, older sister and maternal grandparents. Isabela also often had contact with neighbours and other extended-family relatives, who cared for her several times before enrolment, due to the mother's working hours and the daycare centre's temporary unavailability to receive children. Jussara (Isabela's mother) searched for day care hoping for a more stable care routine, as Isabela stayed with a different family member/person every day. Jussara was finally able to enrol Isabela in a centre when her daughter was six months old. Data collection took place from February to December 2017, following the Brazilian school calendar.

The daycare centre – located in a medium-sized city in the state of São Paulo, Brazil, in a low-income neighbourhood – cared, free of charge, for nearly 230 children from zero to six years. It functioned through a public-private partnership between a non-governmental organization and the municipality, though resources mainly originated from public funds. Service hours operated full time, from 7 am to 5 pm. Isabela was part of the nursery class, where two principal teachers (who had alternating shifts) and two buddy teachers (who stayed the whole day) cared for eighteen attending babies (all younger than one-year-old at admission).

As a transition policy, the centre requested a relative (or someone close to the child) to accompany the baby in the first two days of attendance. During this period, the child's length of stay gradually increased, while the adult's time decreased. In these initial days, caregivers had the opportunity to talk more closely to the family about the child and learn more about detailed background information. In the following days, the baby stayed with caregivers without family members, and by the end of the first week would gradually achieve full staying time. We here shall describe and discuss episodes' excerpts from her first day, and later on from her second month of attendance, intending to highlight locomotor exploration throughout her transition experience.

> On Isabela's first day, the mother comes into the room holding the baby straight up on her lap. Because the child's trunk is erect and supported on its side by the mother, Isabela can have a panoramic view of the environment. The mother walks around the room and shows her daughter the space and toys on the shelf. Then,

she puts Isabela in a sitting up position on the mattress, hands her a toy, and puts a rolled-format pillow behind her back for support, in a manner that allows more autonomy and a more independent role and position in that environment. In turn, Isabela demonstrates tranquility and interest in the space and children, contributing for such actions to be carried out, since she does not protest leaving the lap and having the mother position her in that way.

In this short excerpt, through embodied activity, we can attribute meanings to how the mother conceives and experiences the space and transition to the daycare centre, by the manner she carries her daughter and navigates around the room. With Isabela on her lap, the mother does not turn her daughter to herself, but rather towards the outer environment. When she places her on the mattress, she does not lay her down, but sits her in an upright posture and promotes active attention to the environment, positively mediating the new environment for the child (Amorim, 2010; Fogel et al., 1999).

In the following scenes, during the time that Isabela is sitting, she often slips off the support of the pillow and Jussara helps to get her back up every time. Considering the affordances (Gibson, 1977; Liempd et al., 2018), manipulating a toy allows arms to be outstretched and not used for trunk support; because the mattress is large and soft, it absorbs impact; the pillow allows back support, although its roll format contributes to back slips. Thus, such objects favour certain (but not total) body stability for Isabela to visually explore space and toys manually. When she falls on the mattress, in a supine position, the baby is unable to return to a sitting position without the adult's support (Gibson, 1988), which requires the mother to return her to a sitting posture, and provides new opportunities to the baby in that condition of exploration.

So far, we see Isabela's exploration on day-one taking place through various postural adjustments in a new setting, primarily mediated by her mother. But what happens when peers pitch in? Still on this first day, we highlight a moment of interaction with the peer-age partner that also causes changes in Isabela's body positioning and reconfigures the exploratory scenario.

Figure 7.1 Illustration of first excerpt.

Adolfo (12 months) approaches and leans on Isabela, who was handling a small keyboard, causing her to tip over slightly and fall into a supine position. In this new posture, Isabela has a new visual field that allows a different visual exploration through the 180° movement of the head and neck, as if scanning the surroundings. From this posture, Isabela manages to roll over into a prone position, but struggles to rotate her body, so she can no longer access the toy. To try to catch it, she uses both arms to support the trunk and rotate it. However, the trunk is too heavy for her to accomplish the turning. She kicks her feet and moves her arms up and down, pushing the floor, but there is not enough strength and coordination to cause mobility or displacement of her body. Still, she keeps on reaching for the toy and engages the whole body in reestablishing the manipulation of the object, despite so many struggles. Throughout this movement, Isabela keeps her neck firm, with her head and her eyes focused on the toy, maintaining an expression of furrowed brows.

Peer-infants are distinctive social partners, as they show potential to create new and unusual situations in a more disordered and fleeting way (Rossetti-Ferreira et al., 2010) and may present motor and motivational mirroring in the relationship with the baby. We see some of those elements on the excerpt when, from a peer's action, Isabela is placed in a less familiar posture. However, despite the increased difficulty to reach the toy, she doesn't cease exploration; being in prone contact with the floor stimulates other strategies, such as rotating the body, projecting it entirely towards the object, redistributing body weight and attempting different reaching movements.

Shortly afterwards, the mother arrives. Isabela quickly changes her facial expression to apparent discomfort (arching of eyebrows while moaning) and then turns her head towards Jussara, whimpering. The mother picks her up and sits her on her lap. As first day of attendance, the child has not yet created bonds with the caregivers, so at this point, the mother is the figure reference sought to reposition her. When Jussara takes Isabela on her lap, she says 'You must learn to turn' – 'Like your friend', adds the caregiver Vanessa, who was sitting nearby and observing everything. The mother Jussara, looking at Adolfo says: 'Yeah, you have to teach her how to turn over because she just cries!'.

Figure 7.2 Illustration of second excerpt

As the mother approaches, the baby ceases the exploratory movement and returns to her *old ways*, though that familiar interactive pattern is now (re) signified as something that Isabela must learn to do differently. Also, from a dialogical standpoint (Amorim & Rossetti-Ferreira, 2008b), upon facing a collective reality with more agile babies, both mother and teacher indicate the older peer as a reference when they are talking about Isabela's movement. Their speech seems to contrast her motor performance related to the older peer, concluding that as part of her transition experience in that new context, Isabela should learn to develop more autonomous motricity alongside other strategies besides crying.

In the daily routine that followed, caregivers would regularly leave children on the rubbered-floor having toys at their disposal and used to allow contact among pre-mobile, crawling and walking babies. The nursery module contained a large playroom, with toys, pillows and large objects (e.g. beanbags) on the floor. Resembling overall Brazilian reality, babies spent most of the day in the same open-floor plan room (Meneghini & Campos-de-Carvalho, 1997), and the exchange of environments occurred mostly in the moments of hygiene and feeding. Caregivers would frequently sit Isabela on the playroom's central mattress next to age-peers and hand over a toy for each, revealing their preferential surface and postural (re)positioning for handling the babies (Amorim & Rossetti-Ferreira, 2008a).

Nevertheless, even though stationary sitting with individual playing was frequent, Isabela gradually developed autonomous postural progression from sitting-laying prone, as she learned to direct and balance her body forward, reaching for toys that occasionally were moved by the action of peers, or tossed by teachers. With independent postural progression, Isabela gradually developed belly-crawling, that usually took place in diverse interactions with peers through triadic peer-toy-peer attention (Costa & Amorim, 2018) or joint attention (Tomasello & Carpenter, 2007). The often-displacing object positions by peer or adult in such interactive exchanges led to expanded spatial trajectories, (re)created existing environmental arrangement and produced new locomotor actions.

This way, through interacting with the environment and its participants (Vygotsky, 2010) Isabela gradually became more aware of her broader surroundings and started gazing upon distal objects and room contours, not as evident on the stationary sitting exploration. By having her trunk in contact with the ground and developing pushing forward/backwards by using elbows, hands, arms, knees, feet and legs, she perceived the surface as travelable, and the landscapes explored exceeded the mattress' limits. She was then able to gradually apprehend her environment differently, discover new aims of interest and afford new ways of achieving them. Fast-forwarding to two months later, we briefly discuss another episode that illustrates this situation, now bringing locomotor exploration through autonomous locomotion. In this episode, Isabela was eight months old.

> *Isabela is lying on the mattress, in a prone position, with her elbows on the floor, manipulating a small keyboard. Viviane, a 12-month-old baby, approaches her and gradually pulls the toy close to her and away from Isabela. Viviane, sitting at the edge of the rubber-floor (which borders the mattress), does not take the object at once. She first tumbles it over, grabs one end and slowly drags it; and turns it over in different positions, until she has it on her lap. Accompanying Viviane's movements, Isabela moves gradually and successively, seeking to approach the toy that becomes more and more distant. Though she struggles to belly crawl through the mattress softness and transition to the rubber-floor, her effort is constant. When she reaches the mattress edge, there is a pillow on one side, and Viviane with toys on the other, creating a kind of aperture and challenging Isabela to squeeze in between a narrower space.*

This way, a path and multiple challenges are co-constructed within the spatial (re)arrangements linked to an interactive flow, in which Isabela locomotes in a more far-reaching/challenging exploratory trajectory guided by triadic attention with objects *animated* by peers (Rossetti-Ferreira et al., 2010). The process unfolds: escalating interactive and locomotor engagement; the need for more complex movements means in terms of precision, velocity, alternation; unprecedented achievements of self-mobility exploration (Kretch & Adolph, 2017); and, appropriation (Pol, 1996) of the environment, other partners, and her own body. We are intrigued that the potential conflict does not materialize, indicating that, for Isabela, following the toy displacement seems more compelling than protesting against losing it. Thus, in contrast with the previous episode, her actions this time are not emotional towards the adult, but rather a complexifying of autonomous movement and efforts. Rewinding to the narrow passage scene:

> *Isabela gazes at another keyboard, which now becomes the target of her interest. However, before she moves further, Silvia (caregiver) sits Isabela back on the mattress and hands her that toy. The caregiver also interprets the previous situation, disapproving Viviane taking the object for herself and not sharing it. By placing Isabela sitting up with free hands to manipulate the keyboard, she (re)settles the object attribution and the postural configuration. Isabela is now*

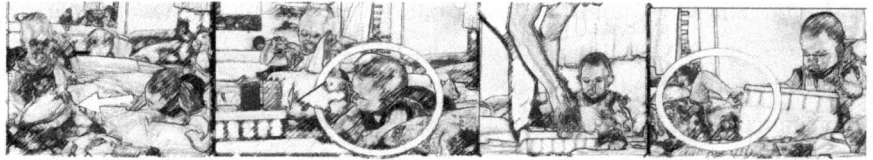

Figure 7.3 Illustration of third excerpt.

sitting, and Viviane is the one who comes crawling, trying to grab the keyboard Isabela is handling. Once she approaches, she lies down sideways. However, because Isabela has her trunk firm and arms/hands released in the sitting posture, compared to Viviane's crawling and posterior lying position, she manages to maintain possession of the keyboard.

In this episode, the (re)positioning of babies promotes different locomotor affordances that unfold in explorative and interactive flow. As inter-postural configuration alternates, a *play of roles* (Oliveira & Rossetti-Ferreira, 1994) is observed due to greater/lesser motor control and object possession, thereby implying different power relationships. The episode confers another transformative sphere of locomotor exploration, disclosing how developing locomotion in parallel with the transition experience of relating to a new context and different partners engenders multiple meanings and means of exploratory actions. Interactions are transformed, relationships are built and practices regarding postural positioning are (re)signified, hence illustrating embodied cultural and social dynamics in the exploratory process.

Final Considerations

This chapter has discussed locomotor exploration within a baby's transition process and experiences to ECEC setting, analysed through a cultural-historical approach and a relational focus. We observed locomotor exploration taking place through the perception-action cycle promoted by multiple interactive arrangements, rather than simple material configuration, revealing greater complexity upon motor acquisitions and developing appropriation of space and bodily affordances. Combining this perspective with cultural-historical theories, we sought to avoid mechanistic and biological determinism associations, as discussed by Del Rio (2002) and Pedersen and Bang (2016), by considering how cultural values, material, historical and economic-political specificities constitute and constrain infants' institutional enrolment, relational dynamics and the opportunities of movement and action through space.

Our hypothesis is that Isabela's multiple-figure care background may have contributed to the absence of overall protest regarding mother's distancing from the very first day, as well as demonstrating interest in unfamiliar people and surroundings. Regarding social relations, conceptions and meanings embodied in action and gesture (Amorim & Rossetti-Ferreira, 2008a; Vygostky, 2000), the mother also seemed to favour this interest in the nursery's surroundings, by directing her daughter towards the environment and supporting postural stability and autonomous activity. It is worth noting that enrolling the child in a day care free of charge was a much-searched solution by the family to guarantee a more stable care routine and some financial relief, so the mother highly valued that moment. Therefore, the case is a counterpoint to claims that ECEC transition disrupts a previous ideal and homeostatic situation and makes us reflect on the experience of so many other children and families who face similar challenges.

On day one, we observed a peer's action transforming exploratory settings and affordances, such that a once-mastered activity becomes novel and challenging in a less familiar posture than that often proposed by the adult's handling. This way, the locomotor transition becomes embodied (Amorim & Rossetti-Ferreira, 2008a) as the baby experiences being positioned differently than at home and developing new haptic and visual strategies thereof.

Once routine settles, we observe caregivers reproducing the same pattern of placing babies with back support and handing them toys. Though adults handle much of body positioning, babies are active and gradually engage in other forms of exploration. Specific affordances support much of these, such as the rubberized floor, ground friction that prevents objects from rolling away very quickly and the mattress preventing falls and providing more confidence in the movement of projecting the body forward to reach the objects.

As a prone position becomes comfortable and frequent, Isabela develops further displacement, and upon her embodied experience, learns to navigate from the mattress – a spot of adult placement – towards the rubber-floor – a landmark of her spatial appropriation. Her initial attempts took place in interactive settings involving older peers, where more complex forms of interaction with the environment were demanded. These included: shared attention promoting shared exploration, object *animated* by the peer generating more keen interest, persistent and articulated movement in a more challenging route and role exchange regarding object possession.

As constitutive contextual practices (Vygostky, 2010), the constant availability of toys, large and small, and the absence of barriers among babies were essential elements to infants' exploration and autonomous activity. Although one-on-one interactions with caregivers were not often and these seemed to favour infants' individual activity, their pedagogical action was materialized in spatial organization, routines and on intervening or not in potentially conflictive situations with peers, as the ones illustrated. Moreover, interactions on day one with a familiar figure on a strange environment seemed to contribute to the baby's spatial locating and a comfortable postural placing for exploration. Finally, embodied conceptions that emerge may enrich the interpretational repertoire of the transition experience regarding babies, their families and caregivers.

Hence, the case has demonstrated infants' curiosity and exploration (Gibson, 1988) being afforded by perception/action cycles that drive movement around a novel space (Gibson, 1966) and allow them to pursuit aims of their interest, to experiment with their bodies and to handle dynamic environmental challenges (Kretch & Adolph, 2017). Though familiarization with the context must be fostered (Ainsworth & Bell, 1970), when it comes to transitions into ECEC settings, this should not imply single focus to emotional reaction nor the assumption of one general family and interactive dynamics.

Through this case study, our work aimed to apprehend the complexity inherently part of the human development – here the baby's exploratory locomotor processes – within a naturalistic collective environment, other than the family house or laboratory. The highlighted context (ECEC institution) represents a contemporary way of infant's care and education, which canalizes diverse elements, structures, partners and relationships, and offers the baby the constitution of different roles and developmental conditions (Rossetti-Ferreira et al., 2007). By following up the transition processes, we sought to analyse the relationship between the singular and the universal aspects, articulating micro and macro affordances, conceptions and interactions regarding the baby's experience (Goes, 2000).

As such, analysis brought considerations of how the structuring of space and relational experiences constrain a baby's locomotor exploration within a socio-cultural-historical context. The study sheds light on how postural positioning and locomotor activity in under one-year-old babies, whether produced by others or by autonomous action, plays out as an inter-corporal process (Amorim & Rossetti-Ferreira, 2008a) and modulates exploratory possibilities and outcomes. Besides, that adults' mediation, spatial organization, peers' interaction and biological aspects simultaneously broaden and limit possibilities (Rossetti-

Ferreira et al., 2007), potentially leading to transformations on such locomotor exploratory processes, through time and experiences. In this sense, our findings may be helpful in understanding how babies explore, make use of and transform locomotor affordances (Liempd et al., 2018) in collective daycare settings within a relational perspective (Sumsion et al., 2014). We thus invite researchers and practitioners to a more refined processual look at the baby's transition and more considerable attention to bodily processes and the constitution of their experience in a new context.

References

Ades, C. (2018). O comportamento exploratório: problemas de definição [The exploratory behaviour: problems of definition]. In P. Izar & P.I.C. Gomide, P. I. C. (Eds.), *Para Além a Dicotomia Inato-Aprendido: Contribuições de César Ades à Psicologia Brasileira* (pp. 9–27). SBP e-Books. http://www.doi.org/10.5935/978-85-61272-03-6.2018B001

Adolph, K. E. (2019). An ecological approach to learning in (not and) development. *Human Development 63*(3–4), 180–201. https://doi.org/10.1159/000503823

Ainsworth, M. D. S., & Bell, S. M. (1970). Attachment, exploration, and separation: Illustrated by the behavior of one-year-olds in a strange situation. *Child Development*, 49–67. https://doi.org/10.2307/1127388

Amorim, K. S. (2010) 'Infant's signification processes: A dialogue with Toomela's focus on case studies'. In S. Salvatore, A. Valsiner & J. Valsiner (Eds.), *Yearbook of Idiographic Science* (Vol 2) (pp. 57–77). Firera & Liuzzo Group.

Amorim, K. S. (2016). Interactions and attachment processes upon infants' transition to daycare in seven countries/cultures: Brazil, Finland, Scotland, Australia, Samoa, New Zealand and USA – Process FAPESP 16/24717-0.

Amorim, K. S., & Rossetti-Ferreira, M. C. (2008a). Corporeidade, significação e o primeiro ano de vida [Embodiment, meaning and the first year of life]. *Arquivos Brasileiros de Psicologia, 60*(1), 67–81.

Amorim, K. S., & Rossetti-Ferreira, M. C. (2008b). Dialogismo e a investigação de processos desenvolvimentais humanos [Dialogism and the investigation on human developmental processes]. *Paidéia (Ribeirão Preto), 18*(40), 235–50. http://dx.doi.org/10.1590/S0103-863X2008000200003

Bowlby, J. (1982). *Attachment and Loss, Vol. I. Attachment*. New York: Basic Books. (Original work published 1969).

Brazil. Ministério da Educação (MEC). Instituto Nacional de Estudos e Pesquisas Educacionais Anísio Teixeira (INEP). (2013). *Censo Escolar da Educação Básica: Resumo Técnico [Census from the basic education: A technical overview]*.

Bussab, V. S. R., & Ribeiro, F. L. (1998). Biologicamente cultural [Biologically cultural]. *Psicologia: Reflexões (im) pertinentes*, 175–93.

Carvalho, A. M. A., Imperio-Hamburger, A., & Pedrosa, M. I. (1998). Interaction, regulation and correlation in the context of human development: Conceptual discussion and empirical examples. In M. C. D. P. Lyra & J. Valsiner (Eds.), *Construction of Psychological Processes in Interpersonal Communication: Child Development within Culturally Structured Environments* (Vol 4) (pp. 155–80). Ablex.

Costa, N. M. S. D., & Amorim, K. D. S. (2018). A co-construção do fluxo locomotor em processos interativos bebê-bebê [Co-construction of locomotor flow in infant-peer interactive process]. *Psicologia em Pesquisa*, *12*(3), 73–83. http://dx.doi.org/10.24879/2018001200300489.

Del Rio, P. (2002). The external brain: Eco-cultural roots of distancing and mediation. *Culture & Psychology*, *8*(2), 233–65. https://doi.org/10.1177/1354067X02008002440.

Fogel, A., Messinger, D. S., Dickson, K. L., & Hsu, H. C. (1999). Posture and gaze in early mother–infant communication: Synchronization of developmental trajectories. *Developmental Science*, *2*(3), 325–32. https://doi.org/10.1111/1467-7687.00078.

Franchak, J. M. (2020). The ecology of infants' perceptual-motor exploration. *Current Opinion in Psychology*, *32*, 110. https://doi.org/10.1016/j.copsyc.2019.06.035.

Gibson, E. J. (1988). Exploratory behavior in the development of perceiving, acting, and the acquiring of knowledge. *Annual Review of Psychology*, *39*(1), 42. https://doi.org/10.1146/annurev.ps.39.020188.000245.

Gibson, J. J. (1966). *The Senses Considered as Perceptual System*. Houghton-Mifflin Company.

Gibson, J. J. (1977). *The Theory of Affordances: Perceiving, Acting and Knowing*. Lawrence Erlbaum Associates.

Góes, M. C. R. (2000). A abordagem microgenética na matriz histórico- cultural: uma perspectiva para o estudo da constituição da subjetividade [The microgenetic approach in the cultural-historical matrix: a perspective for the study of the constitution of subjectivity]. *Cadernos Cedes*, *20*(50), 9–25.

Grossmann, K. E., Grossmann, K., & Zimmermann, P. (1999). A wider view of attachment and exploration: Stability and change during the years of immaturity. In J. Cassidy & P. R. Shaver (Eds.), *Handbook of Attachment: Theory, Research, and Clinical Applications* (pp. 760–786). The Guilford Press.

Keller, H. (2018). Universality claim of attachment theory: Children's socioemotional development across cultures. *Proceedings of the National Academy of Sciences*, *115*(45), 11414–9. https://doi.org/10.1073/pnas.1720325115

Kretch, K. S., & Adolph, K. E. (2017). The organization of exploratory behaviors in infant locomotor planning. *Developmental Science*, *20*(4), e12421. https://doi.org/10.1111/desc.12421

Liempd, H. I. M., Oudgenoeg-Paz, O., Fukkink, R. G., & Leseman, P. P. (2018). Young children's exploration of the indoor playroom space in center-based childcare. *Early Childhood Research Quarterly*, *43*, 33–41. https://doi.org/10.1016/j.ecresq.2017.11.005.

Meneghini, R., & De Carvalho, M. I. C. (1997). Spatial arrangements and groups of young children in day care centers. *Journal of Human Growth and Development*, 7(1), 63–78.

Oliveira, Z. M. R., & Rossetti-Ferreira, M. C. (1994). Coordination of roles: A theoretical-methodological perspective for studying human interactions. In N. Mercer & C. Coll (Eds.), *Teaching, Learning and Interaction – Explorations in Socio-Cultural Studies* (Vol 3) (pp. 217–21). P. del Rio.

Pedersen, S., & Bang, J. (2016). Historicizing affordance theory: A rendezvous between ecological psychology and cultural-historical activity theory. *Theory & Psychology*, 26(6), 731–50. https://doi.org/10.1177/0959354316669021.

Pol, E. (1996). La apropiación del espacio [The appropriation of space]. In L. Íñiguez & E. Pol (Eds.), *Cognición, representación y apropiación del espacio* (pp. 45–62). Publications Universitat de Barcelona.

Rheingold, H. L., & Eckerman, C. O. (1969). The infant's free entry into a new environment. *Journal of Experimental Child Psychology*, 8(2), 271–83. https://doi.org/10.1016/0022-0965(69)90102-7.

Rossetti-Ferreira, M. C., Amorim, K. S., & Silva, A. P. S. (2007). Network of meanings. In J. Valsiner & A. Rosa (Eds.), *The Cambridge Handbook of Sociocultural Psychology* (pp.277–90). The Cambridge University Press.

Rossetti-Ferreira, M. C., Oliveira, Z.M.R., Carvalho, M.I.C., & Amorim, K.S. (2010). Peer relations in Brazilian daycare centres: A new focus for early childhood education. In M. Kernan & E. Singer, (Eds.), *Peer Relationships in Early Childhood Education and Care* (pp. 74–87). Routledge Taylor & Francis Group.

Sumsion, J., Stratigos, T., & Bradley, B. (2014). Babies in space. In L. Harrison and J. Sumsion (Eds.), *Lived Spaces of Infant-Toddler Education and Care: Exploring Diverse Perspectives on Theory, Research and Practice* (pp.43–58). Springer.

Thelen, E. (1995). Motor development: A new synthesis. *American psychologist*, 50(2), 79–95. https://doi.org/10.1037/0003-066X.50.2.79.

Tomasello, M., & Carpenter, M. (2007). Shared intentionality. *Developmental Science*, 10(1), 121–5. https://doi.org/10.1111/j.1467-7687.2007.00573.x.

Vygotsky, L. S. (2000). Manuscrito de 1929 [Manuscript of 1929] *Educação & Sociedade*, 21(71), 21–44. http://dx.doi.org/10.1590/S0101-73302000000200002.

Vygotsky, L. S. (2010). A questão do meio na pedologia [The problem of the environment]. *Psicologia USP*, 21(4).

White, E. J., Rutanen, N., Marwick, H., Souza Amorim, K., Karagiannidou, E., & Herold, L. K. M. (2020). Expectations and emotions concerning infant transitions to ECEC: International dialogues with parents and teachers. *European Early Childhood Education Research Journal*, 28(3), 363–74. https://doi.org/10.1080/1350293X.2020.1755495

Yin, R. K. (2009). *Case Study Research: Design and Methods* (4th edn.). Sage.

8

Transitional Activities: Children's Projects in Finnish Pre-primary Education

Jaakko Hilppö, Teemu Suorsa and Anna P. Rainio

Introduction

We need to start with an explanation. This chapter is in many ways hypothetical. While the arguments advanced are well supported by both theoretical and empirical work done within the broad framework of cultural-historical activity theory, what new we have to offer is still under construction and therefore tentative. In short, we suggest that children in early education, schools, homes and other places come up with and engage in their own projects, activities they have created and that take place in between, within and or the sidelines of more official school, home or free-time activities. These projects can be very short-lived or be sustained over longer periods of time and engaged across multiple different contexts. Furthermore, we suggest that such projects can entail important learning opportunities for the children to expand their knowledge and skill and hence can also be seen as developmentally important. In this sense, we argue that such projects could be understood as examples of *transitional activities*, an intermediate theoretical concept we introduce in this chapter to describe children's engagement between what are typically understood as more developmentally substantial and long-term activities, or leading activities (El'konin, 1972).

Given that our ideas on children's projects and the concept of transitional activities are still quite tentative and abstract (even romantic) we will draw on an example of a children's project from a Finnish pre-primary education group in order to ground and illustrate our ideas. The vignette was collected by a pre-service teacher during a practicum period in a public, municipal kindergarten in the north of Finland. The vignette takes us to the pre-primary education group's gym time and an imaginary trip to Lapland. It serves to illustrate the start of a children's project centred around staging dance performances for friends and other children and adults in the kindergarten.

> *The teachers had planned a gym time for their group. The exercises were embedded in a narrative about travelling to Rovaniemi* [A city in the north of Finland] *and seeing various sights, people and animals that were characteristic to Lapland, like Santa Claus and reindeers. The teachers' educational goal was to familiarize the children with different parts of Finland, Lapland on this occasion.*
>
> *As part of the gym time, the children did cross country skiing* [a popular sport and recreational activity in Finland] *on imaginary tracks across snowy landscapes and saw the northern lights (Aurora Borealis) in the sky. The northern lights were done with different colored scarves hung across the room and a children's song about the northern lights playing in the background.*
>
> *The children were thrilled about their trip to Lapland. After the gym, many of the recited the names of the towns and cities they visited and other really liked the cross-country skiing. One of the children was really inspired by the northern lights, the music and the scarves and started making dance performances with the materials for the other children. At first the performances were for friends only, but later the same friends joined the performances and together the children performed their dances for the rest of the kindergarten.*

What drew our attention in this vignette was how gym time and the imaginary trip to Lapland, a fairly mundane activity in Finnish pre-primary education, seem to have served as an initial scaffold for one of the children's dance project. Moreover, that the dance performances grew both in the number of performances and performers suggests that the kindergarten seemed not only to spark the project, but also support it and allow it to grow. Interestingly, to our knowledge, such self-initiated activities have been less studied within the educational sciences or other fields, although their potential significance for children's learning and development seems apparent (although cf. Crowley & Jacobs, 2002; Van Oers, 1998). As part of a long-term effort to understand and study such activities (Hilppö, 2017), in this chapter we are asking how these self-initiated dance performances (and other children's projects) could be understood and conceptualized from a cultural-historical perspective. Furthermore, we are also interested in exploring what is the potential of these projects, as activities inspired by official educational activities but developed by children on their own right, have for children's learning and development.

Before exploring these questions more deeply (and providing our answers), we have to set the stage and explain our own understanding of the cultural-historical framework and its central elements that are most relevant for our arguments. In the next section, we will elaborate the following three premises, 1) that human activities are object-oriented (Engeström, 1999; Leontiev, 1978) 2) that children's learning and development are structured by the various opportunities offered and demands placed on them by different activities that constitute their everyday lives (Hedegaard et al., 2012); and 3) that the relative importance of various activities for children's development changes between different historical periods and within ontogenesis (Beach, 1995). After this, we will explain and elaborate our notion of transitional activities as an intermediated theoretical conceptualization that helps us to understand children's projects from a cultural-historical perspective. We will close our chapter with a discussion of the role of early childhood educators and the pre-primary education in the emergence of children's projects.

Cultural-Historical Activity Theory as a Framework

A central theoretical premise of the cultural-historical activity theory is that human activities are energized and driven by their object, the fundamental raison d'être or the what for of the activity. In cultural-historical terms, 'the object of an activity is its true motive' (Leontiev, 1978, p. 62). These motives, like healing the ill, producing food or teaching children, represent vital needs of human societies, ones which the society constantly aspires to fulfil to secure its continuation. As such, these objects are understood as being inherently contradictory and complex assemblages of human and material actors that evolve through its inner dynamics but also by being connected to other activities (Engeström, 1987). Furthermore, although objects always appear as tangible things that are worked on, they also transcend their particular manifestations. As Engeström (1999, p. 170) explains:

> The object is not reducible to the raw material given or the product achieved. It is understandable as the trajectory from raw material to product in the emerging context of its eventual use by another activity system. Thus, the object of a hospital may be characterized as the trajectory from symptoms to treatment outcomes in the context of the patient's life activity. The object is projective and transitory, truly a moving horizon. But it is also specific and concrete, crystallized, embodied and re-problematized in every single patient and illness entering the hospital, time and time again.

Importantly, from a cultural-historical activity theory perspective, the object of the activity drives the development of people's skills and competencies (e.g.

Karpov, 2005). For children and adults alike, working to fulfil the requirements of the object calls on them to master new skills and tools, organize, collaborate and learn how to deal with the object. For example, to teach, teachers need to learn how to plan lessons, motivate students, manage teaching materials and master the substance of their curriculum. These demands for peoples' competence are not static, but are in motion and evolve with the society. With the growth of the public-school system and the size of the schools, teachers are more often called to collaborate with other teachers, professionals and parents to manage their students' learning. Moreover, technological advances are also pushing teachers to learn how to teach in an increasingly digital and connected world. In this sense, the object is a moving target, as Engeström (1999) argued.

The second cultural-historical premise central to our chapter is that children's learning and development are structured by the multiple institutions, their objects and associated activities that constitute the children's everyday lives (e.g. Hedegaard, Edwards & Fleer, 2012). Between getting out of bed and going to sleep, children move across many institutions and take part in their activities. At home, this can mean taking part in preparing dinner, playing games or taking care of pets. In pre-primary education, circle time, free play, gym, or making art or crafts, each activity presents opportunities and demands for the children, requiring their engagement, developing and guiding their skills. According to Hedegaard et al. (2012), each institution and its practices have their own cultural-historical tradition, which reflects both the function the institution serves in society as well as the local contingencies the institution has adapted to. By participating in these institutional activities, Hedegaard et al. (2012) maintain, the children take part in the creating conditions for their own learning and development as well maintaining the activities and the institutions themselves (see also, Rogoff, 2003). Importantly, demands and opportunities for learning and development do not emerge just from the activities themselves, but also from the tensions and contradictions between them. For example, the way in which children are required to participate in school might be significantly different to the expectations they face at home or with their peers (Fleer & Hedegaard, 2010; cf. Christensen, 2009). Moreover, these differences in expectations and demands and how intensively they are experienced are relative to the socio-economic, ethnic or other status of the child's family (Phelan et al., 1991). For children coming from a middle class, western cultural background, common educational practices, like the Initiate-Response-Feedback/Evaluation (IRF/E) classroom routine (e.g. Mehan, 1979), are more familiar than to others (e.g. Calarco, 2014).

However, not all activities children engage in during their everyday life are developmentally equal in their impact. Rather, some activities have a more dominant role in shaping and directing children's development than other activities they engage in at the same age and hence conceptualized as *leading activities* (e.g. El'konin, 1972; Leont'ev, 1981). This will be the third cultural-historical premise our work will draw on. Such activities, like socio dramatic play for preschool age children or object-centred joint activity with toddlers have been shown to have a more dominant role in shaping and directing children's development than other activities they engage in at the same age (e.g. Karpov, 2005; Manuilenko, 1975). Accordingly, the succession of leading activities forms the basis for a generalized description of children's developmental pathway from birth to adulthood, its central phases and turning points (El'konin, 1972).

Importantly, this pathway, and the nature of the leading activities within it, is understood within cultural-historical theory as being historically, culturally, and societally situated (e.g. Beach, 1995; Karpov, 2005). In some societies and cultures, children take part in the work activities of their community at an early age (Lancy, 2018). In other societies and cultures, such as western European heritage cultures like Finland, children play and take part in different forms of formal education before transitioning to being employed. Moreover, whether or not an activity can be seen to be leading a person's development depends on the position of the activity in their life course. Beach (1995), based on ethnographical work in rural Nepal, argued that for adult shopkeepers taking part in formal schooling to learn literacy and numeracy, shopkeeping remained their leading activity and which their learning served. For younger villagers, who had not yet entered the work force, studying in school acted as their leading activity.

A central aspect of leading activities is their internal developmental dynamic. Although each leading activity forms its own, stable developmental phase, they also set up children for the next developmental phase (El'konin, 1972). That is, each leading activity contains within itself the prerequisite aspects of the next, developmentally more progressed level. When toddlers learn to manipulate everyday objects, like kitchenware or toys, they also gradually become aware of the various activities and social roles associated with them, like cooking. This readies the children for imitating those activities and roles in role play. Then, as preschoolers, engagement in role play entails controlling and mastering one's own behaviour and thus sets the children up for taking part in formal instructional practices in school (e.g. Bodrova, 2008). More broadly speaking, through engagement with each leading activity the objective, societal worlds of different human activities are gradually disclosed in more nuanced, detailed and transformed forms for the children.

Children's Projects as Transitional Activities

How do these three premises compare to the vignette provided earlier? As with any theory, would it be possible to generate what took place in kindergarten's gym with the three premises? Or, in the spirit of pragmatism (Rorty, 1991), do the premises help us highlight relevant issues for understanding and developing the praxis of pedagogy and its science? In general terms, we think so. The imaginary trip to Lapland served a specific pedagogical goal, learning about different regions of Finland that was motivated by the object of the kindergarten's activities, namely educating and caring for the children. The particular shape these activities took was also contingent on the local history of the kindergarten and how the practitioners and the children together realized the activities with the social and material resources at their disposal. Furthermore, for the children, assuming the role of a traveller on make-believe skies moving across an imaginary snowy landscape could be seen as a manifestation of the leading activity of the preschool period. However, these observations remain at a macroscopic level. While accurate in general, when we look more closely at the emergence of the dance performances and what is said about them, the concepts lose their clarity, or at least grasp them only partially.

This is hardly surprising. In order to make up the core of their respective theories, central premises and related concepts need to be highly generalizable and hence selective in what they highlight. However, this can also be a source of substantial critique. Regarding leading activities, Gutierrez et al. (2019) point out that play as an activity is developmentally significant not just in childhood, but across the lifespan (see also Göncü & Vadeboncoeur, 2017; Holzman, 2009). From their perspective, seeing play as solely the realm of children directs our attention away from how playful interactions can drive the development of youth or adults. It also leaves aside the fact that children's development in institutional settings is connected and relative to adult development and not separate from it (see, i.e. Ferholt et al., 2019; Rainio & Hilppö, 2017; Vygotsky, 1987). Conversely, from our perspective, an overt focus on pretend play as the leading force in early childhood might also direct attention away from other or related activities and their developmental potential. One avenue for solving such discrepancies would be to let go of rigid periodization regarding leading activities, as Gutierrez and her colleagues (2019) have, and instead emphasize that whichever activity leads development at a given time is a matter of empirical investigation. However, this solution runs the risk of overextending leading activity as a conceptual category and losing its conceptual nuance and sensitivity regarding the developmental impact of various activities. An activity can contribute to children's (and adults') development without being developmentally dominant at the same time in the broader picture, as Leont'ev (1965, cited in El'konin, 1972) reminds us.

An alternative strategy would be to develop so-called *intermediate theoretical concepts* (Engeström, 2008, 2016). Such concepts are 'specific enough to be of use in the evaluation of observed phenomena, yet general enough to be incorporated into broader theoretical statements' (Morrow & Muchinsky, 1980, p. 34) and thus also help us to connect more central theoretical premises and concepts to the specific empirical observations. What we argue in this chapter, is that the dance performances, and other similar children's projects, offer good grounds for such a concept, namely *transitional activities*. However, to substantiate this claim and explain our rationale for the term, we need to return to the pre-primary group and explain more about the dance performances and how they were created. The following narrative is told from the perspective of the pre-service teacher who observed the children working on a number of different performances.

> *When I came to the kindergarten, I noticed that some of the children liked to do different performances. Most of the performances were dancing to music. One of the children recruited their friends to dance with them, sometimes the whole pre-primary education group was dancing and sometimes the child performed alone. The performances had many roles. Some made tickets, some were the audience, others were musicians and other dancers. Once a group of eight kids made a performance for the whole kindergarten. They made invitations to each group and posters advertising the performance all over the kindergarten.*

There are several striking elements in the narrative. It seems that northern lights inspired an activity that was not just performing, but entailed setting the performances up and had multiple roles and a different division of labour between them. Moreover, the performances were not just for their own group, but also expanded to include also other groups from the kindergarten, at least as the audience of one of the performances. Importantly, the performances were created, and presumably also organized and directed, by the children. What makes this significant is that while creating similar performances for parents and other groups around major holidays (like Christmas) is a routine activity in Finnish early education, it is dominantly designed and organized by the early childhood educators. Overall, much like in play, creating, engaging and developing the performances arguably created a zone of proximal development for them and enable the children to 'act a head taller' (Vygotsky, 1967).

But a head taller for why? What motivated the children to stretch themselves in this way? When asked for their reasons for performing, the child who had initially started the performances told the observing pre-service teacher that:

> *I do the performances because I like it and I want to do them. They are fun to do. I like when I get to be with my friends and do performances for others. For a performance to be good, you need to rehearse a lot. Although you are a bit scared to perform, it does not matter. If you have trained hard, the performance will go well.*

What is particularly significant in the quote is at the end of the third sentence, 'and do performances for others'. It suggests that while the performances were motivating in themselves, the fact that they were for others was also important. The performances seemed in part to 'aspire to objective productiveness of its activity' (Leon'tev, 1981, p. 366), to create experiences for others as well as for themselves. Discussing similar examples of dramatized and invented games from Russian preschools, Leon'tev suggested that: 'The dramatization-game is thus a possible form of transition to productive activity, namely to aesthetic, activity with its characteristic motive of the effect on other people' (Leont'ev, 1981, p. 352).

For Leon'tev such games and other similar activities represented breakdowns of the leading activity of the preschool period, namely role play. This characterization is problematic for us in three connected ways. First, there are several elements in the dramatization games that come close to pretend play (such as taking up roles) and therefore the line between pretend play and productive activity is in practice more fluid than clear-cut. Second, Leont'ev's view arguably positions other activities as developmentally lesser and deficient in relation to *pure* role playing. Although breakdowns and disruptions are central to cultural-historical theorizing, especially regarding development, characterizing activities like the performances as non-functional downplays rather than highlights their possible developmental role. Finally, the characterization underscores Leon'tev's (and also El'konin's) narrow conceptualization of play and its motivating forces. As Lindqvist (1995) argues, Leon'tev saw play dominantly as stemming from children's unrealized want to take part in activities that adults around them were engaged in and hence took the form of reproducing those activities through role play. This overlooks the fact that play is motivating also in itself, as something real, concrete and immediate for the participants themselves, even if imagined.

If this aspect of play is taken into account, the basis for seeing activities like the performances or other children's projects as breakdowns of play breaks down itself. Productiveness, in the form of aesthetic for oneself and the other players, is already present in the activity.

Instead of breakdowns, we suggest that children's projects and other similar activities could be better conceptualized as *transitional activities*. This would highlight more how such activities seem to entail aspects of conventional role play as well as of productive work towards which the children are stretching themselves. Importantly, this conceptualization would also capture the way in which such activities entail a reversal of roles between children and the adults, especially within institutional contexts. This kind of extended and shared play activities between adults and children have previously been studied and developed as *playworlds*, a specific form of adult-child joint play in the context of education (see Ferholt et al., 2019; Marjanovic-Shane et al., 2011). In the case of the dance performances this would mean highlighting how the dances were sparked by the adult-directed gym activity, but were created and led by the children. In addition, highlighting the transitional nature of the children's projects also emphasizes their possible temporary character and intermediate role in children's development as well as the notion's relation to the concept of leading activities. More generally, characterizing children's projects as transitional activities would also be in line with Vygotsky's conceptualization of human development as achronological and disproportionate (Kellogg & Veresov, 2020). In this sense, borrowing Vygotsky's metaphor (Vygotsky, 1987), children's projects could be described as the smallest crystals of ice that form in water before it turns into solid ice.

Children's Projects as Sites for Agency and Exploration

Water molecules do not self-induce a change in their state, but children's projects do. They emerge through the agency of the children. In Leon'tev's terms, these agentic moments rise from 'an open contradiction' between the child's position in the world of human relations and their experience of their own potential (Leon'tev, 1981, p. 361). What Leon'tev is essentially referring to here is the child's sense of agency (Hilppö, 2016), their first-person experience of themselves as an actor who can engage with their world and push into the opportunities they see as opening for them. Such experiences could emerge in multiple ways in children's everyday life. For example, learning to use a specific tool might prompt various ideas about how it could be used or engaging in a science experiment with one's teacher could generate ideas for re-creating it at home and adding something new to it. In the case of the dance performances, the imaginary trip to Lapland functioned as a formative activity for that experience. In broader cultural-historical terms, such an experience could be seen as particular kind of a *need state* (Bratus & Lishin, 1983; Miettinen, 2005) which through imagination gives rise to transformative agency (Rainio, 2008; Rainio & Hilppö, 2017) and a new motive, the dance performances.

However, the material practice of the new activity is always richer than the plans or ideas that precede it (Engeström et al., 2012; Miettinen, 2005). The idea of the dance performances does not entail all the possible ways in which it could be realized. Hence, pursuing a project like the dance performances means a process of exploration for the children, adventuring into the new activity as an open-ended pursuit. In practice, this exploration means discovering how the project can be realized and what it means for the persons involved, but also discovering what more can be done and what other options for realizing the project are in the world. As Leont'ev (1978) pointed out, the further an activity develops, the more fully the original need that sparked the process is fulfilled. In this sense, while specific goals might be realized through engagement with the project, at the same time new goals and possibilities also appear and need to be explored. In the case of the dance performances, this could be seen with the gradual growth of the project. According to the pre-service teacher's narrative summary above, the performances eventually were not just about dancing to the audience, but also about generating a more encompassing experience with advertisement, tickets and playing music.

But pursuing the unfolding horizon of the project generates exploration also in another, more bounded sense. To highlight this, we must again return to the kindergarten in question and share another quote from the pre-service teacher who observed the development of the dance performances.

> When I got to see a number of consecutive performances, I noticed that the performances started coming together more and more. The kids came up with elements that they needed to do together and at the same time in the performances. They also started to pay more attention to the lyrics of the songs, to sing while dancing and enacting the lyrics.

The fact that the performances were *coming together more and more* suggests that the performances were not static, the same performance each time around, but rather that they developed over time. This development of the children's project, being able to create more coherent, synchronized and deliberately choreographed dance performances, is an indication of learning on part of the children. As Dewey (1910; e.g. Miettinen, 2000) argues, this kind of learning begins when something, a problem, disrupts our engagement with what we are doing and leads into exploring the cause of the disruption and possible solutions to it. This exploration starts with the formulation of a working hypothesis and then testing it, initially via thought experiments and then in action. If the tentative solution does not work, the process of exploring the problem is continued with knowledge gained from the first attempt. If the problem is solved, the participants move forward with the project and the experience of solving the issue turns into a resource for future problem solving. In this sense, given the tentativeness of each potential solution and how the problems are nested within the children's project as a whole, these problem-solving processes could be seen as smaller explorations in themselves (cf., Rantavuori et al., 2016).

The explorations, either in their expanded or more bounded sense, do not emerge solely through the children's transformative acts. In the case of the dance performances, creating them also meant recruiting friends and the adults to work on the performances, as told by the pre-service teacher in her first quote above. Recruiting others highlights the children's relational agency (Edwards, 2005, p. 172), their 'capacity to work with others to expand the object that one is working on and trying to transform by recognizing and accessing the resources that others bring to bear as they interpret and respond to the object'. This relational work is also important in order to stabilize the project as a new activity of the children's lives in early education. As we have argued elsewhere, agency is a complex and contradictory phenomenon (Rainio, 2010; Rainio & Hilppö, 2017). While the enactment of agency can be understood as requiring a level of independency from one's immediate surroundings and standing out from one's community, at the same time it also stems from the community, for example, in terms of the cultural tools and recognition given by the community. In the context of children's projects this means that although children might create and engage in a project on their own, the way in which others receive and recognize the project is similarly significant. Rainio's work (Rainio, 2008, 2010) suggests that dealing with such projects without undermining the agency of the children requires specific efforts and awareness from the teachers and others adults who become involved with the project. This need for pedagogical sensitivity and skill is accentuated even more when the project and its goals are not easy to understand from an adult perspective or push on what adults might regard as appropriate for children to do.

In other words, what is important is how the children's projects impact their social situation of development (Bozhovich, 2009). Are the children able to create new relationships or change the quality of existing ones through the projects? What the case of the performances suggests is that the Finnish kindergartens in general and pre-primary education in specific might potentially be well suited to accommodate children's projects and offer good grounds for their development. Next, we will explore and discuss aspect of the Finnish early education and especially pre-primary education that seem to use relevant for the emergence of children's projects.

Finnish Pre-primary Education as a Context for Children's Projects

Over the recent years, the Finnish educational system has enjoyed intense national and international attention, and the Early Childhood Education and Care (ECEC) sector along with it. This has resulted in multiple descriptions and attempts to characterize its main differences from other national systems (e.g. Einarsdottir et al., 2015; Hujala et al., 2009). In her recent review, Kumpulainen (2018) argues that the Finnish system does not have any one element that makes it unique. Rather, the merits of the Finnish ECEC lie in several intertwined values that permeate the different ECEC services and the educational system as a whole. According to her, these values are 1) the system's principled nature, i.e. the way in which education and care are embedded within the Nordic social welfare state model and its legislation, 2) mutual trust between families, the government, educators and children, 3) child-centred pedagogics and 4) the opportunity to personalize and build individualized support for children's learning and development. Although these values work in concert and form a complete whole, we will elaborate more on the last two which we believe are the most impactful concerning children's projects.

The child-centred nature of Finnish ECEC is well displayed in the current National Core Curriculum. In its opening statements, the curriculum outlines that its mission is to 'promote children's holistic growth, development and learning in collaboration with their guardians' and that 'knowledge and skills acquired in early childhood education and care strengthen children's participation and active agency in the society' (Finnish National Agency for Education, 2016, p. 12). Later, when discussing learning in ECEC settings more specifically, the curriculum states that 'in early childhood education and care, the previous experiences of children, their interests, and their competences are the starting point for learning and in that the curriculums, the 'conception of learning is also based on a view of the child's active agency (Finnish National Agency for Education, 2016, p. 18). In practice, this emphasis has meant that children are invited to participate in creating and assessing activities with the early childhood educators and that their interests and lifeworlds are taken as a starting point for the activities (e.g. Alasuutari et al., 2014; Kangas, 2016). While these educational policies and guidelines have not always translated into professional practices as such (Kangas & Lastikka, 2019; also Paananen, 2017), the child-centred nature of the Finnish ECEC means that children have both the opportunity and the support they might need for creating and engaging in their own projects in pre-primary education.

This opportunity and support are further accentuated by the number of structural elements aimed at securing individualized care and support for learning and development. In addition to families having the several options to choose between the type of care best for their child, Kumpulainen (2018) highlights the individualized education plan (IEP) negotiated between the parents, the child and the early childhood educators as an important tool in this regard. The IEP's goal is to act as a formative bridge between the child's current interests, their possible developmental needs and the ECEC curriculum and help tailor the pedagogical practices for each child (Finnish National Agency for Education, 2016). Again, while the IEPs are not always taken into account in everyday practice and can become stagnant documents (Heiskanen, 2019; Paananen & Lipponen, 2018), they do offer a substantial opportunity to bridge children's lifeworlds and deepen the connections between home and pre-primary education. In relation to children's projects, this means that projects created at home can more easily travel to the early education setting (and vice versa) and children can recruit more materials and support for the projects.

There are also other contributing aspects that make Finnish pre-primary education a formative setting for children's projects. The Finnish pre-primary education, like in other countries, is situated between early education and care services and elementary education, as such a transitional institution itself, and arguably a mix between the care and play oriented kindergarten groups for zero-to-five-year-olds and primary education with is emphasis on formal instruction. For example, approximately 700 hours per year are used for different pre-primary activities, which breaks down to four hours per day (Kumpulainen, 2018). Although only this part of the day is mandatory for all six-year-olds, most of them attend for the full day. In addition, in most cases pre-primary education groups are situated in the kindergarten's facilities (Kumpulainen, 2018). This means that the schedule and daily rhythm have openings and room for self-generated activities during which the children have access to the pre-primary education materials as well as other resources of the kindergarten. Taken together with the trust between adults and children and the other values and associated institutional practices, Finnish pre-primary education could arguably be seen as an open learning environment (Hannafin et al., 2014) in which children can pursue their interests and ideas in a setting that both sparks and supports them. As such, as a learning environment the pre-primary education would exemplify Dewey's notion of a cultivating or development inducing environment in which 'one thing needful in education is secured' (Dewey, 1913, p. 97).

The extent to which primary school practices offer students a possibility to occupy a new social position in their life has a significant impact on how they come to value and engage with formal instruction at school (Bozhovich, 2009). According to Bozhovich (2009), preschool children dominantly strive for a new social position towards the end of their pre-primary education year and if this new position is not realized by what school has to offer to them, they lose their interest in school. One possible way to counter this would be to allow for children to take their projects to primary school and support the projects' growth in a new institutional setting. In primary education, with its different resources and opportunities, children's projects could be taken as a potential nexus where the official school curriculum, children's own interests and their everyday lives could meet.

Conclusions

In this chapter, we have argued the need for a new intermediate concept, transitional activities, to theorize and describe children's self-generated activities, like children's projects, that are relevant for their learning and development, but which fall outside existing conceptualizations within cultural-historical theorizing. To substantiate and ground our argument, we presented a vignette of a children's dance project from a Finnish pre-primary education group. We also argued that the Finnish ECEC, especially pre-primary education, could be seen as a good formative context for different kinds of children's projects and suggested that the projects could also serve children's transition from pre-primary education to primary school.

Our formulations are still tentative and preliminary and as such need to be further substantiated through future work, or refuted altogether. This work could take several directions. One possible avenue could be following children's projects in the everyday life of early education settings and creating comprehensive research designs around them. A central challenge for this work would be identifying children projects as they emerge and following how they are received and how they possibly evolve. Much like with interest-driven engagement (Valsiner, 1992), the projects possibly become visible only after the fact, after they have been created and worked on by the children. Furthermore, if the projects travel and are worked on in other settings, like the children's home, following them might provide an additional challenge. However, collecting more detailed ethnographic data on the projects and how children engage with them would allow for closer-level analysis of how children organize their work on the project and what they learn through their engagement. An additional direction would be to engage in similar efforts in other open learning environments in primary school (see, Hilppö & Stevens, submitted; Hilppö et al., 2016), makerspaces, libraries (Parekh & Gee, 2019) or even in more conventional, but less constrained educational settings like craft education. There are also indications that children's projects and the learning connected to them could be studied in non-western and non-educational contexts (e.g. de Leon, 2015).

While these avenues present enticing prospects, a caveats is also in order. Across educational sectors we are currently witnessing a trend of personalization, increasing accountability and escalating performance pressures (e.g. Chimirri, 2019; Langemeyer, 2006; OECD, 2017). In this climate, uncritical uptake of children's projects runs the risk of turning them from an activity enjoyed in itself into a measure of control and formal educational achievement, one more way of sorting the successful from the failed (Hilppö & Stevens, 2020; Varenne & McDermott, 1999). While daunting, this risk should not deter researchers (us and others) from continuing what we have begun in this chapter. From our perspective, children's projects and other transitional activities can be significant sites for supporting children and letting them freely engage in things that they find interesting and exciting. In times that fill children's lives with other people's agendas and requirements, projects can offer children a possible respite and a chance to grow something more on their own terms. This is a captivating opportunity not just for the children themselves, but also for us adults who live with them.

References

Alasuutari, M., Karila, K., Alila, K., & Eskelinen, M. (2014). Vaikuta varhaiskasvatukseen: Lasten ja vanhempien kuuleminen osana varhaiskasvatuksen lainsäädäntöprosessia.

Opetus- ja kulttuuriministeriön työryhmämuistioita ja - selvityksiä 2014: 13. Opetus- ja kulttuuriministeriö.

Beach, K. (1995). Activity as a mediator of sociocultural change and individual development: The case of school-work transition in Nepal. *Mind, Culture, and Activity*, *2*(4), 285–302. https://doi.org/10.1080/10749039509524707

Bodrova, E. (2008). Make-believe play versus academic skills: A Vygotskian approach to today's dilemma of early childhood education. *European Early Childhood Education Research Journal*, *16*(3), 357–69. https://doi.org/10.1080/13502930802291777

Bozhovich, L. I. I. (2009). The social situation of child development. *Journal of Russian & East European Psychology*, *47*(4), 59–86. https://doi.org/10.2753/RPO1061-0405470403

Bratus, B. S., & Lishin, O. V. (1983). Laws of development of activity and problems in the psychological and pedagogical shaping of the personality. *Soviet Psychology*, *25*(2), 91–103. https://doi.org/10.2753/RPO1061-0405210338

Calarco, J. M. (2014). Coached for the classroom: Parents' cultural transmission and children's reproduction of educational inequalities. *American Sociological Review*, *79*(5), 1015–1037. https://doi.org/10.1177/0003122414546931

Chimirri, N. (2019). Generalizing Together with children: The significance of children's concepts for mutual knowledge creation. In C. Højholt & E. Schraube (Eds.), *Subjectivity and Knowledge, Theory and History in the Human and Social Sciences* (pp. 115–139). Springer Nature.

Christensen, A. D. (2009). Scandinavian Everyday life sociologies: Routines, ruptures and strategies. In M. H. Jacobsen (Eds.), *Encountering the Everyday: An Introduction to the Sociologies of the Unnoticed* (pp. 307–28). Palgrave Macmillan.

Crowley, K., & Jacobs, M. (2002). Building islands of expertise in everyday family activity. In K. Crowley & K. Knutson (Eds.), *Learning Conversations in Museums* (pp. 333–56). Lawrence Erlbaum.

De León, L. (2015). Mayan children's creation of learning ecologies by initiative and cooperative action. In M. Correa-Chávez, R. Mejía-Arauz & B. Rogoff (Eds.), *Advances in Child Development and Behavior* (Vol 49) (pp. 153–84). JAI.

Dewey, J. (1910). *How We Think*. Dover publication.

Dewey, J. (1913). *Interest and Effort in Education*. Riverside Press.

Edwards, A. (2005). Relational agency: Learning to be a resourceful practitioner. *International Journal of Educational Research*, *43*(3), 168–82. https://doi.org/10.1016/j.ijer.2006.06.010

Einarsdottir, J., Purola, A. M., Johansson, E. M., Broström, S., & Emilson, A. (2015). Democracy, caring and competence: Values perspectives in ECEC curricula in the Nordic countries. *International Journal of Early Years Education*, *23*(1), 97–114. https://doi.org/10.1080/09669760.2014.970521

El'konin, D. B. (1972). Toward the problem of stages in the mental development of the child. *Soviet Psychology*, *10*, 225–51. (Original work published 1971). https://doi.org/10.2753/RPO1061-0405370611

Engeström, Y. (1987). *Learning by Expanding: An Activity-theoretical Approach to Developmental Research*. Orienta-Konsultit.

Engeström, Y. (1999). Communication, discourse and activity. *The Communication Review*, *3*(1–2), 165–85. https://doi.org/10.1080/10714429909368577

Engeström, Y. (2008). Enriching activity theory without shortcuts. *Interacting with Computers*, *20*(2), 256–9. https://doi.org/10.1016/j.intcom.2007.07.003

Engeström, Y. (2016). Making use of activity theory in educational research. In G. Dilani, S. P. Gedera & P. John Williams (Eds.), *Activity Theory in Education Research and Practice* (Foreword). Rotterdam.

Engeström, Y., Nummijoki, J., & Sannino, A. (2012). Embodied germ cell at work: Building an expansive concept of physical mobility in home care. *Mind, Culture, and Activity*, *19*(3), 287–309. https://doi.org/10.1080/10749039.2012.688177

Ferholt, B., Nilsson, M., & Lecusay, R. (2019). Preschool teachers being people alongside young children: The development of adults' relational competences in playworlds. In S. Alcock & N. Stobbs (Eds.), *Rethinking Play as Pedagogy: Thinking About Pedagogy in Early Education Series 4* (pp. 17–32). Routledge.

Finnish National Agency for Education. (2016). *National Core Curriculum for Early Childhood Education and Care 2016*. Finnish National Agency for Education.

Fleer, M., & Hedegaard, M. (2010). Children's development as participation in everyday practices across different institutions. *Mind, Culture, and Activity*, *17*(2), 149–68. https://doi.org/10.1080/10749030903222760

Gutiérrez, K. D., Higgs, J., Lizárraga, J. R., & Rivero, E. (2019). Learning as movement in social design-based experiments: Play as a leading activity. *Human Development*, *62*(1–2), 66–82. https://doi.org/10.1159/000496239

Göncü, A., & Vadeboncoeur, J. A. (2017). Expanding the definitional criteria for imaginative play: Contributions of sociocultural perspectives. *Learning & Behavior*, *45*(4), 422–31. https://doi.org/10.3758/s13420-017-0292-z

Hannafin, M. J., Hill, J. R., Land, S. M., & Lee, E. (2014). Student-centered, open learning environments: Research, theory, and practice. In J.M. Spector, M.D. Merrill, J. Elen, M.J. Bishop (Eds.), *Handbook of Research on Educational Communications and Technology* (pp. 641–51). Springer.

Hedegaard, M., Edwards, A., & Fleer, M. (Eds.). (2012). *Motives in Children's Development: Cultural Historical Approaches*. Cambridge University Press

Heiskanen, N. (2019). *Children's Needs for Support and Support Measures in Pedagogical Documents of Early Childhood Education and Care*. [Doctoral Dissertation, University of Helsinki]. JYU Dissertations 139.

Hilppö, J. (2017, August 30th). *Children's Projects: A Proposal for a Research Agenda*. [Poster] 5th International Congress of the International Society for Cultural-historical Activity Research (ISCAR), Quebec.

Hilppö, J., & Stevens, R. (2020). 'Failure is just another try': Re-framing failure in school through the FUSE studio approach. *International Journal of Educational Research*, *99*, 101494.

Hilppö, J., & Stevens, R. (submitted). Productive deviations: Learner agency and interest. *Learning, Culture and Social Interaction*.

Hilppö, J., Stevens, R., Jona, K., Echevarria, R., & Penney, L. (2016). *Productive Deviations as Manifestations of Student Agency in FUSE*. [Paper] 12th International Conference of the Learning Sciences (ICLS), Singapore.

Holzman, L. (2009). *Vygotsky at Work and Play*. Routledge.

Hujala, E., Turja, L., Gaspar, M. F., Veisson, M., & Waniganayake, M. (2009). Perspectives of early childhood teachers on parent–teacher partnerships in five European countries. *European Early Childhood Education Research Journal, 17*(1), 57–76. https://doi.org/10.1080/13502930802689046

Kangas, J. (2016). *Enhancing Children's Participation in Early Childhood Education through Participatory Pedagogy*. [Doctoral Thesis]. University of Helsinki.

Kangas, J., & Lastikka, A. L. (2019). Children's initiatives in the Finnish early childhood education context. In S. Garvis, H. Harju-Luukkainen, S. Sheridan & P. Williams (Eds.), *Nordic Families, Children and Early Childhood Education* (pp. 15–36). Palgrave Macmillan.

Karpov, J. V. (2005). *The Neo-Vygotskian Approach to Child Development*. Cambridge University Press.

Kellogg, D., & Veresov, N. (2020). *The general laws of child psychological development*. In L. S. Vygotsky (Ed.), *LS Vygotsky's Pedological Works* (pp. 85–103). Springer.

Kumpulainen, K. (2018). A principled, personalised, trusting and child-centric ECEC system in Finland. In S. L. Kagan (Ed.), *The Early Advantage 1: Early Childhood Systems That Lead by Example* (pp. 72–98). Teachers College Press.

Lancy, D. F. (2018). Children as laborers. In D. F. Lancy (Ed.), *Anthropological perspectives on children as helpers, workers, artisans, and laborers* (pp. 189–212). Palgrave Macmillan.

Langemeyer, I. (2006). Contradictions in expansive learning: Towards a critical analysis of self-dependent forms of learning in relation to contemporary socio-technological change. *Forum Qualitative Sozialforschung/Forum: Qualitative Social Research, 7*(1). http://dx.doi.org/10.17169/fqs-7.1.76

Leont'ev, A. N. (1965). *Problemy razvitiya psikhi*. (2nd edn.). Mysl'.

Leont'ev, A. N. (1981). *The Development of the Mind: Selected Works of Aleksei Nikolaevich Leontyev*. Marxists Internet Archive.

Leont'ev, A. N. (1978). *Activity, Consciousness, and Personality*. Prentice-Hall.

Lindqvist, G. (1995). *The Aesthetics of Play: A Didactic Study of Play and Culture in Preschools*. [Doctoral dissertation, Uppsala University]. Uppsala Studies in Education 62.

Manuilenko, Z. V. (1975). The development of voluntary behavior in preschool-age children. *Soviet Psychology, 13*(4), 65–116. https://doi.org/10.2753/RPO1061-0405130465

Marjanovic-Shane, A., Ferholt, B., Miyazaki, K., Nilsson, M., Rainio, A. P., Hakkarainen, P., Beljanski-Ristić, L., & Pešić, M. (2011). Playworlds – an art of development. In

C. Lobman & B. O'Neill (Eds.). *Play and Performance, Learning and Development: Exploring Relationship: Play and Culture Series* (Vol 11) (pp. 3–32). The Association for the Study of Play (TASP).

Mehan, H. (1979) *Learning Lessons*. Harvard University Press.

Miettinen, R. (2000). The concept of experiential learning and John Dewey's theory of reflective thought and action. *International Journal of Lifelong Education, 19*(1), 54–72. https://doi.org/10.1080/026013700293458

Miettinen, R. (2005). Object of activity and individual motivation. *Mind, Culture, and Activity, 12*(1), 52–69. https://doi.org/10.1207/s15327884mca1201_5

Morrow, P. C., & Muchinsky, P. M. (1980). Middle range theory. In C. C. Pinder & L. F. Moore (Eds.), *Middle Range Theory and the Study of Organizations* (pp. 33–44). Springer.

OECD. (2017). *PISA 2015 Results (Volume III): Students' Well-Being*. OECD Publishing.

Paananen, M. (2017). *Imaginaries of Early Childhood Education: Societal Roles of Early Childhood Education in an Era of Accountability*. [Doctoral dissertation, University of Helsinki].

Paananen, M., & Lipponen, L. (2018). Pedagogical documentation as a lens for examining equality in early childhood education. *Early Child Development and Care, 188*(2), 77–87. https://doi.org/10.1080/03004430.2016.1241777

Parekh, P., & Gee, E. R. (2019). Tinkering alone and together: Tracking the emergence of children's projects in a library workshop. *Learning, Culture and Social Interaction, 22*. https://doi.org/10.1016/j.lcsi.2019.04.009

Phelan, P., Davidson, A. L., & Cao, H. T. (1991). Students' multiple worlds: Negotiating the boundaries of family, peer, and school cultures. *Anthropology & Education Quarterly, 22*(3), 224–50. https://doi.org/10.1525/AEQ.1991.22.3.05X1051K

Rainio, A. P. (2008). From resistance to involvement: Examining agency and control in a playworld activity. *Mind, Culture, and Activity, 15*(2), 115–40. https://doi.org/10.1080/10749030801970494

Rainio, A. P. (2010). *Lionhearts of the Playworld: An Ethnographic Case Study of the Development of Agency in Play Pedagogy*. [Doctoral dissertation, University of Helsinki]

Rainio, A. P., & Hilppö, J. (2017). The dialectics of agency in educational ethnography. *Ethnography and Education, 12*(1), 78–94. https://doi.org/10.1080/17457823.2016.1159971

Rantavuori, J., Engeström, Y., & Lipponen, L. (2016). Learning actions, objects and types of interaction: A methodological analysis of expansive learning among pre-service teachers. *Frontline Learning Research, 4*(3), 1–27. https://doi.org/10.14786/flr.v4i3.174

Rogoff, B. (2003). *The Cultural Nature of Human Development*. Oxford University Press

Rorty, R. (1991). *Objectivity, Relativism, and Truth: Philosophical Papers* (Vol 1). Cambridge University Press.

Valsiner, J. (1992). Interest: A metatheoretical perspective. In K. A. Renninger, S. Hidi & A. Krapp (Eds.), *The Role of Interest in Learning and Development* (pp. 27–41). Erlbaum.

Van Oers, B. (1998). The fallacy of contextualization. *Mind, Culture, and Activity*, 5(2), 135–42. https://doi.org/10.1207/s15327884mca0502_7

Varenne, H., & McDermott, R. (1999). *Successful Failure: The School America Builds*. Westview Press.

Vygotsky, L. S. (1967). Play and its role in the mental development of the child. *Soviet Psychology*, 5(3), 6–18. https://doi.org/10.2753/RPO1061-040505036

Vygotsky, L. S. (1987). *The Collected Works of L.S. Vygotsky: Problems of General Psychology, Including the Volume Thinking and Speech* (Vol 1). Springer.

Moth Funeral: Exploring Issues of Life and Death in Early Childhood Education

Lasse Lipponen, Jaakko Hilppö and Antti Rajala

Introduction

In the daily flow of activities of kindergarten, many things pass by, and are hardly noticed: a passing feeling, something caught at a glance, an act of kindness. In many cases, even unpleasant events such as missing one's parents, getting hurt, longing for friends or being excluded from play activities, are part of the everyday routines, and as such go easily without any special attention and exploration. Sometimes, however, the daily flow of activities is broken down with something unexpected that inundates the daily routines, with something that calls for more focus, and for expanded exploration. Such unexpected happenings can create opportunities for us to learn about ourselves and others. Sometimes, mundane disruptions in the flow of our daily activity have repercussions at an existential level and can challenge us to reflect on our being in the world.

In this article, relying on sociocultural and cultural-historical theories of human learning (Vygotsky, 1987), we present and analyse how a community of children and adults explores an unexpected, unpleasant and a painful case in Finnish kindergarten. Specifically, based on our ethnographic data, we examine children and adults exploring suffering and death of a moth on a kindergarten playground. This case represents an intensive, information-rich example (Patton, 1990) of how emotions and exploration can be enmeshed in the everyday life of Finnish kindergartens.

According to sociocultural and cultural-historical theories of human functioning, human beings do not live in a vacuum, but our capabilities, emotions and actions (such as exploration) are mediated by cultural tools and activities and their cultural-historical development (e.g. Vygotsky, 1987).

Mediation not only accounts for the structure and content of our actions and experiences, but also for their emergence in the first place. For example, when a child falls down and hurts himself or herself, the words, expressions, tones of voice, objects and embodied actions others use to comfort him or her and the way they distribute this work are culturally mediated, in relation to the child. Moreover, human actions are always encompassed within larger activity systems that also take part in establishing the actions, for example, through the rules and the division of labour (e.g. Engeström, 1987). In different cultural settings, what is seen as an appropriate response to a similar situation might be different and elicit a different set of cultural tools and practices that are used to comfort the child, if it is responded to at all (e.g. Rogoff, 2003). Thus, when we examine exploration, we conceptualize it as a practice, related to material, social conditions and scripts, and taking place on one or more characteristic spaces and timescales. It takes place not only within the individual mind, but also between people, enabled, supported and mediated by socio-material practices and technologies.

To us, being curious, wondering, posing questions, trying to find explanations and understanding, and doing all this collectively, are central parts of exploration. These explorative activities are dependent on the institutional dynamics of personal relations and how practitioners and children interact with artefacts and material conditions (Ødegaard & Hedegaard, 2020). For children as well as adults, exploration always occurs in interaction with the cultural knowledge carried by a social community, which in a sense gives you the glasses through which phenomena are explored and are interpreted. Exploration is often emotionally engaging or emotions may be the prompts for wonder, posing questions and trying to build understanding. Moreover, as Packer and Goicoechea (2000) argue, exploration and learning are not just a matter of coming to know something more or better (epistemology), but importantly also becoming somebody different (ontology) at the same time. Exploring the world around oneself with others and learning about it can therefore also be a process that shapes who you are in the world. According to Ødegaard and Hedegaard (2020), children's exploration and cultural formation are important for their creation of meaningful and compassionate lives, where both the non-human and human worlds on the Earth are the key questions of our time.

This article begins by introducing the role of exploration in Finnish early childhood education and care (ECEC). We then present the importance of suffering and emotions as amplifiers of children's and adults' shared exploration. A section devoted to the *case moth*, including the description of the local context, and the interpretations of our observations follow. We conclude the chapter by discussing the results and their contribution to research on children's exploration, and by elaborating on the pedagogical implications of these results.

The Role of Exploration in Finnish Early Childhood Education and Care

In Finland, all children under school age (children start school when they are seven years old) have a subjective right to early childhood education and care (ECEC). The main aim of Finnish ECEC is to promote children's well-being, growth, development and learning in collaboration with their care takers. In general, the Finnish early childhood education can be characterized in terms of a holistic approach that encourages play, relationship and curiosity. It builds on children's interests, and resists the internationally common approach that centres on school preparation. Furthermore, the Finnish ECEC is characterized by a multi-professional work community with a varying combination of professional qualification levels and job descriptions, as well as cooperation with professionals in other sectors. The cooperative work is usually organized in multi-professional teams (Kopisto et al., 2014).

The Finnish early childhood education has been preparing for and undergoing large-scale reforms in recent years. Previously the role of early childhood education and care has been merely to enable parents to work and support families in upbringing of their children, now the focus has changed to children's right to high-quality ECEC. Secondly, from the beginning of 2013 the administration and steering of ECEC in Finland has moved from under the Ministry of Social Affairs and Health to the Ministry of Education and Culture (Kopisto et al., 2014). Thirdly, ECEC is obligated by two new curricula: National Core Curriculum for Early Childhood Education and Care, 2018 (Finnish National Agency for Education, 2019, implemented for the first time in August 2017) and National Core Curriculum for Pre-Primary Education, 2014 (Finnish National Agency for Education, 2016). These documents are a norm, and obligate ECEC personnel in ECEC centres. The previous curricula were only guidelines. According to Kopisto and others (Kopisto et al., 2014), these transformations in Finnish ECEC highlight a trend towards an integrated education and schooling system in which early childhood and school education form a continuum in terms of operation, administration as well as content.

Finnish ECEC stresses the role of exploration as a central part of pedagogical activities (Finnish National Agency for Education, 2019). Exploration is fostered by creating opportunities for children to ask questions and to wonder. Children's previous experiences and their interests should be the starting point for pedagogical activities and exploration. Children should also have the right to express their opinions, thoughts and emotions, and should be engaged in the planning, implementation and evaluation of daily activities. As stated in the Finnish National Core Curriculum for Early Childhood Education and Care (Finnish National Agency for Education, 2019):

Children must have an opportunity to explore the world with all of their senses and their entire bodies as well as experiment with different working methods. When working, children are encouraged to ask questions and express wonder as well as to explore and solve problems together".

(Finnish National Agency for Education, p. 26)

Exploration and Emotions

Recently, there has been a notable increased interest on emotions in educational research (Dernikos et al., 2020; Madrid et al., 2015), and in early childhood education especially on empathy and compassion (Barton & Garvis, 2019; Jalongo, 2014; Lipponen et al., 2018; Peterson, 2017; Taggart, 2016). Within research on early childhood education, alongside a long tradition of studies focusing on children's emotional development, we have begun to see more diverse theoretical and empirical approaches to studying children's emotional lives and lifeworlds (e.g. Hackett et al., 2015; Taylor & Panici-Ketchabaw, 2017). Yet, according to Madrid et al. (2015; see also Fleer & Hammer, 2013; Vadeboncoeur & Collie 2013), most studies focusing on emotions and children are premised on individualistic assumptions and involve intervention programmes and curricula for promoting emotional skills, and self-regulation strategies for children to express their emotions. Moreover, in these studies emotions are dominantly seen as separate from children's and adults' other cognitive abilities, a position that Vygotsky (1987) already criticized.

Departing from the individualistic, and intervention programme-oriented research traditions, in this chapter, we will conceptualize emotions and exploration from cultural historical point of view. From this point of view, emotions are deeply entangled and situated within cultural and normative practices. They are done by people, anchored in cultural norms, and moral frameworks, and thus, can be done in more or less situationally and culturally appropriate ways. Emotions are relational, about objects in the world (Brinkmann, 2017; Brinkmann & Kofod, 2018).

Case of the Moth: Exploring Suffering and Death in Kindergarten

Our research methodology is based on an ethnographic approach that allows us to study exploration, suffering and emotions as a sociocultural and cultural-historical phenomenon as part of the everyday life of Finnish ECEC (Hammersley & Atkinson, 2007; Hilppö et al., 2019). From this perspective, we focus on mediated actions among the participants. We also examine how different cultural meanings (moral, ethical, ethnicity, diversity) especially in relation to death and suffering, mediate the participants interpretations of and interactions in the situation.

We have been working with our case kindergarten *Shire* for one and a half years from August 2018. Shire is a public kindergarten, and located in one of Finland's largest suburbs. The area is culturally and linguistically very diverse. People who live in the area belong to several different nationalities or ethnic groups. About 35 per cent of the area's population speak a language other than Finnish or Swedish (the other official language is Finland) as their mother tongue. The area includes several racial, religious or cultural groups and, this diversity is manifested in people's cultural assumptions and values, patterns of thinking, behaviours and in ways of communicating. Also Shire is culturally and linguistically very diverse setting, and the children belong to several different nationalities or ethnic groups.

Suffering and death of a moth on a kindergarten playground, the *case moth*, is a rich example of how emotions are not removed or bracketed from exploration, but rather a fundamental part of them. The case presents an example of an episode of spontaneous and serendipitous exploration that is arguably commonplace within early childhood education settings; children (three-to-six-year-olds) are drawn to something they find interesting and this is explored together with the adults. However, what distinguishes the case from a typical daycare situation is that it calls for exploration on the part of the participants at an existential level, on matters of life and death. In the episode, the daily playground routines were interrupted when the children and an educator found a moth from the foyer floor that was wounded and seemingly suffering. Over the episode, initial interest in the moth was turned into shared expressions of empathic concern, then of compassion, and finally of fear and terror when the moth was killed by the teacher. The dramatic moment, and the variety of emotions it prompted and amplified, generated a further need for continuing the exploration into new topics. The narrative is told from the perspective of the second author of this chapter who was present when the interaction in the narrative took place. The narrative is based on field notes that he wrote down immediately after the events.

It had been a cold morning. Although spring was here, the ground had been covered with frost when I had walked to the kindergarten. When we went outside to yard with the children, it was still cool, but not as cold as in the morning. When I came out, I notice a small crowd of children around Marja, one of the teachers. Someone was talking about suffering and killing. I leaned in and saw that Marja – the teacher – was holding something carefully in her hand. A moth. The moth was barely moving. Marja and the group started to walk towards the flagpole at the other end of the yard. A few meters before it, she said that the moth was suffering and it needed to be put down. 'There is no moth hospital where we can take it and cure it.' Killing the moth would help it. I hear her voice shake and I could tell she hesitated when she spoke. One of the children asked her, what suffering meant. Marjo told that the moth had a lot of pain.

After this, Marjo told the children the moth needs a grave, the new flagpole was good. She asked one of the children to dig the grave and another child to get her a stone. The other children were moving around her, some more others less interested in what was happening. When she got the stone, Marja kneeled down and said she was going to squash the moth with a rock. She was holding the moth now on another shovel and up so that everybody could see. All of the children had gathered around her and I noticed they were looking each other and the moth intensively. Marja squashed the moth fast and said that it can't feel pain anymore. Some children seemed more terrified than others. Some moved closer to the shovel. Marja responded by saying that 'The shovel goes around' and circulated the children around her with the shovel so that all could see. Some asked if there was any blood. Marja told that moths don't have blood, more like mucus or slime. The moth was buried in the grave next to the flagpole. Some of the kids gathered pines leaves on top of it. Marja wondered if they needed to sing a hymn and told that in her religion they would sign. She asked if some of the Muslim children if they sung in funerals. They did not know. The conversation moved on in short sentences. When Marja got up, she noticed that the boy in the blue overalls was very upset. I could not tell if he cried or not, but Marja went to him and hugged him, looked him in his eyes and consoled him.

Later, the next day I hear the children, Marja and the other adults had talked about the moth considerably. They had looked at pictures of graves and read a wikipage on moths. They had also asked Samira – a substitute nurse and a Muslim woman – about Muslim funerals and some of the children had told about their experiences and one about how they had buried a mouse near their home with his parents. When I asked how they had found the moth, Marja told me that they had seen it in the group's foyer already the day before and yesterday picked it up to look at it more closely.

Interpreting the Episode

The case of the moth is a good example of how inconspicuous moments may give rise to complex moral and ethical issues, issues of ethnicity and cultural diversity and pedagogy all in one. We will next unpack how they are present in the narrative.

Compassionate Response to Suffering

While there are several emotions present in the narrative, we will centre our discussion on the most dominant of them, compassion and emotions related to it. Compassion, which we understand as taking action to alleviate someone else's suffering or distress (Lipponen et al., 2018; Nussbaum, 1996) can be seen as being constituted by three connected elements: noticing the suffering or distress of the other, feeling empathic concern towards them and acting on that basis to alleviate the suffering. All of these are present in the narrative.

Although the joint interest in the moth and the exploration of its condition did not start with noticing its state or how it was suffering, they figured in early on in the interaction. Marja and some of the children had seen the moth on the foyer floor, picked it up and then noticed its condition. Paying attention to somebody's suffering and making a considered decision that the situation is important and not trivial (Nussbaum, 2001, 2014) potentially call the experience of empathic concern towards the sufferer. Understanding that somebody is possibly suffering can be a powerful motive and leads potentially to a range of different emotional (and other) responses depending on the relationship between the one who suffers and the one who witnesses the suffering (Nussbaum, 2014). We – children and adults – certainly have the opportunity to decide how to respond when we become aware of such situations: whether we ignore the suffering or take action to alleviate the pain. To the very highest degree, whether to act and alleviate or not, is also a moral evaluation we make of people's/or non-humans' suffering: who deserves our alleviation, care and compassion.

In this case, Marja, and possibly the children, see the moth's twitching movements as indication of its pain and treat that pain as something that is relevant for them instead of dismissing it altogether. What is especially significant here is that the moth is included in the participants' circle of care, that is, the entities whose well-being matters personally for them (Nussbaum, 2014). That is, the moth is treated with care and related to on equal grounds with humans, in contrast to the common response to flies or insects that are often seen as annoying, as pests or even disgusting. These actions illustrate how exploration, and especially teacher's actions, led to expanding the circle of concern (Nussbaum, 2014), and compassion from humans towards non-humans.

Paying attention to the moth's distress in this way leads Marja and the children to feel empathic concern (Worline & Dutton, 2017), the need to help the moth somehow. This is evident from the range of different concerted actions they take in the narrative; Marja asking the children get the stone and to dig the grave, the children gathering the pine needles and finally Marja putting the moth down and burying it. These actions and how they are accomplished through interaction well demonstrate the culturally mediated nature of compassion and care. How and when to act with compassion in response to others' suffering always requires interpretation and meaning-making (Dutton et al., 2006).

Overall, as a collective, compassionate response to moth's suffering the kindergarten group's actions arguably parallels how adults work communities have been documented to react in moments of crisis by extracting, generating, coordinating and calibrating resources to direct care and attention towards suffering colleagues (Dutton et al., 2006). The moth is however not the only one who received compassion in the narrative. The dramatic moment of putting the moth down evoked strong emotions, with some children becoming terrified and starting to cry. The same triad of noticing, feeling empathic concern and acting to alleviate the boy's distress is enacted by Marja after the moth is buried. In our case, compassion operated mainly between humans and a non-human, between the sufferer and the one who is trying to alleviate the pain.

Explorations and Transitions

What is also significant in the example is how Marja, the children and others collectively explore different cultural rituals and meanings while they negotiate the appropriate response to the situation. These negotiations are sparked firstly by Marja's and the children's need to act with compassion and secondly by the dramatic moment of putting down the moth. We will discuss both of these moments below and how in and through these negotiations Marja and the children make a transition in their activity from alleviating the moth's suffering to learning more about burial practices and their emotional responses to putting the moth down.

In the moment when Marja and the children realize that the moth is in pain, we can see a complex interplay of the different cultural meanings that are invoked to make sense of the situation and how to act appropriately. The compassionate act, putting the moth down and ending its pain, is first suggested tentatively by someone in the group huddled over the moth. After moving towards the flagpole, the appropriateness of this course of action is affirmed by Marja when in her explanation she closes out other options and restates the need to act. In her words, 'There is no moth hospital where we can take it and cure it.' The complexity of the moment is especially visible from the mixture of determination and hesitation in Marja's conduct. For her, there clearly seems to be a tension between the clear need to alleviate the moth's condition and the course action that seems most suitable as well as her role as the educator in the situation. In a sense, the moral of the situation seems conflictual to her; is it appropriate to kill an animal in front of children, even though the animal is clearly suffering?

The interplay of different cultural meanings and exploration of them is further continued after the moth is put down. The immediate need to alleviate suffering has now passed and Marja and the children transition to a new situation that has more room for such exploration. In addition to trying to determine what type of liquid circulates with the moth, Marja opens up a space to discuss different funeral and grieving practices and tries to solicit the help of the nurse Samira, who has a Muslim background, in this discussion. A diversity of voices and questions are raised in the discussion that ensues. In this discussion, the group explores cultural variation among collective practices of burying and grieving: How is burying conducted in my and your culture and religion? Do they sing in Muslim funerals? Here various cultural norms and moral frameworks provide resources or a script for feeling, expressing, and doing emotions in a certain way. However, as stated by Edwards (2014), a given culture is not experienced the same way by different individuals or even by the same individuals at different times. This view accentuates the importance of opening up spaces for exploring these different norms and associated rituals and meanings. In our narrative, this takes place through Marja's pedagogical actions; by her clearly showing all how she is going to put the moth down, making sure that everyone can see the moth after this, positioning the children as knowledgeable others and reaching out to other potential cultural experts.

What is also significant here is how the exploration sparked by the dramatic event is continued beyond the immediate moment and also expanded to include the whole kindergarten group. In a sense, the direction of moving from an immediate need to help and negotiate over how this should be done to exploring the situation and its personal and cultural meanings and resonances is continued through this transition. Although not all the children of the group were present at the moth funeral, they became part of the exploration when conversations and explorations regarding the moth had continued after returning back inside. This also opened up the possibility of introducing and exploring new cultural meaning related to moths, death and different funeral practices through the use of Wikipedia as a knowledge resource.

Thoughts and Impressions of Case Moth

In this chapter, we have presented and analysed an unexpected, and a painful case in Finnish kindergarten, and how a community of children and adults engages in exploring it. The case, suffering and death of a moth on a kindergarten playground, is based on our ethnographic data, collected in Finnish multicultural kindergarten. The case is an intensive, information-rich example of how emotions and exploration are intertwined in the everyday life of Finnish kindergartens.

Overall, the case moth exemplifies well how seemingly trivial activities may play a powerful role and carry important meanings or strong messages, and may give rise to complex issues of morality, ethnicity, diversity and pedagogy all in one. The case also shows how dramatic events can powerfully trigger a transition in the activity to enable joint exploration (see also Matusov, 2009). Although these aspects are analytically separable, as shown, they are highly intertwined, and form a complex whole in the flow of everyday life in early childhood education.

Participating in an exploration of a dramatic event, to which there is no ready answer, can be a valuable learning experience for both children and adults. For example, extending compassion beyond humans is a significant pedagogical and also a moral act. The teacher Marja's hesitation in the situation suggests that this extension of the sphere of concern involves a transition in the way the group is orienting to bugs. If we want to prevent cruel attitudes and behaviour towards animals, we need to educate children to respect and treat those who are different from them with kindness, and dignity. From previous research we know that one feels more empathy and compassion for those who are most important to one's well-being. It is more difficult to feel compassion when there are differences between people including status, culture, religion, language, skin colour, gender or age (Goetz et al., 2010). Globe's ecological situation requires overcoming human-centred approach and extending compassion and responsibility to non-human nature. We need to educate children to understand that we are always entangled in and dependent on nature.

In Finnish ECEC, children are guided to value diversity in the local community, recognizing the right to one's own language, culture, religion and world view as a fundamental right. Among others, the diversity of people, genders and families is explored. The goal is to educate children to understand that all people are different but equal. Equal and equitable treatment of all children as well as protection against discrimination are requirements. As demonstrated, the case of moth sparked off a conversation about the cultural practices and rituals of suffering and funeral. It is a concrete example, that Finnish early childhood education and care are part of culturally transforming and diverse Finnish society, where cultural diversity should be perceived as a resource.

The Finnish ECEC is based on an integrated approach to care, education and teaching, the so-called educare model, with particular emphasis on pedagogy. In spirit of Finnish early childhood education and care, the dramatic moment of exploration is a good example of combination of care and education: children are taught about cultural rituals of funerals and burying, and simultaneously, the moral achievement of extending concern to non-humans, to take care of the vulnerable and suffering moth. Finally, we agree with Vadeboncoeur and Collie (2013) that experiences where emotions and learning with and about them enmesh should be recentred in education.

References

Barton, G., & Garvis, S. (Eds.) (2019). *Compassionand Empathy in Educational Contexts.* Palgrave Macmillan.
Brinkmann, S. (2017). The culture of grief. https://www.kommunikation.aau.dk/digitalAssets/268/268233_the-culture-of.grief.pdf

Brinkmann, S., & Kofod, E. H. (2018). Grief as an extended emotion. *Culture & Psychology, 24*, 160–73. https://doi.org/10.1177/1354067X17723328

Dernikos, B., Lesko, N., McCall, S. D., & Niccolini, A. (2020). *Mapping the Affective Turn in Education: Theory, Research, and Pedagogy*. Routledge.

Dutton, J. E., Worline, M. C., Frost, P. J., & Lilius, J. M. (2006). Explaining compassion organizing. *Administrative Science Quarterly, 51*, 59–96. https://doi.org/10.2189/asqu.51.1.59

Edwards, A. (2014). Learning from experience in teaching: A cultural historical critique. In V. Ellis, & J. Orchard (Eds.), *Learning Teaching from Experience: Multiple Perspectives, International Contexts* (pp. 47–61). Bloomsbury.

Engeström, Y. (1987). *Learning by Expanding: An Activity-theoretical Approach to Developmental Research*. Orienta-Konsultit.

Finnish National Agency for Education (2016). *National Core Curriculum for Pre-Primary Education 2014*. Finnish National Agency for Education.

Finnish National Agency for Education (2019). *National Core Curriculum for Early Childhood Education and Care 2018*. Finnish National Agency for Education.

Fleer, M., & Hammer (2013). Emotions in imaginative situations: The valued place of fairytales for supporting emotion regulation. *Mind, Culture, and Activity, 20*, 240–59. https://doi.org/10.1080/10749039.2013.781652

Goetz, L., Keltner, D., & Simon-Thomas, E. (2010). Compassion: An evolutionaryanalysis and empirical review. *Psychological Bulletin, 36*, 351–74. https://doi.org/10.1037/a0018807

Hackett, A., Seymour, J., & Procter, L. (Eds.). (2015). *Children's Spatialities: Embodiment, Emotion and Agency*. Palgrave Macmillan.

Hammersley, M., & Atkinson, P. (2007). *Ethnography: Principles in Practice*. Routledge.

Hilppö, J. A., Rajala, A., & Lipponen, L. (2019). Compassion in children's peer cultures. In G. Barton, & S. Garvis (Eds.), *Compassion and Empathy in Educational Contexts* (pp. 79–95). Palgrave Macmillan.

Jalongo, M. R. (2014). *Teaching Compassion: Humane Education in Early Childhood*. Springer.

Kopisto, K., Salo, L., Lipponen, L., & Krokfors, L. (2014). Transformations and tensions in Finnish early childhood education and care. In L. R. Kroll & D. R. Meier (Eds.), *Educational Change in International Early Childhood Contexts: Crossing Borders of Reflection* (pp. 141–54). Routledge.

Lipponen, L., Rajala, A., & Hilppö, J. (2018). Compassion and emotional worlds in early childhood education. In C. Pascal, T. Bertram, & M. Veisson (Eds.), *Early Childhood Education and Change in Diverse Cultural Contexts* (pp. 168–78). Routledge.

Madrid, S., Fernie, D., & Kantor. R. (2015). Introduction to reframing emotions. In S. Madrid, D. Fernie & R Kantor (Eds.), *Reframing the Emotional Worlds of the Early Childhood Classroom* (pp. 1–15). Routledge.

Matusov, E. (2009). *Journey into Dialogic Pedagogy*. Nova Science Publishers.

Nussbaum, M. (1996). Compassion: The basic social emotion. *Social Philosophy and Policy, 13,* 27–58. https://doi.org/10.1017/S0265052500001515

Nussbaum, M. C. (2001). *Upheavals of Thought: The Intelligence of Emotions.* Cambridge University Press.

Nussbaum, M. C. (2014). Compassion and terror. In M. Ure & M. Frost (Eds.), *The Politics of Compassion* (pp. 89–207). Routledge.

Ødegaard, E., & Hedegaard, M. (2020). Introduction to children's exploration and cultural formation. In E. Ødegaard & M. Hedegaard (Eds.), *Children's Exploration and Cultural Formation* (pp. 1–10). Springer Open

Packer, M. J., & Goicoechea, J. (2000). Sociocultural and constructivist theories of learning: Ontology, not just epistemology. *Educational Psychologist, 35,* 227–41. https://doi.org/10.1207/S15326985EP3504_02

Patton, M. Q. (1990). *Qualitative Evaluation and Research Methods.* SAGE Publications, Inc.

Peterson, A. (2017). *Compassion and Education: Cultivating Compassionate Children, Schools and Communities.* Springer.

Rogoff, B. (2003). *Cultural Development of Human Development.* University Press.

Taggart, G. (2016). Compassionate pedagogy: The ethics of care in early childhood professionalism. *European Early Childhood Education Research Journal, 24,* 173–85. https://doi.org/10.1080/1350293X.2014.970847

Taylor, A., & Pacini-Ketchabaw, V. (2017). Kids, raccoons, and roos: Awkward encounters and mixed affects. *Children's Geographies, 15,* 131–45. https://doi.org/10.1080/14733285.2016.1199849

Vadeboncoeur, J. A., & Collie, R. J. (2013). Locating social and emotional learning in schooled environments: A Vygotskian perspective on learning as unified. *Mind, Culture, and Activity, 20,* 201–25. https://doi.org/10.1080/10749039.2012.755205

Vygotsky, L. S. (1987). Thinking and speech (N. Minick, Trans.). In R. W. Rieber & A. S. Carton (Eds.), *The collected works of L. S. Vygotsky: Problems of general psychology* (Vol 1) (pp. 39–285). Plenum Press. (Original work published 1934).

Worline, M., & Dutton, J. E. (2017). *Awakening Compassion at Work: The Quiet Power That Elevates People and Organizations.* Berrett-Koehler Publishers Inc.

10

Micro-transitions in Outdoor Playtime in Kindergarten: Conditions for Children's Exploration and Cultural Formation

Åsta Birkeland, Hanne Værum Sørensen and Min He

Introduction

Transitions are an important aspect of children's lives. Transitions can relate to significant changes in the lives of children, such as when a child, for the first time in his or her life, attends an early childhood education institution. Later, children experience another major transition when they, at the age of five or six, leave this early childhood education institution to attend school. These transitions between qualitatively different institutions have a major influence on children because the child attends different institutional settings with different cultures, traditions, values and norms, as well as different demands and anticipations (Hedegaard, 2008a, 2009; Hedegaard & Fleer, 2019). As Hedegaard and Fleer observed, 'Children's transitions into different institutions, such as when starting school, have always been an important topic in research and something that is of great interest to families as they support the transitioning child into the different institutions they attend and life course events they experience' (2019, p. 1). Extensive research on children's transition from kindergarten to school exists (Cavada-Hrepich, 2016; Hedegaard & Munk, 2019; Winther-Lindqvist, 2019), as well as research on the daily transition between home and kindergarten (Kousholt, 2011, 2019), focusing on the different demands and expectations of these two spaces.

Children also experience numerous micro-transitions during their everyday lives in kindergarten,[1] transitions that require adjustment to expectations and demands in different settings (Hedegaard & Fleer, 2019). These micro-transitions are important sites of children's engagement, where they must understand and adapt to the institution's motives and leading activities (Leontiev, 2005). However, these micro-transitions have received limited attention in research (Cavada-Hrepich, 2019; Devi et al., 2019). Different early childhood education institutions have different practices and procedures when shifting between activities. The institutional demands and expectations in these situations differ as well (Birkeland, 2019; Birkeland & Sørensen, 2021). For instance, when moving from indoor to outdoor activities, the conditions and demands during the transition depend on what is valued in the kindergarten. Some kindergartens consider children's competency in smooth and efficient transitions a key skill, while other kindergartens value other aspects of transitions, such as competencies in independently dressing properly for the current weather conditions (Birkeland, 2019; Birkeland & Sørensen, 2021). These micro-transitions seem to be more important than previously described in the research and deserve more attention in early childhood education research. Additionally, these micro-transitions have implications for children's flexibility and adjustment to activities with different expectations and demands. Micro-transitions differ in different cultural contexts and, as such, provide traces of cultural formation ideals.

Consequently, this chapter examines micro-transitions within the outdoor activity setting in kindergarten, i.e. going from indoor to outdoor activities and vice versa, as well as some of the numerous shifts between activities in the activity setting of outdoor playtime. The activities in the outdoor activity setting have different traditions in different national contexts, and thus, they are interesting to study from the perspective of micro-transitions. We aim to identify how micro-transitions in kindergarten provide opportunities for children's participation, enactment and engagement in meeting demands in activity settings, and we highlight the dialectical interplay between institutional transitions and children's exploration and cultural formation. The research question we pose is as follows: how do the micro-transitions related to the activity setting of *outdoor playtime* interplay with children's exploration in institutional settings with different traditions related to community policies and values?

This research uses a cultural-historical approach and draws on Hedegaard's (2009) concepts of development and cultural formation as an individual, institutional and societal process and Hedegaard and Fleer's (2019) concept of transition. Furthermore, we use Bakhtin's (1981, 1986) concept of the chronotope of the threshold (constructions of a liminal space-time event) as a metaphor for the micro-transitions. We highlight examples of transitions in two kindergartens situated in China and one in Norway. The research methods are participant observations, videos and photos taken on the playgrounds, and interviews with the teachers. The dialectical interplay between the micro-transitions and children's engagement in outdoor activities is the unit of analysis.

Theoretical Perspectives on Micro-transitions

The theoretical framework of this study is based upon a cultural-historical research tradition of understanding children's cultural formation from a *wholeness perspective*, that is, as a dynamic and dialectic process between the person's activities, intentions and motives; institutional traditions and practices; societal demands and material conditions (Hedegaard, 2009, 2012, 2019). Within this perspective, children are viewed as active agents participating in and interacting with their surroundings (Hedegaard, 2012; Leontiev, 2005; Vygotsky, 1998) and 'contributing to transformative communal practices' (Stetsenko, 2017, p. 34).

Institutional practices in kindergarten create conditions for the activity settings and the children's learning and development. This practice must be seen as working towards connecting and fulfilling societal traditions, values and expectations regarding an education for kindergarten children. Cultural ideas take form in the interactions between everyday practices, but these ideas relate to values and meanings far beyond the institution (Gulløv & Højlund, 2003).

Activity settings are planned and organized situations or shared activities in the pedagogical practice of kindergarten in which children are expected to participate (Hedegaard, 2012), such as outdoor playtime. Analysing and conceptualizing what is occurring in an activity setting means investigating the societal and institutional conditions for the activity setting, together with the demands on children and kindergarten teachers in the social situation.

The conditions for micro-transitions in kindergarten are shaped at different levels (Hedegaard, 2008a, 2014), including the societal, the institutional and the personal levels, as well as the dialectic relationships between these levels. An additional dimension of nature was added in Sørensen and Birkeland's study (2020), highlighting how climate, weather and air quality also provide the conditions for children's outdoor activities.

In micro-transitions, as in other activities, demands and motives interact in the activity setting. The children must identify what matters in different situations and different places[2] and adapt to specific rules of conduct and normative expectations (Fleer, 2019). Teacher-organized games may constitute a breach of basic social rules in a different activity, such as child-initiated play (Fleer, 2019). In changing participation from one activity to the next, both demands and motives change, as well as relations. Transitions within activity settings indicate different teacher roles, different interactions and sometimes, new positions in different transitions (Fleer, 2019). Corsaro et al. (2002) frame the transition as a process of interactions between people, and they regard transitions as 'always collectively produced and shared with significant others' (p. 325). They argue strongly against models of transition that focus primarily on the individual or a set of individual variables.

The micro-transitions in kindergartens are social constructions of space-time (chronotope) that are continuously negotiated and enacted by teachers and children. Over time, participants learn the routines of a kindergarten and come to expect and orient themselves to activities happening in the same order and around the same time each day and week (Brown & Renshaw, 2006; Ritella et al., 2020). Spatial-temporal features are central in educational episodes and activities: the episode or event involves actions and interactions occurring in some order, in certain places, and at a certain time (a moment, hour, day, week, year or era). In this sense, chronotope can be seen as an analytical tool to use in explicating the relationships between people and events in their worlds (Morson & Emerson, 1988).

Micro-transitions can be considered *the chronotope of the threshold* (Bakhtin, 1981, 1986). There is something different going on before and after one step over the threshold. In this sense, the threshold is a liminal space, meaning a transitory, in-between state or space characterized by indeterminacy, ambiguity, hybridity and the potential for subversion and change (Skoglund et al., forthcoming). So it is, also, for micro-transitions. This *chronotope of the threshold* essentially describes the state of being 'connected with the breaking point in life, the moment of crisis, the decision that changes a life' (Bakhtin, 1986, p. 248). In our context, the crisis is related to resistance and ambiguity for children crossing the threshold, for example, when changing from one activity to another or from one activity setting to another. Some children will hesitate, others may resist and still others may have no doubts in trespassing across the threshold and looking for possibilities to explore, i.e. social experiences and environments.

These micro-transitions are routinized in different ways and have more or less clear expectations and demands for the participants when moving from one spot to another on the playground or from one well-defined activity to another. These are structured by the teachers or by the children themselves. As such, some micro-transitions can be clearly framed, whereas other micro-transitions may be more subtle concerning expectations and demands. Some children may, in these transitions, struggle to understand the expectations and demands and what is considered *right* and *wrong* in the social situation (Sørensen, 2021).

Micro-transitions, as chronotopes, are imbued with values and meanings and create different conditions for children's exploration and cultural formation (van Eijck & Roth, 2010). Exploration involves investigation and examination, testing opportunities, challenging rules and offering resistance (Ødegaard, 2020). The concept illustrates the importance of dialogical engagement on the part of kindergarten teachers. Although the teachers may have a plan for their activities, they are still attentive and open to a focus shift when the children are distracted by their experiences in the situation (Ødegaard, 2020). It is interesting to enquire into how micro-transitions in the outdoor activity setting provide opportunities for children to investigate, examine, test opportunities, challenge rules and offer resistance.

Methodological Approach: Studying Micro-transitions Related to the Outdoor Playtime in Three Kindergartens

We are three researchers located in Norway, China and Denmark, working together across continents, with experiences and a shared interest in researching transitions in outdoor playtime in different countries and cultures. We focus on the importance of outdoor playtime for children three to six years old. To examine opportunities and resistances related to transitions in outdoor playtime in kindergartens, we have made a case study of three kindergartens situated in China and Norway, with different institutional expectations and demands. We do not seek results that are representative of societies or institutions in general; we intend to learn about how micro-transitions related to outdoor playtime in kindergartens create conditions for children's exploration and contribute to their cultural formation.

The Sample of Kindergartens

The three kindergartens in our study emphasize children's access to outdoor activities. One of the Chinese kindergartens, the D-kindergarten, is a public kindergarten in a district of Beijing. The D-kindergarten emphasizes new demands in the curriculum guidelines by providing more outdoor time for children, approximately two hours daily. The outdoor activities vary, including gardening, animal care, physical exercises, child-initiated play, teacher-organized games and outdoor project work. In addition to activities in the outdoor play area, the kindergarten organizes projects on a farm connected to the kindergarten and environmental projects in the local surroundings. The kindergarten has 300 children aged two to six years in nine classes.

The A-kindergarten is part of a new kindergarten concept in China, one receiving attention nationally and internationally. This is a public kindergarten in a county in Zhejiang province. All the kindergartens in the county have emphasized outdoor play as the main activity since 2000. This is a major change in Chinese early childhood education because many kindergartens have not paid much attention to outdoor play, although it is included in the new curriculum guidelines. Outdoor play is the local policy choice in the county and is regulated by the Chinese national guidelines on kindergarten education, in which play is suggested as the basic activity for young children. The kindergarten has 500 children aged three to six years.

The O-kindergarten is a Norwegian kindergarten situated on the outskirts of Bergen. The O-kindergarten is an *outdoor kindergarten*, building on a solid fundament of outdoor-life values and traditions. This means that the children and the kindergarten teachers spend most of the day outside, approximately eight hours during the summer and around six hours in the cold and dark season. Three to four times per week, they go on trips to other play spaces, i.e. parks, sport areas or natural settings, to play, ski, ice skate or mountain walk. One day every week, all through the year, they go by the kindergarten bus to a forest nearby the kindergarten and spend the day, from around 9.30 to 14.30. The O-kindergarten has their own spot there, in the natural terrain, with a forest, a grassy area, a small creek and large rocks and stones. They also have a lavvo[3] with a fireplace inside and a round bench, where they can sit and eat lunch inside. The kindergarten has ninety children, aged one to six years, organized into six groups.

Participants

In the Chinese D-kindergarten, thirty middle-class, four-year-old children and their two kindergarten teachers participated. In the Chinese A-kindergarten, thirty middle-class, four-year-old children and their three teachers participated.

In the Norwegian O-kindergarten, the oldest twelve children and two kindergarten teachers participated. All children were four to five years old.

Empirical Material and Analysis

The empirical material was produced through fieldwork with participant observations, video recordings, photos, interviews with kindergarten managers and teachers, and conversations with children and teachers in 2017, 2018 and 2019. Our analysis in this chapter draws particularly on the participant observations and video recordings.

In the analysis of the video observations, we built on the methodological approach formulated by Hedegaard (2008b). We started with a common-sense analysis, exploring what is at stake in the observed micro-transition situation. What kind of situation is it? What demands and expectations do the kindergarten teachers have regarding children's participation in the micro-transition? How do children participate and what kind of exploration do they engage in during the micro-transition?

The next analytical level was the situated practice level, in which the analysis focused on how the micro-transitions are embedded in and part of the everyday life and pedagogical practice in kindergarten. The analytical questions, or categories, were as follows: What kind of routines can we observe in the micro-transition, and what meaning do the routines have in the process of children's cultural formation in kindergarten?

When these two first levels of analysis were completed, a thematic analysis showed certain patterns in the pedagogical practices and provided an overview of the empirical study. For example, what is the connection between the demands and expectations on the part of kindergarten teachers regarding children's participation, children's cultural formation and societal values and traditions in each kindergarten?

Ethical Reflections

The study is built on a thorough knowledge of young children's learning and development in early childhood education, as well as insight into the legislation and purpose of the researched institutions in China and Norway. We respect children's integrity, safety and well-being, as well as the children's and kindergarten teachers' right to be anonymous in our research. We were ready to leave the role of researcher and take on the role of responsible adult in every situation during our research (Sørensen, 2014). The Norwegian Centre for Research Data, NSD, has approved the ethics of the study, and the Chinese kindergartens gave permission according to their ethical standards. If the research is planning to collect data in a natural situation, not via experiments, measurements or a questionnaire, there is no need to apply for consent. However, the researchers needed to be sure of the nature of their research.

Micro-transitions in the Outdoor Activity Setting

In this section, we will present and analyse some examples of micro-transitions from our observations in the outdoor activity setting in the three kindergartens. Our research question is as follows: how do the micro-transitions related to the activity setting of outdoor playtime interplay with children's exploration in institutional settings with different traditions related to community policies and values? Sub-questions in the analysis are as follows: what are the expectations and demands during the transitions? What are the teacher's and children's roles in the transitions? What do the children explore?

We have chosen examples of micro-transitions from each of the three kindergartens. These examples are representative of the micro-transitions in each of the three institutions and are not taken as representative of all kindergartens in China or Norway. The examples involve both children and teachers.

Transitions in the D-Kindergarten

In the outdoor activity setting in the D-kindergarten, one of the Chinese kindergartens, we can identify certain distinct micro-transitions, chronotopes of the threshold as the time and space in-between indoor and outdoor collective physical activity, in-between collective physical activity and teacher-initiated games, in-between teacher-initiated games and child-initiated play, and, finally, in-between child-initiated play and moving indoors. In the following, we will present two of these micro-transitions that exemplify different expectations for and demands on the children and offer different conditions for exploration: the transition from indoor to outdoor activities and the transition from teacher-organized games to child-initiated play.

Transition from Indoors to Outdoors

The children have finished their morning indoor activities, and the teacher puts on music. This is the same kind of music used every day to mark the transition to going outdoors. All the children go to the corridor after having visited the bathroom. They put on their coats and take their bottles of water. Then, they line up in the corridor behind the head teacher to wait for everyone to get ready. Some of the children are standing quietly, waiting. Others are eagerly talking and having fun with one another. There are no observations of resistance among the children. No one seems to protest going outdoors. Quite to the contrary, they look excited and eager to go. They walk collectively in two parallel lines down the stairs. The teacher reminds them to keep to the right side, where painted footprints indicate on what side of the stairs the children are supposed to walk. The children seem familiar with these rules and the procedure of the transition. The entire process takes only a few minutes and is efficient. The children collectively pass the threshold from indoors to outdoors.

Transition from Collective, Teacher-Initiated Games to Child-Initiated Play

The children have finished their collective exercises and the collective, teacher-organized games. Now, it is time for child-initiated play activities, and the children are told by the teacher which area of the playground they are supposed to use. This morning, they are supposed to use the big open space and the sand area. There is no music to accompany this transition. The children immediately walk to the different areas at an individual pace. Some of the girls walk towards the open area, where the teachers have placed some materials to climb and balance on. One of the girls tries out some of the items, jumping and climbing, and then joins another girl. After a few minutes, the two girls approach the shelter, where there is different play equipment, and fetches some plastic animals they can ride on. After a few minutes of riding, the two girls suddenly take some of the material for climbing and jumping and go to a place on the outskirts of the open space and start a role play. The teacher follows the children to the open space but is not in the front and does not give any instructions.

Analysis of the Micro-transitions in the D-Kindergarten

The two examples of micro-transitions in the D-kindergarten give different impressions. The transition from indoors to outdoors has a collective pulse, with clear signs and expectations for the children to be efficient and play by the rules, such as putting on their coats, picking up their water bottles, walking in line behind the teacher and walking on the right side of the stairs. The teacher is the leader, giving instructions to the children on how to walk outdoors. The micro-transition from teacher-initiated to child-initiated play has another character. In this transition, there are no common signs, such as music, and no reminders from the teachers about how to walk to the play area. The micro-transition is more open for children's initiatives and takes more time. It is accepted by the teacher that the children explore some of the equipment before they settle down with the role play.

These two examples illustrate a micro-transition that is collective and quite efficient, as well as a more individualized transition to child-initiated play. The children are familiar with the institutional expectations and demands of the different micro-transitions, and they adjust to the different routines. The institutional expectations seem to be efficiency and cooperation with the collective group and the group pulse, as in the example of walking from indoors to outdoors. The expectation of the teacher is to be a visible leader, making sure that the children will come out rather efficiently, and to be ready for the collective physical training. Other classes are supposed to attend this activity as well and should not need to wait for this group to come. However, there are different expectations for the children and teachers in the transition between teacher-organized games to child-initiated play. The teachers expect the children to walk at their own pace and decide what they want to play, how to play and with whom. The institutional expectations for the teachers are that they provide play materials for children. Otherwise, the expectations for the teacher are to be laid-back in this micro-transition, quite in contrast to the chronotope mentioned above. The teacher is expected to observe and let the children take their time to explore and find their play area and playmates. Both the teachers and the children seem to adjust to the variety of expectations in these two micro-transitions. The two situations provide different conditions for children's enactment and engagement.

Transitions in the A-Kindergarten

The A-kindergarten, another Chinese kindergarten, has a different schedule from the D-kindergarten. As in the D-kindergarten, this kindergarten uses the collective transition from indoors to outdoors, accompanied by music.

However, the outdoor activity time is less divided into distinct parts, such as collective physical activity, teacher-organized games and child-initiated play. In the following, we present examples of the transition from collective physical movements to child-initiated play and the transition from child-initiated play to indoor activities.

Exploring Peer Relations

After the physical movement activity, the children begin to prepare their outdoor activity clothes: a thin plastic rain suit, which is to some degree waterproof and easy to clean if it gets dirty with pigment, soil or leaves. These clothes make children free to play in the water, sand and painting areas outdoors. There is a small area outdoors for changing clothes and shoes for each class. The children sit down on benches or upended buckets to put on their boots and clothes. They manage themselves during the entire process, taking out their own rain clothes and boots, sitting down to take off their ordinary shoes, and then, putting on their rain-proof pants, boots and raincoat. Most of the children can do this themselves; a few need assistance, mainly from their nearby peers. Some of the children seem to lack skill in buttoning up their water clothes, so they needed to ask for help from others. They try it by themselves first, but if they do not manage it, they ask for help from their peers. The teacher does not provide aid if it is not necessary. All the children were busy getting dressed, so the children that needed help had to observe and explore who was skilled at dressing, who was almost finished getting dressed and who was willing to provide help. These children were asked to help, and we could not observe any refusals among the children. One girl helped two boys. This girl looked around after she finished clothing herself. It seemed as if she was checking who needed help. One of the youngest children had limited verbal communication. He held the two button sides with his fingers and walked towards a classmate to show that he needed help. His classmate looked at him for a second and understood that the young boy needed help. We can see that both those who needed help and those who provided help are attentive to others.

Exploring Materials

Some children put on their clothes slowly, but no one hurries them. The teachers allow them to dress at their own pace. During this time, one of the children initiates a playful episode with the boots. Other children model the first child.

They put their two palms in their boots and announce loudly, 'Look at me. I'm a dinosaur. A dinosaur is coming!' and crawl with their palms in the boots, which attracts even more children to imitate them. The teacher announces, 'All the dinosaurs, go to the dinosaur land to prepare for later play.' She suggests they put on their clothes in the bench circle, and the children go there as if they are giant dinosaurs. One of the children continues to play by himself, bending down to put his head into a plastic frame, muttering something and putting the plastic frame on his head to pretend he is a brave fighter or monster.

Exploring Basic Rules

There are several micro-transitions from the outdoor to the indoor activity setting. The teachers use music and song as signs, as well as words like 'near the end time' and 'five minutes to clean-up', to remind the children in advance about the transition time. Then, the music 'time to stop work' announces that playtime is over. The children return the materials to the shelves. This is the beginning of the transition from outdoor play to indoor activities. Some children instantly realize that it is time to collect the materials and put them back in the shelter. Other children still enjoy playing. With the other children busily collecting and returning materials nearby, they gradually join the group to return the materials.

However, one of the children still wants to continue his play, although the other children have left the playground. This boy is in the sandpit, focusing on digging in the sand and walking in the water. He is left alone when the other children walk inside. The teacher kindly asks him to go back to the classroom and reminds him that otherwise, he will be late for the next section, which is lunchtime. The boy ignores the teacher's advice and does not reply. He keeps digging canals and watching the water flow into the sand. Then, the teacher says, 'Come back when you have finished. Do not stay too late. We will start to eat lunch soon'. He nods and continues to explore the water and sand, digging more canals and dams. After almost ten minutes, one of the teachers comes out to talk to him: 'Have you finished now? Can you go back with me?' He nods to confirm, and the teacher asks him, 'Do you need me to accompany you to the water faucet?' He washes his hands and takes the tools to the shelter, then follows the teacher to the classroom. In this example, the teacher gives the boy a chance to follow his interests. At the same time, the teacher kindly reminds him about the rules. The boy is well aware of the rules and the time schedule.

Analysis of the Micro-transitions in the A-Kindergarten

From the aforementioned cases in the A-kindergarten, we can see that the atmosphere is quite relaxed, unhurried and loosely organized, which allows for flexibility and diversity in children's initiatives. The transitions seem to be based on well-known routines. Although the transitions from indoor to outdoor activities are done with a collective pulse, there is still room for the children's independence and autonomy in their decisions to follow the group or to work on their own projects. The children are allowed to find their own pace in getting dressed, taking part in collective activities and getting ready to go indoors.

The expectations of and demands on the children in this institutional setting are clearly connected to the philosophy of the kindergarten in this community. The teachers in the A-kindergarten seem to use this short time as a meaningful situation for the children in terms of cultivating their independence and acceptance of peer assistance. The principal told us that they permit this kind of 'left alone playing' among children. Usually, some children will go back to the classroom about fifteen minutes later than the others. She explained that they respect the children's play. The children will return to the classroom voluntarily because they have had the satisfaction of playing for a longer time and because they are hungry and ready to eat lunch.

The teachers in the A-kindergarten let the children do what they like to do. They provide opportunities for different activities but do not push the children. The teachers seem to be confident that the children will find their way and that they should be more relaxed regarding safety issues than most Chinese kindergartens. Instead of giving instructions, the teacher takes part in dialogues with the children and goes into an imaginative world with them. They also have confidence in the skills of the children, allowing them to explore dressing, water and sand activities by themselves. The transitions in this kindergarten offer opportunities for children's enactment and engagement by providing time to explore, as in the situation of getting dressed, the dinosaur play and the sand and water play.

Transitions in the O-Kindergarten

From the outdoor kindergarten, we have chosen to present two micro-transitions. First, the indoor get-ready-to-go-outside routines in the morning and second the walk from the bus to the spot in the forest.

Indoor Get-Ready-to-Go-Outside Routines in the Morning

Some children eat their breakfast, gathered around a small table, with the kindergarten teacher at the end of the table; she is making small talking while she serves milk and helps the children if they need it. The atmosphere is calm but active; children arrive, and the teacher welcomes them. Parents give messages to the kindergarten teacher and say goodbye to their children. The kindergarten teacher is like the conductor of an orchestra: she is in the middle of the activities, aware of all that is happening around her. When the second kindergarten teacher arrives, she joins in, and the theme of the activities changes to focus on the preparations to go outside. One of the kindergarten teachers asks the children to use the bathroom and get dressed and ready for the trip. Some children get dressed and ready quickly, while others need more time. After a while, all the children are outside with their backpacks on. One of the kindergarten teachers gathers the children in a circle and explains a more detailed plan for the day.

Walk from the Bus to the Spot in the Forest

There is a two-kilometre walk on small paths from the bus parking area to the location in the forest. The children carry their small backpacks, and the kindergarten teachers carry their big ones. No one complains about the heavy load to carry. The children seem to be familiar with the path; they walk and talk with each other and with the kindergarten teachers about what they expect to see on the way. 'Is there more water in the creek today than last week? Will the two horses be close by the fence when we pass them, so we can give them some grass?' When they arrive at the destination, a large natural area for play and exploration, all the backpacks are set into the *lavvo*, and the children disappear to play.

Analyses of the Micro-transitions in the O-Kindergarten

The transition from the kindergarten to the forest went through many minor processes, in which the children and teachers followed some well-known routines: arriving at the kindergarten, eating breakfast, playing, getting ready to leave on the bus and the quite long walk through nature and farmland to the forest, where more playing, eating and exploration are possible. Some of the oldest children are eager to come outside and hurry to get ready. They dress themselves independently due to years of training and their motive orientation to engage in outdoor activities with friends.

According to the kindergarten teachers and the manager, it is important to motivate the children to be outdoor and train their independency in getting dressed and ready to go out. In addition, this is in line with Norwegian traditions and culture. Physical activities like mountain walking, skiing and dealing with transport on water were necessary in the past because these were the only ways of moving from one place to another in Norway due to the topography, climate and weather. This is something children are expected to learn in the O-kindergarten.

Summing up

As illustrated in the examples above, the micro-transitions structure time and space differently and influence children's adjustment to a variety of rules, demands and expectations. In the D-kindergarten, the expectation in the micro-transition from indoors to outdoors was an expectation of interdependency, exemplified by adjusting to the collective movement of the group, being efficient, and making sure to bring the necessary belongings and equipment. The expectation in the micro-transition from collective games to free play was an expectation of independency and agency, exemplified by choosing activity and playmates without further instructions. In the A-kindergarten, the expectations and demands in the preparation for free play were to develop skills in dressing and be autonomous but still ask peers for help. In the micro-transition for the left-behind boy, the expectation of the teacher was to follow the institutional schedule but still provide opportunities for negotiation according to individual interests. The expectations in the O-kindergarten are to develop skills in dressing and being prepared for outdoor life, as well as managing patience in moving to the area for play.

In the micro-transitions, the children experienced and explored a variety of teachers' and children's roles. As illustrated in the D-kindergarten, the children experienced the teacher as the leader and instructor when they moved collectively from indoors to outdoors. They also experienced a more laid-back and observing teacher during the transition between collective games and free play. In the A-kindergarten, the children experienced the observing and playful teacher in the transition between physical training games and the free play situation. In the example of the left-behind child, the child experienced the teacher as a negotiator and supporter of play and a reminder of the daily schedule and rules. In the O-kindergarten, the children clearly experienced the teacher as a role model in the activities intended to prepare for leaving the kindergarten for the forest trip.

The framing of time and space provided different conditions for the children's opportunities to participate, explore, negotiate and interplay with the institutional demands and expectations in the three kindergartens. Some of the micro-transitions were short, only a few minutes, and had the character of a clear break, such as the transition from indoors to outdoors in the D-kindergarten (and in the A-kindergarten, although this was not used as an example). Other micro-transitions were more like an activity itself, such as the boy exploring the sandpit in the A-kindergarten and the walk from the bus to the forest in the O-kindergarten.

Discussion

Our concern in this study has been the institutional traditions of micro-transitions as exemplified by three kindergartens situated in China and Norway. The micro-transitions studied in this chapter are all examples of framing time-and-space in-between activities. As such, micro-transitions are like borders, a moment of breaking and a turning point in-between events, a chronotope of the threshold (Bakhtin, 1986) involving action in some order, in certain places, and at a certain time of the day. The micro-transitions in all three kindergartens were routinized through signals, such as words and music, a change of place, a change of clothes, a change in the teacher role and the children's roles, and a change in interactions.

However, in most of the examples, this framing of time and space was not a fixed entity but a dynamic social construction of space and time continuously negotiated and enacted by the children and teachers. As such, the spatiotemporal matrix is produced and productive rather than a passive background for ongoing activity – like creative spaces (Ritella et al., 2020). The micro-transitions provide opportunities for children to negotiate, explore and challenge the limits, rules and institutional expectations and demands, as well as for teachers to be dialogically engaged (Ødegaard, 2020).

The examples from the three kindergartens illustrate how the micro-transitions provide a diversity of structuring and framing for time and space in the everyday practice in kindergarten (Bakhtin, 1986). As such, the micro-transitions are not unified and universal but depend on institutional expectations and demands influenced by values and traditions (Hedegaard,

2012). In the micro-transitions between the indoor and outdoor activity settings, we identified major institutional differences between the Chinese and Norwegian kindergartens. In both Chinese kindergartens, this transition was characterized as a collective and teacher-directed movement accompanied by music. The micro-transition was efficient and predictable but offered little space for exploration. On the other hand, this way of organizing the micro-transition resulted in less waiting time and more time for play and exploration when the children came outdoors.

The institutional practice in most Chinese kindergartens is conditioned by a large number of classes and children in comparison with Norwegian kindergartens. This demands a high degree of interdependency within the institution. In addition, the scheduled hot lunch prepared by a special staff and the fixed sleeping time for all children influence institutional interdependency. In the D-kindergarten, institutional interdependency was even more emphasized because the kindergarten organized collective physical activities for several classes at the same time outdoors. The children were not supposed to wait for one another, and this resulted in limited time for the micro-transition from indoors to outdoors. Adjustment to joint collective movements is valued within this perspective.

This is quite in contrast to the O-kindergarten, which allowed the children to take their time in getting ready to go outdoors. The time schedule in the Norwegian kindergarten is less fixed than in the two Chinese kindergartens due to having fewer classes and no sleeping time for this age group. Most of the days, the children are served cold lunch, which can be more flexible in terms of a time schedule. Independence in getting dressed is a valued skill in the kindergarten, where children go outdoors in spite of heavy rain, snow, wind and cold weather. However, it is not just the skill of getting dressed that is emphasized but also the skill of taking care of themselves by getting properly dressed according to the weather conditions. The institutional practice in the O-kindergarten is built on the Norwegian outdoor tradition, and the teachers are experienced outdoor-teachers. Consequently, it is both an explicit and taken-for-granted expectation in the kindergarten that children will learn to get dressed, get ready to go outdoors, carry their own backpack and do it more and more independently through the years in kindergarten. This is an important time for the exploration of self-protection and skills, as well as the need to take time. Consequently, the Norwegian children must have patience in order to wait for other children to get ready.

Other micro-transitions connected to the outdoor activity setting in the three institutions seem to be more similar and open to children's investigation, examination and testing, as well as giving room for focus shift when the children were distracted. Examples from all three kindergartens illustrate influences from the national curriculum guidelines and framework plan emphasizing children's agency and engagement. The expectations of children in the micro-transition in the outdoor activity setting are clearly open to children's initiatives and autonomy. When the children were not hurried, they had the opportunity and were even encouraged by the teachers to explore their own skills; their relationships to their peers, play materials, rules and expectations; and their own motivations and desires. The institutional expectations were related to children's initiatives and being flexible in different situations.

Our study underlines that seemingly unimportant and routinized micro-transitions require attention within institutional practices because they provide conditions for children's exploration and cultural formation.

Notes

1 The early childhood education and care institutions for children aged 3–6 years are called *You'eryuan* 幼儿园 (kindergarten) in China and are full-time institutions. The educational institutions for children in Norway are called *Barnehage* (kindergarten). These are full-time institutions for children aged 1–6 years. In this chapter, we use kindergarten as a common name for the early childhood institutions in China and Norway.

2 'In ancient Greece, *plateia* ($\pi\lambda\alpha\tau\epsilon\iota\alpha$, street) was a central place for feasts, celebrations, events and meetings. Plateia is not some position, not an empty space, but an area that becomes a significant because of the events, meetings, feasts that "take place" in the place, which thereby comes into existence as place by virtue of the event. All subsequent uses of the word in all languages – e.g., Ger. *Platz*, Fr. *place*, Sp. *plaza*, It. *piazza* – refer us to locations where people meet and significant events occur' (Van Eijck & Roth, 2010, p. 889).

3 A *lavvo* is a specially designed tent, large and circular, traditionally used by the indigenous Sami population for more than 2,000 years.

References

Bakhtin, M. M. (1981). *The Dialogic Imagination: Four Essays by M. M. Bakhtin* (M. Holquist, Ed.; C. Emerson & M. Holquist, Trans.). University of Texas Press.
Bakhtin, M. (1986). *Speech Genres and Other Late Essays*. University of Texas Press.

Birkeland, Å. (2019). Temporal settings in Kindergarten: A lens to trace historical and current cultural formation ideals? *Journal of European Early Childhood Education and Care Research*, 27(1), 53–67. https://doi.org/10.1080/1350293X.2018.1556534

Birkeland, Å., & Sørensen, H.V. (2021). Time regulation as institutional condition for children's outdoor play and cultural formation in kindergarten. In L. T. Grindheim, H. V. Sørensen & A. Rekers. (Eds.), *Outdoor Learning and Play: Pedagogical Practice and Children's Cultural Formation*. Springer.

Brown, R., & Renshaw, P. (2006). Positioning students as actors and authors: A chronotopic analysis of collaborative learning activities. *Mind, Culture and Activity*, 13(3), 247–59. https://doi.org/10.1207/s15327884mca1303_6

Cavada-Hrepich, P. (2016). Starting First-year Primary: Children's Transitions in Classroom Learning Activities. [PhD thesis, University of Copenhagen].

Cavada-Hrepich, P. (2019). Transitioning from play to learning: Playfulness as a resource in children's transition. In M. Hedegaard & M. Fleer (Eds.), *Children's Transitions in Everyday Life and Institutions* (pp. 145–66). Bloomsbury.

Corsaro, W.A., Motenary, L., & Brown Rosier, K. (2002). Sena and Carlotta: Transition narratives and early education in the United States and Italy. *Human Development*, 45(5), 323–48. https://doi.org/10.2304/rcie.2008.3.3.250

Devi, A., Fleer, M., & Li, L. (2019). Transition between child-initiated imaginative play and teacher-initiated activity: An analysis of children's motives and teachers' pedagogical demands in a preschool context. In M. Hedegaard & M. Fleer (Eds.), *Children's Transitions in Everyday Life and Institutions* (pp. 207–26). Bloomsbury.

Fleer, M. (2019). Children and teachers transitioning in playworlds: The contradiction between real relations and play relations as a source of children's development. In M. Hedegaard & M. Fleer (Eds.), *Children's Transitions in Everyday Life and Institutions* (pp. 185–206). Bloomsbury.

Gulløv, E., & Højlund, S. (2003). *Feltarbejde blandt børn. Metodologi og etik i etnografisk børneforskning*. Gyldendal.

Hedegaard, M. (2008a). A cultural-historical theory of children's development. In M. Hedegaard & M. Fleer (Eds.), *Studying children: A Cultural-historical Approach* (pp. 10–30). Open University Press.

Hedegaard, M. (2008b). Developing a dialectic approach to researching children's development. In M. Hedegaard & M. Fleer (Eds.), *Studying children: A cultural-historical approach* (pp. 30–46). Open University Press.

Hedegaard, M. (2009). Children's development from a Cultural-Historical approach: Children's activity in everyday local settings as foundation for their development. *Mind, Culture and Activity*, 16(1), 64–81. https://doi.org/10.1080/10749030802477374

Hedegaard, M. (2012). Analyzing children's learning and development in everyday settings from a cultural-historical wholeness approach. *Mind, Culture and Activity*, 19(2), 127–38. https://doi.org/10.1080/10749039.2012.665560

Hedegaard, M. (2014). The significance of demands and motives across practices in children's learning and development: An analysis of learning in home and school.

Learning, Culture and Social Interaction, 3(3), 188–94. https://doi.org/10.1016/j.lcsi.2014.02.008

Hedegaard, M. (2019). Children's perspectives and institutional practices as keys in a wholeness approach to children's social situations of development. In A. Edwards, M. Fleer & L. Bøttcher (Eds.), *Cultural-Historical Approaches to Studying Learning and Development* (pp. 23–41). Springer.

Hedegaard, M., & Fleer, M. (2019). Children's transitions in everyday life and institutions: New conceptions and understandings of transitions. In M. Hedegaard & M. Fleer (Eds.), *Children's Transitions in Everyday Life and Institutions* (pp. 1–18). Bloomsbury.

Hedegaard, M., & Munk, K. (2019). Play and life competences as core in transition from kindergarten to school: Tension between values in early childhood education. In M. Hedegaard & M. Fleer (Eds.), *Children's Transitions in Everyday Life and Institutions* (pp. 21–46). Bloomsbury.

Kousholt, D. (2011). *Børnefællesskaber og familieliv. Børns hverdagsliv på tværs af daginstitution og hjem*. Dansk Psykologisk Forlag.

Kousholt, D. (2019). Children's everyday transitions: Children's engagements in life contexts. In M. Hedegaard & M. Fleer (Eds.), *Children's Transitions in Everyday Life and Institutions* (pp. 145–166). Bloomsbury.

Leontiev, A. N. (2005). Study of the environment in pedological works of L.S. Vygotsky. A critical study. *Journal of Russian and East European Psychology*, 43(4), 8–28. https://doi.org/10.1080/10610405.2005.11059254

Ministry of Education (2001). *Guidelines for Kindergarten Education Practice - Trial Version* (in Chinese). Ministry of Education.

Morson, G.S., & Emerson, C. (1988). *Rethinking Bakhtin: Extensions and Challenges*. Northwestern University Press.

Ødegaard, E. E. (2020). Dialogical engagement and the co-creation of cultures of exploration. In M. Hedegaard & E. E. Ødegaard (Eds.), *Children's Exploration and Cultural Formation: International Perspectives on Early Childhood Education and Development* (Vol 29) (pp. 83–104). Springer Open.

Ritella, G., Rajala, A., & Renshaw, P. (2020). Using Chronotope to research the space-time relations of learning and education: Dimensions of the unit of analysis. In *Learning, Culture and Social Interaction*. https://doi.org/10.1016/j.lcsi.2020.100381

Skoglund, R.I., Hu, A., & Birkeland, Å. (forthcoming, 2020). Student teachers' dialogical formation in an international program within Kindergarten teacher education. In Paulsen, Koefoed, Brömssen, Jacobsen, Petersen & Garsdal. *Global Challenges – Rethinking Education: Society, Culture and the Anthropocene Seen from a Scandinavian Point of View*. Routledge: Manuscript submitted for publication.

Sørensen, H. V. (2014). Ethics in researching young children's play in preschool. In M. Fleer & A. Ridgway (Eds.), *Visual Methodologies and Digital Tools for Researching with Young Children* (pp. 193–212). Springer.

Sørensen, H. V. (2019). Studying children's friendship activities ethically using the 'Interaction Based Observation Method'. In A. Edwards, M. Fleer & L. Bøttcher (Eds.), *Cultural-Historical Approaches to Studying Learning and Development* (pp. 279–292). Springer.

Sørensen, H. V. (2021) Children's play and social relations in nature and on kindergarten playground: Examples from Norway. In L. T. Grindheim; H. V. Sørensen & A. Rekers (Eds.), *Outdoor Learning and Play: Pedagogical Practice and Children's Cultural Formation*. Springer.

Sørensen, H. V., & Birkeland, Å. (2020). Children's explorative activities in kindergarten playgrounds: A case study in China and Norway. In M. Hedegaard & E. E. Ødegaard (Eds.), *Children's Exploration and Cultural Formation: International Perspectives on Early Childhood Education and Development* (Vol 29) (pp. 47–63). Springer Open.

Stetsenko, A. (2017). *The Transformative Mind*. Cambridge University Press.

Van Eijck, M.W., & Roth, W.-M. (2010). Towards a chronotopic theory of 'place' in place-based education. *Cultural Studies of Science Education*, 5(4), 869–98. https://doi.org/10.1007/s11422-010-9278-2

Vygotsky, L. S. (1998). *Child psychology: The Collected Works of L. S. Vygotsky* (Vol 5). Kluwer Academic and Plenum Publishers.

Winther-Lindqvist, D. (2019). Becoming a school-child: A positive developmental crisis. In M. Hedegaard & M. Fleer (Eds.), *Children's Transitions in Everyday Life and Institutions* (pp. 47–70). Bloomsbury.

Index

Note: Page references with letter 'n' followed by locators denote note numbers.

affordance 43, 46–8, 62, 148, 150–1, 153, 157–60
agency 1, 7, 10–11, 14–15, 45, 171–5, 211, 214
alternative pathways 107–10, 111–12

celebration 8, 10, 35–6, 43, 48, 53, 57, 60–1, 63, 214 n.2
child development 1–2, 6, 8, 10–11, 14, 21–5, 30, 35, 45–6, 63, 73, 76, 98, 117, 120–1, 139–41, 165, 167–8, 171
children's social situation 8, 46, 72–3, 92, 100, 117, 123–6, 141, 174, 199, 201
Chinese early childhood education 8, 10, 69–82, 87–8, 91–3, 198, 201–4, 206, 209, 212–13, 214 n.1
co-exploration 7–10, 42, 46, 63, 63 n.1
collaborative exploration 8–9, 43, 45–6, 49–51, 55–8, 61–3, 63 n.1
compassion 184, 186, 188–93
cultural formation 4, 7, 13, 19, 35, 42–4, 46, 49, 55, 61, 70, 74–6, 79–81, 88, 91–3, 136, 139–40, 184, 198–9, 201, 203, 214
cultural-historical 1–2, 6, 12, 21–2, 43–4, 71, 98–101, 110, 141, 149, 151, 159, 164, 172, 187, 198–9
cultural-historical theory 4, 10–11, 13–14, 45, 62, 98, 120–1, 157, 163, 165–8, 176, 183

defectology 98
demands 5, 10–11, 15, 21–4, 29, 35, 72–4, 76, 88–9, 93, 97, 99–101, 104–5, 107, 112, 124, 126–7, 130, 139, 149, 158, 165–6, 197–204, 206, 209, 211–13
developmental transitions 97–8, 117
disability 9–10, 97–9, 101–12
diversity 1, 8–9, 44–5, 53, 55, 57, 63, 101, 187, 189, 191–3, 209, 212

education 1, 4, 7–8, 12, 14, 19–25, 30, 35, 41–5, 58, 61–3, 69–70, 72, 77, 82, 87–8, 99, 103–4, 106–12, 119, 122, 138, 141, 149, 159, 163–7, 169, 171, 173–7, 185–7, 192–3, 197–8, 200, 202–3
educational experiment 70–9, 82, 88–93
embodiment 4, 10–12, 48, 51, 76, 87, 150, 153, 157–9, 184
emotions 6, 12–13, 48, 62, 183–4, 186–93
English early childhood education 45, 79
expectations 8, 29, 49, 89, 98, 120, 132, 166, 197–201, 203–4, 206, 209, 211–14
exploration 1, 4, 6–15, 19, 21, 23–4, 30, 32, 35–6, 41–3, 45–50, 57, 59, 61–2, 70–80, 82–3, 86–93, 99–103, 105, 107–8, 110–12, 118, 121, 125–6, 136–8, 140–1, 148, 150, 153–6, 158–9, 171–4, 183–93, 198, 201, 203–4, 210, 213–14

father-child interactions 12, 117–18, 120–1, 123, 125, 127, 137, 141
father involvement 118–20, 138–9, 141
Finnish early childhood education 13–14, 163–4, 169, 174–6, 183–6, 192–3

incongruence 98–9, 105, 107, 110–12
Indian early childhood education 11–12, 117–19, 131–4, 138–41
infants 12, 23, 46, 147–9, 151, 158–9

leading activities 14, 22, 72–3, 131, 163, 167–71, 198
local 7–10, 14, 22, 25, 30–1, 35, 41–4, 46, 48–55, 57–63, 69–70, 92, 106–7, 166, 168, 185, 193, 202
locomotor exploration 12, 149–57, 159

microgenetic 6, 11, 14, 117, 151
micro-transitions 11, 13, 43, 62, 117–18, 120–1, 124–6, 128–32, 136–8, 141, 197–201, 203–6, 208–14
moral 82, 186, 189–3
motive orientation 72–3, 76, 82, 85–6, 88–9, 92, 100–1, 210
motives 4, 6, 8–9, 13, 21, 24, 29, 36, 45, 74–5, 87, 90–2, 97, 99–112, 117, 121, 124, 130, 132, 134, 136, 138, 165, 170, 172, 189, 198–200

national celebration 8, 48, 57, 61, 63
Norwegian early childhood education 8–10, 13, 53, 60–1, 117–18, 198, 201–4, 212–13, 214 n.1

outdoor playtime 13, 198–9, 201, 204

participatory design 42, 44, 49
peer interaction 12, 159
play 1, 4–8, 10, 12, 14–15, 19, 21–32, 34–6, 41–2, 45–7, 52, 54, 57, 69–83, 85–93, 119, 121, 131, 136, 139, 155, 159, 166–8, 170–2, 175, 183, 185, 192, 200, 202, 205–11, 213–14
preschool 5, 6, 20–5, 30–2, 35–6, 36 n.1, 43, 72–3, 76, 92, 122, 127, 167–8, 170, 176

radical-local 19, 21–3, 30, 36

social opportunities 97, 99, 101, 107, 110, 112
societal demands 10, 70, 73, 79, 91, 199

transition 1–15, 19, 22, 35–6, 42–5, 49–55, 57, 59, 61–3, 70–4, 90, 93, 97–103, 107, 110, 119, 132, 150–3, 155, 157–60, 170, 176, 190–3, 197–8, 200–1, 204–13

wholeness perspective 199

young adult 98, 100–1, 111

www.ingramcontent.com/pod-product-compliance
Lightning Source LLC
Chambersburg PA
CBHW062217300426
44115CB00012BA/2102